GRAMMAR
by DIAGRAM

second edition

GRAMMAR
by DIAGRAM

UNDERSTANDING ENGLISH GRAMMAR THROUGH
TRADITIONAL SENTENCE DIAGRAMING

second edition

Cindy L. Vitto

broadview press

LIBRARY AND ARCHIVES CANADA CATALOGUING IN PUBLICATION

Vitto, Cindy L
      Grammar by diagram: understanding English grammar through traditional
      sentence diagraming/Cindy L. Vitto.—2nd ed.

Includes index.
ISBN 1-55111-778-9

1. English language—Grammar. 2. English language—Sentences. 3. English language—Usage. I. Title.

PE1380.V58 2006   428.2   C2006-901730-1

BROADVIEW PRESS is an independent, international publishing house, incorporated in 1985. Broadview believes in shared ownership, both with its employees and with the general public; since the year 2000 Broadview shares have traded publicly on the Toronto Venture Exchange under the symbol BDP.

North America
Post Office Box 1243,
Peterborough, Ontario, Canada K9J 7H5

Post Office Box 1015
2215 Kenmore Ave.,
Buffalo, New York, USA 14207
tel: (705) 743-8990; fax: (705) 743-8353

EMAIL customerservice@broadviewpress.com

UK, Ireland, and continental Europe
NBN International
Estover Road
Plymouth, PL6 7PY, UK
TEL (01752) 202300; FAX (01752) 202330;
EMAIL enquiries@nbninternational.com

Australia and New Zealand
UNIREPS University of New South Wales
Sydney, NSW 2052
TEL 61 2 9664099; FAX 61 2 9664520
EMAIL infopress@unsw.edu.au

We welcome comments and suggestions regarding any aspect of our publications–please feel free to contact us at the addresses above or at broadview@broadviewpress.com.

This book is printed on paper containing 100% post-consumer fibre.

Cover design by Black Eye Design
Typeset by Liz Broes, Black Eye Design

Printed in Canada

10 9 8 7 6 5 4 3 2 1

GRAMMAR
by DIAGRAM

UNDERSTANDING ENGLISH GRAMMAR THROUGH
TRADITIONAL SENTENCE DIAGRAMING

second edition

Cindy L. Vitto

broadview press

LIBRARY AND ARCHIVES CANADA CATALOGUING IN PUBLICATION

Vitto, Cindy L
      Grammar by diagram: understanding English grammar through traditional
      sentence diagraming/Cindy L. Vitto.—2nd ed.

Includes index.
ISBN 1-55111-778-9

1. English language—Grammar. 2. English language—Sentences. 3. English language—Usage. I. Title.

PE1380.V58 2006   428.2   C2006-901730-1

BROADVIEW PRESS is an independent, international publishing house, incorporated in 1985. Broadview believes in shared ownership, both with its employees and with the general public; since the year 2000 Broadview shares have traded publicly on the Toronto Venture Exchange under the symbol BDP.

North America
Post Office Box 1243,
Peterborough, Ontario, Canada K9J 7H5

Post Office Box 1015
2215 Kenmore Ave.,
Buffalo, New York, USA 14207
tel: (705) 743-8990; fax: (705) 743-8353

EMAIL customerservice@broadviewpress.com

UK, Ireland, and continental Europe
NBN International
Estover Road
Plymouth, PL6 7PY, UK
TEL (01752) 202300; FAX (01752) 202330;
EMAIL enquiries@nbninternational.com

Australia and New Zealand
UNIREPS University of New South Wales
Sydney, NSW 2052
TEL 61 2 9664099; FAX 61 2 9664520
EMAIL infopress@unsw.edu.au

We welcome comments and suggestions regarding any aspect of our publications–please feel free to contact us at the addresses above or at broadview@broadviewpress.com.

This book is printed on paper containing 100% post-consumer fibre.

Cover design by Black Eye Design
Typeset by Liz Broes, Black Eye Design

Printed in Canada

10 9 8 7 6 5 4 3 2 1

CONTENTS

ACKNOWLEDGMENTS

I had no idea, when the first edition of *Grammar by Diagram* became available, that I would be hearing from people in various parts of the world who had questions, comments, and suggestions about the text. I owe a special thanks to many of those readers, especially Becky Cargile (who sent me pages of suggestions, shared some of her own excellent teaching strategies and exercises, and became a kindred soul to whom I could turn whenever I had doubts about continuing with the second edition); Scott Meyer, a law student who read the text so closely, with such a finely attuned ear and sharp eye for detail, that he deserves credit for smoothing out many sentences that I hadn't realized were capable of improvement; Judge James Bentivegna and Denis Costrum, who shared with me verb tables they had drawn up for themselves as a way of remembering verb voice, tense, and aspect. In addition to the many informal readers of the text, I also owe thanks to the anonymous readers selected by Broadview Press to evaluate *Grammar by Diagram*. Their clear and constructive comments have led to definite improvements for the second edition.

As was the case with the first edition, I also thank the students at Rowan University who have toiled through the text—whether with Barbara Patrick, Donna Jorgensen, or myself at the head of the class—and have given me valuable feedback. Also, once again I am happy to acknowledge my family, especially my husband and daughter, George and Elizabeth, along with Mindy, Kristy, and Erin. Without them, I would not have the impetus to bring this work to completion. Without them, there would be no poetry in the deep structure of my life.

Finally, I would like to acknowledge the influence of the many fine teachers of literature and language that I have been privileged to know. While working on the final changes for the second edition, I was obliged to make a trip to my home town of Parsons, West Virginia. Thanks to our friends Jane and Jack McGuigan, I was able to peruse the holdings of the Tucker County Historical Society, visit the building that used to be Parsons High School, and reminisce about the devoted teachers I had known there and elsewhere. My visit reminded me of just how important teachers are, at every stage of one's life, and how—just as children eventually take over the parental role—our own students often come to take over the teaching role. To all of my teachers (including my students) and to my parents, who somehow instilled in me a love of learning even though they had little formal education themselves, I dedicate this book.

INTRODUCTION

To grasp the concept of grammar as a discipline, we need a frame of reference—a basic overall perspective plus definitions for several key terms. The overarching principle is that grammar, in the purest sense, is a method of describing the way people actually use language, in both spoken and written forms. There is no one "right" way to describe language, and in fact the history of grammar illustrates that through the centuries the English language has been analyzed from various perspectives—for example, as if it were an offshoot of Latin and should therefore be manipulated to follow certain rules of that language, as a tool for moving up the social ladder, as a way of explaining basic operational rules not only of English but of all human language. One way of approaching the most recent developments in the field is to note that many specialists employ the plural, "grammars," indicating that not all who speak English follow the same rules, but that no one set of rules is inherently superior to any other. And that, perhaps, is what often comes as the biggest shock to those who enter a serious course of study in English grammar: the notion that grammar does not come stocked with a rigid set of "rights" and "wrongs," and, even more surprising, that linguistic experts do not all describe the language in exactly the same way, using the same terms. This is not to imply, of course, that there are no standards, but to remind us all that any grammar textbook is, to some extent, set up in an arbitrary fashion, and usually set up to reinforce a particular variety of the language—the "prestige" dialect favored by educated individuals in positions of academic, political, and social leadership. In fact, modern English itself has evolved from a particular dialect of Old English and then Middle English. Before we proceed to analyze the grammar of our language, let's take a few moments for an overview of its history.

A BRIEF HISTORY OF THE ENGLISH LANGUAGE

What language might we be speaking today if not for the various twists and turns of history that led us to modern English? We might be speaking a language with the distinctly musical accents of Gaelic and Welsh, two languages still spoken in the United Kingdom. We might be speaking something that would sound like German, Dutch, or a Scandinavian language. We might even be speaking French. Instead, we are in some ways speaking a mixture of all these languages, and we call it English. To understand the evolution of our language, we need to grasp the impact of a series of invasions on the island that today we call England.

The original inhabitants of this island, the **Celts** (the builders of Stonehenge), spoke a language derived from what scholars call Indo-European, an ancient language whose existence we postulate from similarities among certain words found in several modern languages. The Celts received an exploratory visit from the Roman general Julius Caesar in 55 BC and then, beginning in 43 AD, were subject to a series of attacks by invading Roman legions. Eventually the Celts and Romans came to live somewhat peacefully together, but when Rome itself came under attack from barbarians, the Roman soldiers left to defend their homeland, leaving the Celts relatively defenseless.

About 449 AD, small tribes of people that we know today as **Angles, Saxons, and Jutes** sailed across the North Sea from Denmark and Germany. The Jutes had originally been asked by Vortigern, a Celtic king, to help repel two other tribes that had been causing trouble for the Celts; however, the Jutes themselves, along with the Angles and Saxons, soon became the invaders. The most successful resistance to the Angles, Saxons, and Jutes was organized by a Celtic chief by the name of Artorius, apparently the real-life model for the legendary King Arthur. Eventually the Anglo-Saxons (as the tribes came to be known) set up seven distinct kingdoms of their own, while the Celts moved to the west and north, with some sailing off to northern France, where the Breton dialect is spoken today. Now that they had effectively taken over the island, the Anglo-Saxons called the Celts "wealas," meaning "foreigners." From "wealas" comes the name "Wales," the area of England where many of the Celts settled and where today Welsh remains a living language. The Anglo-Saxon language, or **Old English**, absorbed only about a dozen Celtic words, most of them describing geographical structures, such as "crag" (a steep, rugged rock or cliff) and "tor" (a high, steep hill).

The Anglo-Saxons spoke an inflected language, meaning that word order is not important because the forms of the words in a sentence indicate the function of each word. For example, the word "cyning" (king) becomes "cyninges" to mean "of the king" and changes to "cyninge" to mean "for the king." Furthermore, "cyning" serves as the subject form, while a different form—"cyningas"—indicates that the word is used as the object of a verb. As you can see, modern English is not an inflected language; unless we were forming a plural or a possessive, we would use simply "king" and then rely on prepositions and/or word order to grasp the use of the word within the sentence.

When Christianity took hold in England beginning about 597 AD, Latin took over as the prestige language—the tongue used for administrative, legal, and religious purposes. Christianity added many words to the Anglo-Saxon or Old English language; for example, the Latin word "evangelium" (good news) became "godspell" in Old English and eventually "gospel" in modern English.

Beginning about 750 AD, the Anglo-Saxons, who had driven out the Celts, now found themselves struggling against invaders from what is today Sweden, Norway, and Denmark. Viking raids began in earnest in 793, when monasteries in the north of England were sacked for their gold and silver, and by about 850 half of the country belonged to the **Vikings**. In 871, a newly crowned Anglo-Saxon king named Alfred managed to raise a small army and defeat a band of Danes, resulting in a treaty that established an area known as the Danelaw, where the Danes agreed to settle. With the Danes in the north and the Anglo-Saxons in the south, Alfred used this time of comparative peace to draw his people together and to rebuild monasteries and schools, using Old English to accomplish his tasks. He also commissioned the writing of the *Anglo-Saxon Chronicle*, a "diary" of historical events in English. At the same time that Alfred was assuring the continuance of the English language, border contacts between the Danes and the Anglo-Saxons were leading to a simplification of Old English word endings and also the incorporation of Norse words that have resulted in such words as modern English "dirt," "sky," "birth," "die," and "want." It is Alfred's West Saxon dialect of Old English which forms the foundation of modern English.

The final major invasion of England occurred in 1066, when a French duke who subsequently became known as William the Conqueror led his forces across the English Channel to defeat the Anglo-Saxon forces under King Harold. The **Norman Conquest of 1066**, memorialized in the famous Bayeux Tapestry, is arguably the single most important event for England historically and linguistically. Although Anglo-Saxon continued to be spoken, French and Latin were now the languages of those in power, and it would be about 300 years before another English king would actually speak English. As had happened with the Danes, though, contact between the Normans and the Anglo-Saxons eventually led to the reappearance of English, this time with few inflections and a greatly enriched vocabulary of words derived from French. The language changed so much that today we call the English spoken from about 1100 to about 1500 **Middle English**. From among several dialects of Middle English, one evolved into modern English: the East Midlands dialect (spoken in and near London, and the dialect in which Geoffrey Chaucer wrote).

Beginning in the 1500s and continuing into the late 1600s, the English language went through another major phase, what scholars term "**early modern English**," the language of the King James Bible and Shakespeare. During this period, which encompasses what is known in British literary history as the Renaissance, English added more than 10,000 new words, mostly from Latin, Greek, French, Spanish, and other languages. A thirst for classical learning, the advent of the printing press, world exploration, and an expansion of literacy all contributed to this era's bold experimentation with language.

Today we speak **modern English**—having dropped words such as "thee," "thou," "thy," "thine," and indirect requests such as "prithee" that mark early modern English—but it is clear that our language continues to evolve. We have incorporated words from other languages (such as Spanish "burrito," Italian "papparazi," Japanese "karaoke"), made up words of our own (such as "smog" and "laser"), and invented new uses for familiar words (such as "mouse" and "port" for computer users). Perhaps because English has withstood so many invasions and proved its ability to incorporate new words and new concepts, it has become the world's **lingua franca**, the language used for international communication.

THE MEANING AND HISTORY OF GRAMMAR

Having had a glimpse of the rich history of English, we turn now to consider the history of its grammar. Grammar is a subset of a larger discipline, linguistics. Linguistics includes the study of sounds (phonetics), how those sounds make meaning (morphology), how words are strung together into meaningful sentences (syntax), how any language operates according to a finite set of rules (grammar), how certain rules tend to be preferred by educated users of the language (usage), and how language must be carefully constructed and scrutinized for meaningful communication (semantics). In addition, linguists study spelling (orthography), the derivation of words (etymology), the use of arbitrary signs to facilitate communication (semiotics), the interaction of culture and language (sociolinguistics), the interaction of psychology and language (psycholinguistics), the historical evolution of a language, the process by which native speakers of one language learn to use another language, and other facets of language study too numerous to mention.

According to the *Oxford English Dictionary*, the word "grammar" is derived ultimately from a Greek form meaning "of or pertaining to letters or literature." This is an apt root since in classical Greek and Latin "grammar" included the study of literature as well as of language. We can trace our modern word from the Greek form, to Latin *grammatica*, to the Old French *gramaire*. Since, in the Middle Ages, grammar referred almost exclusively to the study of Latin and thus to a knowledge reserved for a relative few, *gramaire* became associated with the occult, so much so that the word *gramaire* could mean either a grammar book or a sorcery book. Even today simple magic is sometimes referred to as "glamour," reflecting an association with "grammar," and the word "gramarye" can be found in the dictionary with the definition "magic."

Much more important than its association with the occult, though, is the central importance of grammar in the medieval curriculum of higher education. The seven liberal arts were organized into a *quadrivium* (arithmetic, geometry, astronomy, and music) and the foundational *trivium* (grammar, logic, rhetoric).

By the middle of the seventeenth century, the study of grammar in England became firmly associated with the exercise of reason and even of moral conduct. Several developments pushed forward the study of language, and the prestige of that study: the Royal Society for the Improvement of Knowledge, founded in 1664, took on language as one of its interests; Samuel Johnson published the first comprehensive dictionary of the English language in 1755, establishing the basic format still followed by lexicographers (Johnson humorously defined a lexicographer as a "harmless drudge"); and in 1762, Robert Lowth's *Short Introduction to English Grammar* set the tone for approaching grammar through a study of right and wrong, an attempt to stop what he perceived as a rapid decline in linguistic standards. His approach prevailed until the mid-twentieth century.

On the whole, today we can divide the study of English grammar into two movements, with two diametrically opposed emphases. Through the nineteenth and early twentieth centuries, following the lead of Lowth and others like him, the principal emphasis of grammar instruction was **prescriptive**; that is, grammarians concentrated not so much on how native speakers actually used the language as on how they *should* use the language. Typically, they made their decisions on the basis of Latin grammar, since for centuries Latin had been the lingua franca (language used in common) of educated people. They ignored the fact that English was not derived from the same mother tongue as Latin but instead was a **Germanic** language, with roots in common with such languages as German, Dutch, and the Scandinavian tongues.

Beginning in the 1950s, propelled especially by the work of Noam Chomsky, the emphasis of grammar study (and eventually, of grammar instruction) shifted from prescriptive to **descriptive**. That is, linguists now acted less as grammar police and more as anthropologists, describing nonjudgmentally the way native speakers actually use the language. Working inductively, using actual language as data, Chomsky isolated basic operational rules. He worked out a system to describe **kernel sentences**, the patterns from which almost all of our sentences are generated, as well as ways to describe how we transform those basic patterns into more sophisticated ones (thus the term **transformational grammar**).

Chomsky's work did much to shift linguistics from a prescriptive to a descriptive mode, a change that has created some controversy, at least as it has filtered into the popular press and into the classroom. Descriptive grammar recognizes that educated speakers do set accepted standards (**standard English**, or, when written, **standard edited English**). However, those standards are subject to change, and, even more important, those standards are not inherently superior to any other version of the language. Within any country where English is spoken (and it is now the most widely used language in the world), **dialects** of the language exist based on geographic area, on social class, on ethnic heritage. The most versatile users of English are actually, in some sense, bilingual—or even multilingual. They can move swiftly and smoothly from, say, a dialect spoken within the home to a slightly different dialect spoken in the neighborhood to standard English spoken at work. They can pepper their language with **idioms, figurative language**, and **slang**, yet sit down to write a formal business letter that a prescriptive grammarian would find faultless.

At this point you may be wondering, "If there is no superiority to standard English, why have I spent so many hours in school studying grammar rules? Is there no such thing as 'good grammar'? No such thing as 'right' or 'wrong' when it comes to language?" The answer is that there is no *inherent* superiority to standard English. In theory, all dialects are equal, and all dialects are logically organized according to a set of discernible rules. (In fact, the rules of a given dialect are often more logical than the rules of standard English.) In practice, however, our social mobility and economic success frequently depend upon our ability to communicate with the greatest number of people, and so fluency in standard English *is* essential for most of us.

ORGANIZATION OF THE TEXT

This text is designed to suit both descriptive and prescriptive goals of language instruction, with descriptive and prescriptive (usage) chapters interwoven throughout. We begin with a descriptive approach in the first three chapters. Chapter 1 takes the traditional eight parts of speech as a useful foundation for grammar instruction. You should realize, though, that many texts begin with phonetics and morphology—units of sound and of meaning—rather than jumping immediately to whole-word units. In addition, keep in mind that there is no magic to the phrase "eight parts of speech." Other texts may describe five parts of speech, or eleven, or skip this concept altogether. Even though all linguists will be describing the same phenomena, there are many ways to do this. Chapters 2 and 3 move from words to whole sentences, describing ten basic sentence patterns in English. Again, keep in mind that other texts may specify a different number of sentence patterns, or not find the concept useful at all. Chapter 4 shifts to usage, addressing problems of adjective and adverb form and use, since these are the problems we can address at the level of a simple sentence.

Next, building on the ten basic sentence patterns, Chapters 5, 6, and 7 discuss how to combine and expand them into compound, complex, and compound-complex sentence structures. Chapter 8 then takes up usage issues that often arise in the more complicated sentence structures—issues of subject-verb agreement and pronoun case, agreement, and consistency. Chapter 9 offers a relatively brief description of the English verb system, followed by a discussion of verbals in Chapter 10 and usage problems related to verbs and verbals in Chapter 11.

Chapters 2, 3, 5, 6, and 7 make extensive use of traditional sentence diagraming, a technique of visualizing the way that all the words in a sentence relate to one another. Although various systems of sentence diagraming have been developed, this text uses the Reed-Kellogg format, devised by Alonzo Reed and Brainerd Kellogg for their book *Higher Lessons in English*, first published in 1877. The Reed-Kellogg system is the one public schools are most likely to adopt. Immediate-constituent, or "tree," diagraming is another popular diagraming system but one usually found only in college-level texts. Because many readers of this text may have had experience with traditional diagraming, or may find themselves teaching in lower-grade classrooms, or may be tutoring their own children, we will concentrate on the Reed-Kellogg system.

As you begin working your way through this book, however, you may question what benefits traditional sentence diagraming can offer you. Wouldn't it be simpler to drop it altogether? What if this system of analyzing sentences just doesn't work for you? Typically, anyone encountering sentence diagraming for the first time either loves it or hates it; neutral reactions are rare. Should you fall into the "I hate this" category, keep in mind that diagraming is an extremely useful tool for sentence analysis and relatively easy to learn. Diagraming allows us to grasp a sentence spatially, to see its various parts clustered together as a whole. Rather than working your way through a sentence word by word, you will learn to see it as one or more units, eliminating what is not essential in order to pinpoint the elements that give the sentence its structure and meaning. You may also find, as many of my students have, that knowing how to diagram will improve your writing, will give you a teaching tool if you are helping others analyze sentences, and may even land you a job. One student being interviewed for a job as a software programmer diagramed a sentence on demand and was hired on the spot, despite the fact that other applicants had more extensive experience with computers. The interviewer considered sentence diagraming an excellent way to assess logic skills. In addition, the current emphasis on grammar in the elementary and secondary classroom, as well as on standardized tests, bodes well for the return of diagraming to the standard language arts curriculum.

The final two chapters of this book provide the finishing touches for English sentences: how to punctuate for clarity and how to transform for effect and variety. The remainder of the book contains a complete answer key (invaluable if you are using this text on your own or if you are enrolled in a grammar course where, typically, there simply isn't time for an instructor to check or grade exercises) and a set of six appendices: (1) a set of exercises dealing with the key elements of descriptive grammar but without answers, for the benefit of instructors who asked for extra practice material without an answer key; (2) verb conjugations; (3) irregular and troublesome verb forms; (4) a summary of the functions of clauses and verbals; (5) a recap of diagraming structures; and (6) a list of commonly confused words.

A NOTE FOR STUDENTS AND GENERAL READERS

If you are a native speaker of American English, as you work your way through this text you may have difficulties "taking apart" a language that you know so intimately. Like a computer, your brain has been programmed to put words in particular orders, to change verb tenses, to form plural or singular subjects and effortlessly choose the verb form that will agree. Looking at the language more analytically may make it seem temporarily foreign to you. Be aware that this may happen—and that throughout your course of study you may find yourself, in the midst of leisure reading, recognizing a participle or some other structure you never consciously thought of before. You may even find yourself diagraming sentences in your sleep. This phase will pass, but in the meantime enjoy the experience of becoming a "scientist" of your own language.

Allow me to issue one caution about using this book: refer to the answer key in the back of the book with care. If you check your answers at each step, sentence by sentence, you may be using the answer key as a crutch, as a substitute for your own learning. Once you understand the information that underlies each exercise, complete the exercise before checking your answers. If you do not use the answer key responsibly, you may well find that you have cheated yourself of real learning. In fact, if you are using this book in the context of a class, you might panic when you face a test and suddenly have no answer key as a backup. Finally, feel free to question the answer key; bring up in class discrepancies between the answer key and your own sense of a given sentence. In my own classes, this sort of question has often resulted in rich discussion.

You should also be aware that, by its nature, a grammar book makes use of carefully controlled sentences. As you know, English in actual use is filled with exceptions to the usual rules, with idioms, with slang, with structures that are much more complex than you would typically find in a textbook like this one. Now that you will be paying more attention to everyday language, bring to class a few intriguing sentences that surpass the boundaries of what you have learned.

A NOTE FOR TEACHERS

If you have chosen to use this book within a grammar or composition course, quite likely it is one of a few or even several texts your class will be working with. This text is designed, as much as possible, for independent use; I have attempted to make the commentary and examples clear and have provided answers for all of the exercises (except those in Appendix 1). Please refer your students to the cautionary note (in the section above) regarding responsible use of the answer key. Because many readers of the first edition used this text independently, without a teacher as a guide, I have maintained a complete answer key but have added a set of extra practice exercises, without answers, as Appendix 1. Having a complete answer key for the main text makes it possible to find various ways to integrate this text into a course:

1. Ask students to purchase the text before the course begins and assign the sections that will be most helpful as prerequisite knowledge. At a minimum, students should be able to complete Chapter 1 without help, and many students will be able to complete the first four or five chapters without difficulty. In addition, because most students have some difficulty with punctuation, you may wish to assign Chapter 12 as pre-course study.

2. Assign pertinent sections from this text as your course progresses. You can do this on a whole-class basis ("Everyone must complete the comma rules section of Chapter 12 by tomorrow") or make assignments for individual students based on their own needs as you evaluate their writing samples.

3. Use the text as a whole, progressing in whatever order best suits your needs. Although I have interwoven descriptive and prescriptive chapters, for example, you may decide to concentrate on one or the other.

4. Because this is unabashedly a traditional approach to grammar, using traditional sentence diagraming, you may wish to pair this text with one utilizing a more contemporary, more theoretical approach—for example, one that deals more intensively with transformational-generative grammar, or one that uses tree diagraming. Students might begin with this volume in order to review what they have probably already learned at some point and to orient themselves before going on to higher levels of grammar study.

5. Finally, some classes will benefit from using this volume as their only or primary text. Students who need a thorough review of traditional grammar—for example, either for remedial purposes or for teacher-training purposes—will benefit from in-depth coverage.

A final note: I have adhered primarily to MLA format (or have clearly specified deviations from it) in order to facilitate the text's usefulness in English courses. Although in no way will this text substitute for the *MLA Handbook* (for example, I do not address citation format), neither will it conflict with MLA style. In particular, Chapter 12, "Punctuation and Capitalization," complements the *MLA Handbook* by addressing how to set up and punctuate both short and long quotations.

CHANGES IN THE SECOND EDITION

Although no drastic changes have taken place in the second edition, thanks to the helpful comments of several readers I have clarified various points, added a few exercises, and corrected errors (and no doubt created new ones along the way, for which I take full responsibility). I have also, as much as possible, eliminated the use of dependent clauses or verbals in exercises in the chapters preceding those topics. This change will allow students to use many of the exercises to gain more diagraming practice. For those familiar with the first edition, the most noticeable changes will be the inclusion of a brief section on the history of the English language in the introduction, conformity with the most recent edition of the *MLA Handbook*, and substantial changes in the appendices. The first appendix provides additional exercises for Chapters 1, 2, 3, 6, 7, and 10—the chapters that introduce the most important descriptive components of language study. To accommodate several instructors' request for a limited amount of material without an answer key, Appendix 1 does not provide answers. The second appendix, verb conjugations of *see* and *be*, should help flesh out the range of possible verb forms. I have dropped appendices from the first edition that seemed redundant in order to add more helpful material, but I have also retained four of the original appendices.

Working my way through the text to prepare a second edition has forcefully reminded me that no piece of writing is ever "done"; *Grammar by Diagram* remains a work in progress, and because of that I encourage readers with questions or comments to contact me by e-mail at vitto@rowan.edu.

The Eight Parts of Speech

Words are the basic building blocks of any language. One way to begin analyzing a language, then, is to classify each word as belonging to a distinct category and to determine how the categories work together to make meaning.

Most of you are probably already familiar with the traditional way of classifying English words—the eight parts of speech. Just for fun, see if you can list all eight in the spaces below. (If you're like most people, you'll remember only six or seven! Check your answers by turning to the Summary of Key Concepts at the end of this chapter.)

1. _____

2. _____

3. _____

4. _____

5. _____

6. _____

7. _____

8. _____

As neat and tidy as this organizational system seems, though, we must beware of assuming that each word in English can be tucked neatly into one of these categories and remain there. Part of what makes English such a dynamic language is that the same word can be used as more than one part of speech. Consider the word "water," for example, in the following sentences:

The *water* in the birdbath was filthy. (water = noun)

The children *water* the sunflowers every day. (water = verb)

The *water* sign is Aquarius. (water = adjective)

In addition, linguists certainly do not agree that using the traditional eight parts of speech—based on Latin instruction from earlier centuries—is suitable for describing the English language. There is no magic to the number "eight"; indeed, some texts prefer to make two large divisions in the language, between open classes of words (those to which new words can be added—nouns, verbs, adjectives, adverbs) and closed classes (pronouns, conjunctions, prepositions). Other texts might prefer to categorize words into seven, eleven, or some other number of categories.

What remains constant is that English words do fall into recognizable categories, even if experts label and group those categories differently. Those categories are defined by two qualities: **form** (the way a word looks or can be changed to look) and **function** (the way a word operates within a larger unit to help make meaning).

Although we will use the traditional eight parts of speech as our starting point, then, keep in mind that these categories are flexible. Also, by necessity you will find a number of terms in this chapter that have not yet been introduced in the text. Examples are provided to give you an inductive sense of those terms for now, and you will find them defined in more detail in later chapters. Once you have completed this text, you should (ideally) reread this first chapter because you will then be able to make more connections between form and function, and among the various parts of speech, than you can at this point.

1 ● NOUN

Asked to list the eight parts of speech, almost everyone begins with the noun—not surprising if we think of how infants begin to speak. With very limited language, they produce nouns as a way to ask for what they want and as a way to begin to make sense of the world around them. "Cup," "milk," and "juice" are examples of nouns that may be among the first words a baby consistently offers to the family.

Definition of a Noun

A noun is a person, place, thing, or idea.

Categories of Nouns

Nouns are often categorized as **abstract** (intangible entities such as justice, love, philosophy) or **concrete** (tangible entities such as house, tree, computer). Nouns are also **proper** (if individualized and therefore capitalized, such as the Declaration of Independence) or **common** (if designating membership in a generic group and therefore uncapitalized, such as "declaration" or "independence"). Finally, nouns are either singular or plural, leading to two additional categories: **regular** and **irregular** nouns, **countable** and **uncountable** (mass) nouns. The plurals of regular nouns end in *s* or *es* (e.g., "coats," "buses"). Irregular nouns either change their form altogether to indicate a plural number (e.g., "mouse" becomes "mice") or remain unchanged (e.g., "sheep"). Countable (or count) nouns indicate entities that can be numbered; mass nouns indicate entities that, although understood to be plural in some sense, cannot actually be counted. For instance, we can count five cookies, but we cannot count the flour and sugar used to make the cookies—although, of course, we can measure the flour and sugar in terms of cups, since "cup" is a count noun.

Identifying a Noun

Nouns are often preceded by noun-markers called determiners (possessive nouns or pronouns, demonstrative pronouns, indefinite pronouns, interrogative pronouns, or articles). Even if the noun is not preceded by a determiner, you can insert one as a test; if the phrase makes sense, the word that follows the determiner is a noun.

POSSESSIVE NOUNS OR PRONOUNS	John's house, his house
DEMONSTRATIVE PRONOUN (this, that, these, those)	that house
INTERROGATIVE PRONOUN (what, which, whose)	which house
ARTICLE (a, an, the)	the house

This test works equally well with abstract nouns, which are sometimes the hardest to identify: her anger, this silence, the peace.

Another test, although it does not work equally well with all nouns, is to make the word either plural or possessive. "Cabinet" is a noun if you can make it plural ("cabinets") or possessive ("the cabinet's handle").

A final test is to substitute a pronoun for a noun:

Mark composed the *song.*

He composed *it.*

EXERCISE 1.1

Underline the nouns in the following passage.

> The governess insisted that the children should not be allowed to indulge their whims. She instructed the butler, Percy Shaw, to ignore their complaints; as she put it, "These spoiled darlings need to learn the meaning of discipline!"

see answer key, p. 373

2 ● PRONOUN

Definition of a Pronoun

A pronoun is a word that takes the place of a noun.

Categories of Pronouns

Pronouns fall into a variety of categories, beginning with the fact that we can divide pronouns as a whole into two large classes: **personal pronouns** (those that indicate first, second, or third person, singular or plural, with masculine, feminine, or neuter gender) and **impersonal pronouns** (those that do not reflect these characteristics). Nominative, objective, reflexive or intensive, and possessive pronouns fall into the category of personal pronouns; indefinite, reciprocal, interrogative, demonstrative, and relative pronouns are impersonal.

PERSONAL PRONOUNS

Nominative or subjective pronouns: the form used for the subject of a sentence or for the subjective complement.

SUBJECT — *She* is here.

SUBJECTIVE COMPLEMENT — Who is *she*?

Objective pronouns: the form used for the direct object, indirect object, or object of a preposition. A quick method for native speakers of English to determine the objective form is to use the pronoun that naturally follows the preposition "to": "to me," "to her," "to him," "to us," "to them."

DIRECT OBJECT — Joe understands *me*.

INDIRECT OBJECT — Sally bought *him* a present.

OBJECT OF PREPOSITION — The company will do anything for *them*.

Reflexive or intensive pronouns: the form used to refer back to the antecedent (a noun or pronoun used earlier in the sentence). Reflexive pronouns are necessary for clarity of meaning; intensive pronouns are optional forms used for emphasis.

REFLEXIVE — Perry found *himself* alone in the room.
The children locked *themselves* in the bathroom.

INTENSIVE — The children *themselves* painted this mural. (Here, "themselves" is an intensive pronoun because it is used solely for emphasis.)

These categories—nominative or subjective, objective, and reflexive or intensive—are personal pronouns because they relate to the three "persons" of English grammar, as outlined below. The fourth category of personal pronoun, the possessive, appears separately because it has more than one inflection. In other words, in addition to showing person, number, and gender, the possessive pronoun also indicates by its form whether it is a free-standing pronoun or a determiner preceding and modifying a noun.

Nominative or Subjective	SINGULAR	PLURAL
FIRST PERSON	I	we
SECOND PERSON	you	you
THIRD PERSON	he, she, it	they

Objective	SINGULAR	PLURAL
FIRST PERSON	me	us
SECOND PERSON	you	you
THIRD PERSON	him, her, it	them

Reflexive or Intensive	SINGULAR	PLURAL
FIRST PERSON	myself	ourselves
SECOND PERSON	yourself	yourselves
THIRD PERSON	himself, herself, itself	themselves

Possessive pronouns: the form used to show possession of a noun. Possessive pronouns have two forms, depending on whether they are acting as free-standing pronouns or as determiners before a noun. As determiners they act as adjectives because they provide more information about the noun that follows.

Pronoun form	SINGULAR	PLURAL
FIRST PERSON	mine	ours
SECOND PERSON	yours	yours
THIRD PERSON	his, hers, its	theirs

Determiner form	SINGULAR	PLURAL
FIRST PERSON	my	our
SECOND PERSON	your	your
THIRD PERSON	his, her, its	their

Her book is on the table. (determiner)

The book is *hers*. (possessive pronoun)

The cat licked *its* paw. (determiner)

Notice that "its" is the one possessive pronoun that causes problems; if you insert an apostrophe, you've created a contraction meaning "it is" or "it has"; without an apostrophe, you have the possessive form. Perhaps it will help if you remember that the pronoun "his" is possessive but never takes an apostrophe; "its" follows the same model. **Personal pronouns never use an apostrophe to signal possession.**

It's [It is] correct to write "its" for possession.

Another way of avoiding this problem is to remember that contractions are inappropriate in most formal writing; therefore, it is seldom suitable to use "it's."

IMPERSONAL PRONOUNS

Unlike the personal pronouns, the impersonal pronouns that follow cannot be inflected (changed) to reflect first, second, or third person; singular or plural; or masculine, feminine, or neuter. Indefinite and reciprocal pronouns can, however, be inflected to become possessive in form.

Indefinite pronouns: used to take the place of a noun which cannot be named specifically. The indefinite pronouns you may be most familiar with begin with "any," "some," "every," or "no":

anyone	someone	everyone	no one
anybody	somebody	everybody	nobody
anything	something	everything	nothing

Words that specify a number or amount also qualify as indefinite pronouns, such as "enough," "many," "each," "both," "none," and the cardinal numbers ("one," "two," and so on).

Anybody can learn the eight parts of speech.

She studied *nothing* but grammar.

Many of the flowers have already bloomed.

Twenty of the students gave *each* of the teachers a little *something* as a parting gift.

Indefinite pronouns can appear in possessive form:

Someone's car was parked in the mud.

Reciprocal Pronouns: indicate reciprocity, either singular ("each other," meaning only two) or plural ("one another," meaning more than two).

They love *each other*. (This sentence indicates two people in love.)

They love *one another*. (This sentence indicates more than two people, perhaps a loving family.)

Reciprocal pronouns can also be used as determiners (adjectives) when in the possessive:

Nate and Sheena get on *each other's* nerves.

In our family, we have learned to put up with *one another's* foibles.

Interrogative pronouns: "who," "whom," "whose," "which," and "what" when used to begin a question.

What is the name of this object?

Which is the painting that you just bought?

Whose is this?

"Whose," "which," and "what" function as adjectives (determiners) when they immediately precede a noun. Notice the difference between the free-standing pronouns above and the same forms used as determiners below:

What object is on the table?

Which painting did you just buy?

Whose bicycle is this?

Certain words that may at first glance seem to fall into the same category as interrogative pronouns—"when," "where," "why," "how"—function as adverbs, not pronouns.

Demonstrative pronouns: used to point out a specific noun. There are only four demonstrative pronouns: "this," "that," "these," "those." Demonstrative pronouns are interesting because they indicate proximity in English. In the sentences below, notice that "this" and "these" indicate closeness to the speaker, while "that" and "those" indicate distance. Some dialects of English emphasize this difference by adding "this here" or "that there."

This is a dirty shirt.	*That* is a clean shirt.
These are dirty shirts.	*Those* are clean shirts.

Note that demonstrative pronouns function as adjectives (determiners) when they precede a noun.

These clothes are dirty. ("These" is a determiner, not a pronoun, in this sentence.)

These are dirty. ("These" is a demonstrative pronoun here.)

Relative Pronouns: begin a relative, or adjective, clause. (We will learn more about relative clauses in Chapter 5. Briefly, a relative clause is a group of words containing a subject and a verb and used to modify the noun that precedes the clause.) The relative pronouns are "who" (and its variants "whoever," "whom," "whomever," and "whose"), "which," and "that."

The police officer *who* helped us was extremely courteous.

That piano, *which* has been in storage during the winter, needs to be tuned.

Do not trust a wild animal *that* has been caged.

Identifying a Pronoun

You will probably not have much trouble identifying pronouns if you remember that they take the place of nouns. Although with some categories of pronouns, and some sentence structures, this can become complicated, the basic test for a pronoun is to substitute a noun. If the sentence makes sense, you've found a pronoun.

Subjective Pronoun:	*He* jogs every day. (*Mike* jogs every day.)
Objective Pronoun:	Mary gave *her* a lollipop. (Mary gave *the child* a lollipop.)
Reflexive or Intensive Pronoun:	Eleanor made *herself* sick with worry. (Eleanor made *Eleanor* sick with worry.)
Possessive Pronoun:	*Her* mother is learning Spanish. (*Jenna's* mother is learning Spanish.)
Indefinite Pronoun:	I doubt that *anyone* can do better. (I doubt that *George* can do better.)
Reciprocal Pronoun:	The children waved good-bye to *one another*. (The children waved good-bye to *their friends*.)
Interrogative Pronoun:	*Whom* did Steve call for advice? (In this case, rearrange the wording: Did Steve call *Bill* for advice?)
Demonstrative Pronoun:	I would like to buy *that*. (I would like to buy *the computer*.)
Relative Pronoun:	The employees preferred a supervisor *who* could be objective. (In this case, isolate the relative clause and substitute a noun for the relative pronoun: *Melissa* could be objective.)

EXERCISE 1.2

Underline the pronouns in the following passage. Then see if you can take the next step and categorize each pronoun as well.

"That is not acceptable," proclaimed the schoolmaster, rocking himself emphatically back and forth on his heels. "I want to know the person who is responsible for this suggestion. Should students have the right to determine their own grades?

It is a preposterous idea! I will assign grades to you as I see fit, and anyone wishing to argue with me may do so. Grades are my prerogative. You will not grade yourself, nor will you grade one another. Who would ever think of such a thing?"

1. _____   2. _____
3. _____   4. _____
5. _____   6. _____
7. _____   8. _____
9. _____   10. _____
11. _____   12. _____
13. _____   14. _____
15. _____   16. _____
17. _____   18. _____
19. _____

see answer key, p. 373

3. ● VERB

Verbs are the most complex of the eight parts of speech. As you will see in the following two chapters, it is essential to identify verbs and to classify them in order to determine the function of other elements in the sentence.

The most basic classification of a verb requires us to label it as either **active** or **passive**. An active verb indicates that the subject of that verb is performing the action; a passive verb indicates that the subject is not performing the action and is therefore "passive." Passive verbs always consist of at least two words, a form of the *be* verb followed by the past participle (the verb form that would follow the auxiliary "have").

Active: Monique *threw* the ball.

Passive: The ball *was thrown* by Monique.

We will discuss passive verbs (and passive sentences) in a later chapter. For now, the rest of our discussion on verbs is limited to active verbs.

Definition of a Verb

A verb shows either action or state of being (existence). Note that sometimes the "action" does not involve physical motion, as in "we *slept*" or "Bill *considered* the idea."

Categories of Verbs

By definition, verbs fall into two large categories: **action** or **state of being (existence)**. These categories can be further subdivided, as illustrated below:

ACTION VERBS		STATE OF BEING (EXISTENCE) VERBS	
↙	↘	↙	↘
Transitive Verbs	Intransitive Verbs	*Be* Verbs	Linking Verbs

Action verbs fall into two categories:

1. **Transitive** verbs are followed by an object indicating who or what receives the action.

> He *kicked* the ball.
>
> She *waved* her hat.

2. **Intransitive** verbs are not followed by an object. A transitive verb can often serve as an intransitive verb when you simply delete the object:

> He *kicked*.
>
> She *waved*.
>
> The children *ran* through the yard.

State of being verbs fall into two categories:

1. **As the most irregular verb in English, *be* has a variety of forms: am, is, are, was, were, being, been.**

> They *were* happy.

For quick reference, the most common forms of the *be* verb are conjugated below:

PRESENT TENSE	I am	we are
	you are	you are
	he, she, it is	they are
PAST TENSE	I was	we were
	you were	you were
	he, she, it was	they were

PERFECT ASPECT (PRESENT / PAST)	I have / had been you have / had been he, she, it has / had been	we have / had been you have / had been they have / had been
PROGRESSIVE ASPECT (PRESENT / PAST)	I am / was being you are / were being he, she, it is / was being	we are / were being you are / were being they are / were being

2. **Linking verbs can be replaced by a form of *be* without substantially changing the meaning of the sentence.**

"They *seemed* happy" is basically equivalent to "They *were* happy."

Note that all of the verbs of sense can be used as linking verbs:

The soup *tasted* good.

The soup *smelled* good.

The soup *looked* good.

The soup *sounded* good when you suggested it.

The soup *felt* good on such a cold day.

The following sentences illustrate other common linking verbs:

I *become* sleepy around midnight.

People *seem* intelligent when they think before they speak.

Moments of happiness *appear* frequently in the life of a secure child.

Senior citizens *remain* valuable community members.

Leaves *turn* red, orange, and yellow in the fall.

The nights *grow* shorter before the summer solstice.

Notice that linking verbs can often function as action verbs, depending on the sentence:

The farmer *grew* sad as he talked about his childhood. (linking verb because you can replace "grew" with "was"—The farmer *was* sad as he talked about his childhood.)

The farmer *grew* corn. (transitive verb because you cannot replace "grew" with "was" and because an object follows the verb.)

An essential characteristic of the *be* and linking verbs is that, by themselves, they cannot complete the thought of the sentence. Whenever we use a *be* or linking verb as the main verb of the sentence, we must follow it with an adjective that modifies the subject or with a noun or pronoun that renames the subject—hence the term "linking verb," since the verb links an adjective, noun, or pronoun to the subject. With the *be* verb, the element that follows may also be an adverb of time or place.

Carla is happy.   (The adjective "happy" modifies Carla.)

Carla is a lifeguard.   (The noun "lifeguard" renames Carla.)

Carla is here.   (The adverb "here" specifies where Carla is.)

Note that normally it would be impossible to use "Carla is" as a complete sentence. Similarly, it would be impossible to use a linking verb without completing the sentence with an additional element. "Carla seems" is not a sentence, but "Carla seems happy" does express a complete thought.

Verb Phrases

Verbs often appear in phrases, making it more difficult to determine which category of verb you are dealing with. **When you see a verb phrase, the last word in the phrase determines whether you have an action or a state of being verb.** The last word in the verb phrase is the main verb; the other verbs, those leading up to the main verb, are called auxiliaries or helping verbs. They allow us to express various shades of meaning, including tense (when the action or existence indicated by the verb took place).

Four types of verbs can be used as auxiliaries:

1. **modals**   (shall, should, will, would, can, could, may, might, must, have to, had to, ought to)

2. **forms of *have***   (has, have, had)

3. **forms of *be***   (am, is, are, was, were, being, been)

4. **forms of *do***   (does, do, did)

(We will discuss *do* separately, since it operates differently from the others.)

Note in the following sentence how a modal, a form of *have*, and a form of *be* all precede the main verb. **These auxiliaries always appear in the same order:**

modal + *have* + *be* + main verb

The toddler *should have been eating* at the table.

When faced with a verb phrase such as this one, how do we determine the category of the verb? **The main verb, not the auxiliaries, determines the category of the verb as a whole.** In the example above, "eating" is the main verb. We classify it as an action verb because it denotes action on the part of the subject ("toddler") and is clearly not a *be* or linking verb. Further, it is not followed by an object. (The noun "table" is not the object of the verb but the object of the preposition "at.") We can therefore classify "eating" as an intransitive verb, and by extension the entire verb phrase "should have been eating" is intransitive.

Once we move from parts of speech to sentence patterns (Chapters 2 and 3), identifying the category of the verb in the sentence will help you determine the pattern of the sentence. When faced with a verb phrase, then, you can determine how to categorize the verb by using a decision tree:

1. Are there auxiliary or helping verbs—a modal, a form of *have*, and/or a form of *be*? If so, eliminate these components of the verb phrase in order to locate the main verb, the last word of the verb phrase.

2. Does the main verb show a state of being or existence? If so, is the main verb a form of *be* or is it a linking verb? (Remember that the test of a linking verb is that it can be replaced by a *be* verb without substantially changing the meaning of the sentence.) Sentence patterns 1, 2, and 3 contain a form of *be* as the main verb; sentence patterns 4 and 5 use a linking verb.

3. If the main verb is not a *be* or linking verb, then it must be an action verb. If the verb shows action, is it intransitive (with no direct object following the verb) or is it transitive (followed by an object—a noun or pronoun that answers the question "whom?" or "what?" following the verb)? Sentence pattern 6 contains an intransitive verb; sentence patterns 7, 8, 9, and 10 build upon a transitive verb.

Let's look at a few examples to see how this works:

Geraldine *has been dancing*.
"Has been dancing" is an action verb because of the final word, "dancing." You can further classify it as intransitive because no object follows the verb.

The manager *is being* unreasonable.
"Is being" is a state of being verb and belongs to the *be* category because of its final word, "being."

My sister *is feeling* happy.
"Is feeling" is a state of being verb and belongs to the linking verb category; its final word, "feeling," does not show action and the sentence could be rephrased as "My sister is happy."

My sister *is feeling* her boyfriend's biceps.
Here, "is feeling" is an action verb and is transitive because it is followed by an object, "biceps." It would not make sense to rephrase the sentence as "My sister *is* her boyfriend's biceps," so "feeling" is not used here as a linking verb.

The fourth type of auxiliary, forms of *do*, appears in special circumstances. We use this auxiliary when we phrase a question from a sentence that contains no other auxiliaries, when we make a positive statement negative, and when we want to add emphasis.

STATEMENT WITHOUT AUXILIARY	Courtney likes chocolate.
QUESTION FORMATION	*Does* Courtney like chocolate?
NEGATIVE STATEMENT	Courtney *does* not like chocolate.
EMPHATIC STATEMENT	Courtney *does* like chocolate.

Note that if the original sentence already contains an auxiliary ("Courtney *has* always liked chocolate"), then there is no need for the auxiliary *do* ("*Has* Courtney always liked chocolate?").

Identifying a Verb

If you can locate the subject of a sentence (who or what the idea of the sentence is about), you will probably be able to identify the verb—the words that indicate the subject's action or state of existence.

EXERCISE 1.3

In the sentences below, identify the italicized verbs as belonging to one of the following categories:

[A] State of being verb—*be* verb

[B] State of being verb—linking verb

[C] Action verb—intransitive (no object)

[D] Action verb—transitive (object follows verb)

_____ 1. I *felt* the torn material.

_____ 2. I *felt* sorry about the mistake.

_____ 3. The cadet *sounded* angry.

_____ 4. The cadet *sounded* the trumpet.

_____ 5. A comet *has been* in the sky.

_____ 6. Everyone *has been looking* for hours at the unusual sight.

_____ 7. The beach *has been looking* lovely.

_____ 8. The beach *has* an irresistible allure.

_____ 9. My neighbor Janelle *has acted* in a few low-budget films.

_____ 10. Because of her experience, she *acts* rather snobbish now.

_____ 11. The most expensive items *were* in a locked cabinet.

_____ 12. Two customers *were waiting* patiently.

_____ 13. They *were buying* a retirement gift for a beloved colleague.

_____ 14. They *seemed* nervous about making the best choice.

_____ 15. They finally *selected* a jeweled kaleidoscope.

see answer key, p. 374

EXERCISE 1.4

Underline the verbs and verb phrases (including helping verbs) in the following passage. Then, above each verb or verb phrase, identify the type of verb by using the following symbols: [T] for transitive, [INT] for intransitive, [BE] for any form of the verb "to be," or [L] for linking verb.

The hands of the clock were moving slowly while Gretchen walked to town. She had a serious look on her face as she approached the shop where her mother had worked for the past ten years. Today she would enter the shop for her final good-bye before she was on her way to America. As she pushed open the heavy door, she did not weep. Instead, she smiled so that she might appear happy and confident.

see answer key, p. 374

4. ● ADJECTIVE

Definition of an Adjective

An adjective is a word that modifies a noun or a pronoun.

Categories of Adjectives

An adjective usually answers one of three questions: (1) which one? (2) how many? (3) what kind?

1. **which one?**

> I like *my* car.

> She wants *that* house.

Notice that this category, as mentioned earlier, includes words that are more properly called determiners (because their presence "determines" the presence of a noun to follow). Determiners come in many varieties, such as possessive nouns, possessive pronouns, demonstrative pronouns, indefinite pronouns, interrogative pronouns, and reciprocal pronouns in possessive form. Possessive nouns can even have their own determiners. Notice the difference between "I read *her* letter" and "I read *her mother's* letter."

The three articles—"a," "an," and "the"—constitute another set of determiners answering the question "which one?" We classify articles as indefinite ("a" or "an") and definite ("the"). "A" and "an" are variants; use "an" before a word beginning with a vowel or before a silent or an unvoiced letter. Thus we would say "*a* historical document" if we pronounce the initial "h" but "*an* herbal remedy" if we take the "h" in "herbal" to be silent. Likewise, we say "*a* university degree" because, even though "university" begins with a vowel, it does not begin with a vowel sound.

> Sara ordered *a* cake for *the* party.
> (The indefinite article indicates no particular specification of cake, but the definite article indicates a specific party.)

> Sara ordered *an* anchovy pizza to be delivered in *an* hour for *a* friend of hers.
> (Use "an" before words beginning with vowel sounds.)

Note that "the" is occasionally used not as an article but as an adverb, in a sentence such as "She runs the fastest" or a phrase such as "the sooner the better" or "none the worse for wear."

2. **how many?**

> I want *no* excuses.

> She drank *three* cups of tea.

> *Almost* everyone arrived on time.

3. **what kind?**

> They chose a *purple* carpet for the *Victorian* house.

Placement of Adjectives

Single-word adjectives almost always occur in two slots in the sentence, either before the noun (or pronoun) being modified or after a *be* or linking verb. The adjective that follows a verb is called a **predicate adjective** or a **subjective complement**; adjectives preceding nouns are labeled **attributive**.

> The *red* scarf is in the closet.

> The scarf is *red*.

Like verbs, adjectives can occur in phrases. When they do, they typically follow the order given above—which one, how many, and what kind:

> She paid for *the three china* figurines.

EXERCISE 1.5

Underline the adjectives, including articles, in the following sentences.

The choppy blue waters of the normally quiet lake battered Michael's worn old boat. As a veteran of many fierce storms, it looked both defiant and triumphant as high waves slapped against its chipped bow.

see answer key, p. 374

5 ● ADVERB

Definition of an Adverb

An adverb modifies a verb, an adjective, or another adverb, as demonstrated below:

She smiled [verb] *discreetly*.

She is *quite* discreet [adjective].

She smiled *very* discreetly [adverb].

Categories of Adverbs

Single-word adverbs usually answer one of three questions: (1) how? (2) when? (3) where?

1. **how? in what manner? under what condition?**

She walked *quickly*.
(Many adverbs in this category end with –ly. Not all words that end in –ly, though, are adverbs; "friendly" "neighborly," "curly," "burly," and "surly," for example, are always adjectives, even though they end with –ly.)

The word "not" also fits under this category as an adverb because it creates a negative condition:

She is *not* walking.　　　She is *not* happy.

2. **when?**

She walked *yesterday*.

3. **where?**

She walked *here*.

Adverbs also take the form of larger groups of words, known as phrases and clauses. These extended adverbs, besides answering the questions above, can also answer the question **"why?"** or **"for what purpose?"**

> She walked *to improve her health*. (infinitive phrase used as adverb)
>
> She walked *because she enjoyed the exercise*. (adverb clause)

Identifying an Adverb

In many cases, one of the best ways to identify an adverb is to use the **test of movability**. If you can move the word (or phrase or clause) in question without changing the meaning of the sentence, it is probably an adverb.

> She walked quickly.
>
> She quickly walked.
>
> She walked yesterday.
>
> Yesterday she walked.
>
> She walked to improve her health.
>
> To improve her health, she walked.
>
> She walked because she enjoyed the exercise.
>
> Because she enjoyed the exercise, she walked.

As you can see, though, this test is not infallible. In the following example, moving "here" results in an awkwardly phrased sentence, yet "here" is clearly an adverb because it specifies where she walked.

> She walked here.
>
> *Here she walked.

(An asterisk indicates a structure that violates the grammatical rules or the idiomatic flow of English.)

EXERCISE 1.6

Underline the single-word adverbs in the following passage.

> Sarah and Manuel sat forlornly on the porch steps. They talked very quietly as they considered what life would now be like. With their grandmother's death, life had changed irrevocably forever, and they could not bear going inside.

see answer key, p. 375

6 ● PREPOSITION

Definition of a Preposition

A preposition is a word that relates a noun or pronoun to the rest of the sentence. The noun or pronoun is known as the **object of the preposition.**

Consider the following sentence:

I walked _____ the door.

Unless we fill in the blank with a preposition, the sentence simply does not make sense. But once we insert a preposition, many spatial possibilities can be expressed. Here are just a few:

I walked *through* the door.
      into
      behind
      out
      around

Prepositions can also express concepts of time and of condition:

The child fell asleep *during* the intermission.

Paulette married Pierre *despite* his quick temper.

Sometimes, rather than a single-word preposition, a prepositional idea is expressed in an idiomatic phrase of two or three words, followed by the object:

According to Paulette's mother, Pierre has a quick temper.

On account of his temper, Pierre has been *out of* work.

Categories of Prepositions

Every prepositional phrase, once identified, acts as either an adjective or an adverb. (On rare occasions, a prepositional phrase may also function as a noun, as in "The best time for a short phone call is *before lunch*.") When you are looking for the subject and verb of a sentence, it helps if you first identify and then eliminate the prepositional phrases. In almost all cases, they merely distract you from finding the essential information contained within a sentence.

The motto *on the wall* is inspirational.

In this case, the prepositional phrase is an adjective, even though it may initially seem to be an adverb because in a sense it indicates where the motto is. Here the primary purpose of the prepositional phrase is to indicate *which* motto is inspirational. If you can locate the subject and verb of this sentence—"motto is"—you'll notice that the prepositional phrase separates them. **When you see this pattern of subject, prepositional phrase, and verb, the prepositional phrase is almost always an adjective modifying the subject.**

We hung the picture *on the bedroom wall.*

Here the prepositional phrase acts as an adverb because it indicates *where* the picture was hung, not *which* picture. Notice that the prepositional phrase could also appear at the beginning of the sentence without changing meaning; remember that adverbs are usually movable but adjectives are not.

> The boys drew the graffiti *on the wall.*

In this sentence, the prepositional phrase could be either an adjective, specifying which graffiti, or an adverb, explaining where the boys drew. Out of context of surrounding sentences, it is impossible to determine if this prepositional phrase is functioning as an adjective or an adverb. The sentence could be rephrased, though, to clarify the function of the prepositional phrase:

> Although we did not know who had drawn the graffiti on the sidewalk, we knew that the boys had drawn the graffiti *on the wall.* (Here the prepositional phrase serves as an adjective to distinguish the graffiti on the sidewalk from the graffiti on the wall.)

> After considering the best location for their message, the boys decided to draw the graffiti *on the wall.* (Here the prepositional phrase serves as an adverb to specify *where* the graffiti had been placed.)

Identifying a Prepositional Phrase

Remember that prepositions do not occur in isolation but as part of a phrase. When you see a word expressing time, location, or condition that is followed by a noun or a pronoun, you have a prepositional phrase. Most prepositions are short words, as you'll see from the list of common prepositions below. In addition, since the majority of prepositions indicate spatial location, you can generate a representative list for yourself by choosing a noun as object and placing prepositions before it: in the cloud, under the cloud, over the cloud, through the cloud, within the cloud, on the cloud, below the cloud, across the cloud, beyond the cloud, on top of the cloud, next to the cloud, beside the cloud, past the cloud, and so on.

A List of Common Prepositions

about	behind	for (when it does not	past
above	below	mean "because")	since
according to	beneath	from	through
across	beside	in, inside	throughout
after	between	instead of	to
against	beyond	into	toward
along	but (when it means	like	under
among	"except")	near	until
around	by	of	up
as	despite	off	upon
at	down	on	with
because of	during	out, out of, outside	within
before	except, except for	over	without

Placement of Prepositions

Common wisdom is that a sentence should not end with a preposition, and this is usually true (especially when the preposition is unnecessary, as in "Where are you *at*?") On the other hand, it is better to end with a preposition than to contort a sentence. Winston Churchill has left his mark on this grammatical issue. When a civil servant revised one of Churchill's sentences to eliminate a preposition at the end, Churchill reportedly responded, "This is the sort of English up with which I will not put." Consider your audience when deciding whether or not to end a sentence with a preposition. In formal contexts, you may wish to rephrase the sentence; for everyday use, end the sentence with a preposition if it sounds natural and if the preposition is not redundant.

EXERCISE 1.7

Underline the prepositional phrases in the following passage. Then identify each prepositional phrase by writing above it either [ADJ] for a prepositional phrase used as an adjective or [ADV] for a prepositional phrase used as an adverb.

The barking dog chased the frantic squirrel around the house and under a bush. It

was a scene of pathetic comedy. For several moments the squirrel's escape seemed

hopeless, but fortune suddenly reversed itself. The dog collapsed in exhaustion, and

we breathed a sigh of relief.

see answer key, p. 375

EXERCISE 1.8

The following sentences end with a preposition. Rewrite each sentence so that the preposition appears earlier in the sentence. Consider which version sounds more natural and which version would be more appropriate for formal occasions.

1. Dylan is the one that Luigi always seeks advice from.

   _____

2. Animal rights is an issue I care deeply about.

   _____

3. Which flavor of ice cream are you going to ask for?

_____

4. Rochester is the man Jane Eyre fell in love with.

_____

see answer key, p. 375

7 ● CONJUNCTION

Definition of a Conjunction

A conjunction is a word that connects words, phrases (groups of words that do not contain both a subject and a verb), or clauses (groups of words that do contain subjects and verbs). Three conjunctions you are likely to recognize are *and, but,* and *or.*

Helen *and* Mary are close friends.

The confused cat sped through the door *but* stopped in the hallway.

You can memorize the eight parts of speech, *or* you can struggle throughout the rest of this course.

Categories of Conjunctions

Conjunctions come in many varieties, and we'll take them up in more detail later. For now, here's a quick overview:

1. **Coordinating conjunctions:** If you remember the acronym **FANBOYS**, you can easily memorize all of the coordinating conjunctions:

for (meaning "because")	and	nor	but
or	yet	so	

The Jones family has visited London, *so* this year they are traveling to Munich.

2. **Subordinating conjunctions:** These conjunctions join an adverb clause to the main clause of a sentence. Although the list that follows is not complete, here are some of the most common subordinating conjunctions:

after	if	until
although	once	when, whenever
as	since	where, wherever
because	so that	whereas
before	though	whether or not
even though	unless	while

You may notice that several of the subordinating conjunctions can also be found in the list of common prepositions. When followed by a noun as object, the word is a preposition; when followed by a subject and verb, the word is a subordinating conjunction. Occasionally the same word can function as an adverb as well. In the sentences below, all of the italicized structures impart the same sense of "when," but the grammatical structure of each one differs.

Before the game, we placed bets on the winner. (*Before* is used here as a preposition because it is followed by an object, "game." The prepositional phrase as a whole serves as an adverb.)

Before the game began, we placed bets on the winner. (*Before* is used here as a subordinating conjunction, preceding the subject-verb unit of "game began.")

We had never seen such a game *before*. (*Before* is used here as an adverb answering the question "when.")

3. **Correlative conjunctions:** These conjunctions occur in pairs: both/and, either/or, neither/nor, not only/but also, and whether/or.

Neither the steaks on the grill *nor* the chicken in the oven looked appetizing.

4. **Conjunctive adverbs:** These "hybrids" are adverbs that do the work of conjunctions by following a semicolon that joins two complete sentences. Whereas the semicolon indicates the joining of the two sentences into one, the conjunctive adverb expresses the logical relationship between the ideas of the two sentences. Some of the most common conjunctive adverbs are words often labeled as "transitions" in writing courses:

accordingly	in conclusion	nonetheless
additionally	in contrast	on the contrary
also	indeed	on the other hand
consequently	in fact	otherwise
finally	instead	still
furthermore	likewise	then
hence	meanwhile	therefore
however	moreover	thus
in addition	nevertheless	

Kristina has studied grammar for several years; *therefore*, she should become an excellent copy editor.

We will encounter conjunctive adverbs in more detail in Chapter 5.

EXERCISE 1.9

Underline and identify the conjunctions in the passage below.

Although Lady Grimshaw offered us both tea and coffee, we refused to take advantage of her hospitality, for the hour was late; however, we agreed to return within a few days.

1. _____   3. _____

2. _____   4. _____

see answer key, p. 375

8 ● INTERJECTION

Definition of an Interjection

An interjection is a word used to express emotion at a low, moderate, or high level. The interjection is probably the least used part of speech, at least in writing. It is often difficult to determine if an interjection is part of a sentence or if it constitutes a sentence on its own.

Well, you're wrong again.

Wow! What a car!

Because the interjection does not perform an essential grammatical function but instead is used to add extra "flavor" to a sentence, we will not need to discuss it further in this book.

SUMMARY OF KEY CONCEPTS IN CHAPTER 1

As traditionally defined, there are eight parts of speech:

1. **Noun** — person, place, thing, or idea

    TESTS: can be made plural or possessive
    a pronoun can substitute for a noun

2. **Pronoun** — takes the place of a noun

    CATEGORIES: personal (nominative or subjective, objective, reflexive or intensive, possessive)

    impersonal (indefinite, reciprocal, interrogative, demonstrative, relative)

3. **Verb** — shows either action (transitive or intransitive) or state of being (*be* verb or linking verb) of the subject of the sentence

    last verb in a verb phrase determines whether verb is an action or state of being verb; may be preceded by a modal, and/or a form of *have*, and/or a form of *be*, or a form of *do*

4. **Adjective** — modifies a noun or pronoun

    answers (1) which one? (2) how many? (3) what kind?

5. **Adverb** — modifies a verb, an adjective, or another adverb

    answers (1) how? in what manner? under what condition? (2) when? (3) where?

    TESTS: can often move within a sentence without changing meaning

    adverbs that answer the question "how?" often end in −ly

6. **Preposition** — relates a noun or pronoun (the object of the preposition) to the rest of the sentence; every prepositional phrase acts as either an adjective or an adverb

    TEST: must be followed by a noun, pronoun, or noun phrase

7. **Conjunction** — connects words, phrases, or clauses

    CATEGORIES: coordinating, subordinating, correlative, conjunctive adverbs

8. **Interjection** — expresses emotion

CHAPTER 1 EXERCISE

I. Label each word in the passage below as a part of speech.

Use the following abbreviations:

[N] noun

[P] pronoun

VERB: [V-T] transitive verb
            [V-INT] intransitive verb
            [V-BE] *be* verb
            [V-L] linking verb

[ADJ] adjective

[ADV] adverb

[PREP] preposition

[CONJ] conjunction

[INTER] interjection

A strangely familiar portrait faced me during my dinner at the ancestral estate.

Because I am not usually superstitious, I felt upset by the effect of that experience.

Oh, that portrait gave me nightmares for days, but they finally stopped when I

investigated the history of the house and its owner. The subject of the portrait was

an ancestor of mine and had fallen to a grisly death in the previous century.

This type of exercise, common in schoolrooms through the early twentieth century, is known as "parsing." This is the last time you will be directed to parse sentences; instead, you'll learn to identify the most important words in the sentence and categorize them by function (subject, object, etc.). In addition, you'll learn to diagram sentences in order to illustrate spatially the relationship of each word to other words in the sentence.

II. In the sentences below, indicate the part of speech of each italicized word. Be able to explain how you determined your answer.

   1. Every student needs to buy the required *book* for this course.

2. We asked the travel agent if she could *book* us on the next flight to Baltimore.

_____

3. The *book* value of the classic car was astounding.

_____

4. We looked *up* at the stars.

_____

5. Please do not *up* the price of this car.

_____

6. We saw the flashing lights of an ambulance *up* the street.

_____

7. The town has been steadily growing *since* last summer.

_____

8. The town has been steadily growing *since* the economy has boomed.

_____

III. Write a sentence that includes at least six of the eight parts of speech. Once you have done this, can you meet the ultimate challenge, writing a sentence with all eight parts of speech included?

_____

_____

_____

_____

IV. The English language depends to a great extent upon prepositions. Can you describe where you live in a short paragraph of five to seven sentences without including any prepositions?

_____

_____

_____

_____

_____

_____

see answer key, p. 375

Basic Sentence Patterns for
Be and Linking Verbs

After completing Chapter 1, you know that one way to analyze sentences is to label each word as a part of speech. But we are now going to move beyond parsing to more useful methods of sentence analysis.

LOCATING AND LABELING ESSENTIAL SENTENCE PARTS

Not all words within a sentence are equal; while some are essential for basic meaning, others are optional. In Chapters 2 and 3 we will learn to identify essential sentence parts and to call them by terms that other grammarians would recognize.

CATEGORIZING SENTENCES ACCORDING TO BASIC PATTERNS

Grammarians of the twentieth century came to realize that the English language (indeed, all languages) could be described simply by categorizing the limited number of sentence patterns used by the speakers of the language. Although these patterns can be transformed in various ways, expanded upon, and combined, a grasp of the most basic patterns is extremely helpful. You should be aware that grammar texts may vary in the number of basic sentence patterns they describe, or in exactly how they describe the patterns. What is most important is to understand that the number of basic sentence patterns is finite, and that this foundation allows us to build more and more complex sentence structures. Chapters 2 and 3 will introduce you to ten basic patterns that will fit almost all English sentence structures. Chapter 2 will address the first five patterns, those using state of being or existence verbs. In the first three sentence patterns, the main verb is a form of *be*, while the remaining two structures contain linking verbs. In Chapter 3 we will move on to action verbs, with one sentence pattern determined by an intransitive verb and the remaining four patterns built around a transitive verb.

DIAGRAMING

A third way to analyze a sentence is to utilize a diagraming technique. Diagraming allows us to see a sentence spatially, to place each word in its appropriate place as though sentence parts were pieces of a jigsaw puzzle. In the late nineteenth century, scholars developed a number of ways to sketch out a sentence visually. Eventually the Reed-Kellogg system of diagraming, now known as traditional diagraming, became the most popular visual representation of a sentence and the only nineteenth-century system to endure to the present. Alternative methods of diagraming have since been developed. Currently a popular method is "tree diagraming" (illustrated below), in which a sentence is split into smaller and smaller branches to reflect the relationship of each branch to the rest of the "tree":

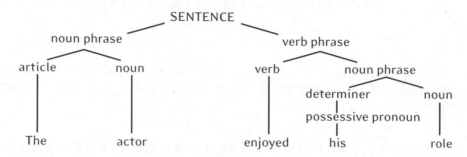

Diagraming is logical and especially helpful for visual learners, who can see the sentence in non-linear fashion, with sentence elements spatially related to one another. In addition, kinetic learners, puzzle lovers, and those with a penchant for putting things in their place typically find diagraming simultaneously challenging and satisfying. Diagraming forces us beyond rote memory of grammar definitions, beyond repetitive grammar and usage exercises, into the realm of application, where every word in a sentence must take its place in the diagram.

In this text we will concentrate on traditional diagraming. Although it does have some limitations, traditional diagraming is a sophisticated tool for sentence analysis. Manipulating individual words forces us to analyze each word as a part of speech, to isolate the essential sentence parts, and to determine the relationship of the essential sentence parts to one another. A distinct advantage of traditional diagraming is that it is the method most often used in schools. You may find it familiar, even if you had limited exposure to it as a student, and it will be helpful to prospective and practicing teachers (including parents helping children with homework) as another tool for language instruction. Even if the official curriculum does not require it, teachers and students often find that traditional diagraming is an excellent supplementary tool for understanding how sentences are constructed.

Our method in this chapter will be to integrate all three methods of sentence analysis. We begin by categorizing a sentence into its basic sentence pattern, describing its essential parts, and diagraming it. However, you do not need to follow the steps in this order for accurate sentence analysis. Many students begin by diagraming the sentence, using that as a tool for determining the essential sentence parts, and then pinning down the sentence pattern. Here, for handy reference, is an overview of the ten basic sentence patterns we will describe, along with an example for each:

1. **subject – *be* verb – adverb of time or place**
   The king is here.

2. **subject – *be* verb – predicate adjective (subjective complement)**
   The king will be generous.

3. **subject – *be* verb – predicate noun (subjective complement)**
   The king is a friend.

4. **subject – linking verb – predicate adjective (subjective complement)**
   The king seems unhappy.

5. **subject – linking verb – predicate noun (subjective complement)**
   The king became a tyrant.

6. **subject – intransitive verb**
   The king coughed.

7. **subject – transitive verb – direct object**
   The king proclaimed the news.

8. **subject – transitive verb – indirect object – direct object**
   The king gave Anne Boleyn his love.

9. **subject – transitive verb – direct object – adjective (objective complement)**
   The king considered Anne beautiful.

10. **subject – transitive verb – direct object – noun (objective complement)**
    The king considered Anne a beauty.

Notice that these formulas identify only the essential elements of a sentence. Typically, a sentence will also contain many "extras," necessary for semantic but not grammatical reasons. In other words, although "The king proclaimed the news" is an example of a Pattern 7 sentence, most sentences in English will contain many additional words that impart meaning but are not essential in terms of grammar:

> In 1534 *the king*, Henry VIII, *proclaimed* with joy *the news* of his divorce from Katherine of Aragon.

For more convenient reference, we'll use shorthand formulas for the ten basic sentence patterns. We will also break the ten patterns into two groups, with sentences built around *be* and linking verbs grouped together in this chapter, and sentences built around action verbs (intransitive and transitive) in the following chapter. Notice how the formulas below can help you see the correspondences between certain patterns. Patterns 2 and 4, and Patterns 3 and 5, are identical except for the type of verb, and Patterns 8, 9, and 10 build in different ways upon the sentence kernel of Pattern 7. Patterns 1 and 6 stand out as being different from all the others.

1. **s – *be* – adv/tp**	2. **s – *be* – pa**
3. **s – *be* – pn**	4. **s – lv – pa**
5. **s – lv – pn**	6. **s – itv**
7. **s – tv – do**	8. **s – tv – io – do**
9. **s – tv – do – adj**	10. **s – tv – do – n**

Before we begin breaking sentences into essential components, however, let's take a quick look at how **each sentence first breaks into two parts, the complete subject (what the sen-**

tence is about) and the complete predicate (what is being said about the subject). The complete subject includes the simple subject (typically a noun or pronoun) and all of its modifiers; the complete predicate includes the verb and all of its complements, objects, and modifiers. In the sentences below, a vertical line separates the complete subject from the complete predicate. The simple subject and the verb are italicized.

The *box* of tissues on the counter | *had become* soggy from the leaking roof.

No one in the room | ever *understood* a word of the teacher's lecture.

EXERCISE 2.1

Follow four steps for each sentence below:

[A] Draw a vertical line between the complete subject and the complete predicate.

[B] Circle all prepositional phrases. You will never find the simple subject or the verb of a sentence within a prepositional phrase, and so eliminating prepositional phrases will help you locate the subject and verb. Also, although exceptions do occur, usually prepositional phrases function as adjectives or adverbs that are non-essential grammatical elements.

[C] Underline the simple subject once and the verb twice.

[D] Cross out all remaining non-essential words in the sentence, leaving only those words necessary for a grammatically complete sentence conveying the basic intended meaning. (Skip this step if it seems too difficult. We will be distinguishing between essential and non-essential words as we work our way through the ten basic patterns one at a time.)

1. Photographs of children in various settings adorn the walls of the gallery.

2. I have improved my writing skills.

3. Gratitude and self-discipline are signs of maturity.

4. The people of the village were angry about the increased taxes.

5. The clerk in our office should have been aware of the growing technical difficulties of the job.

see answer key, p. 377

Once we understand that each sentence breaks into two parts, and that each part is built around a simple subject and a verb, we are ready to take a closer look at the ten basic sentence patterns.

PATTERNS 1, 2, AND 3 • THE "BE" PATTERNS

PATTERN 1:   s – *be* – adv/tp
PATTERN 2:   s – *be* – pa
PATTERN 3:   s – *be* – pn

The most important feature of the first three patterns is that they all contain the *be* verb; that is, some form of the verb *be* (am, is, are, was, were, being, been) is used as the main verb. Remember that *be* can also be used as a helping verb, but to qualify for one of these three patterns, the *be* form must come *last* in the verb phrase.

He *must be going* to a nearby college. ("Be" serves as a helping verb because the final word in the verb phrase is "going," an action verb.)

His college *must be* nearby. (Here "be" is the final word in the verb phrase and so the sentence contains a *be* verb.)

Remember that any sentence with *be* as its main verb must have some element to follow in order to complete the idea of the sentence. In Pattern 1, *be* is followed by an adverb that indicates the time or the place in which something or someone exists.

The king is *here*.

The king is *on the throne*. (Remember that a prepositional phrase can function as an adverb, so you may find a prepositional phrase, not a single-word adverb, completing the idea of the *be* verb.)

Patterns 2 and 3 complete the *be* verb with a **subjective complement** (an element that "completes" the subject by modifying or renaming it). There are **two types of subjective complements**: **predicate adjectives** and **predicate nouns** (also known as predicate nominatives). **Pattern 2 completes the idea of the sentence with a subjective complement in the form of a predicate adjective.** The adjective modifies the subject of the sentence. (If "modifies" is a confusing term for you, then replace it with "points back to" or "describes" the subject of the sentence. "Modifies" is the term preferred by linguists because it indicates that our understanding of one word is changed by the influence upon it of another word.)

The king is *happy*.

The king is *in a good mood*. (Remember that a prepositional phrase can function as an adjective, so in this pattern you may find a prepositional phrase, not a single-word adjective, completing the idea of the *be* verb.)

Pattern 3 completes the idea of the sentence with a subjective complement in the form of a predicate noun. The predicate noun *renames* the subject of the sentence.

The king is *Henry VIII*.

EXERCISE 2.2

See if you can determine whether the following sentences follow Pattern 1 (s – *be* – adv/tp), Pattern 2 (s – *be* – pa), or Pattern 3 (s – *be* – pn). To locate the subject and verb, it will help if you circle prepositional phrases first. **You will never find a subject or verb of a sentence inside a prepositional phrase**. At the same time, remember that a prepositional phrase *can* serve as an adverb or a predicate adjective to complete the idea of the *be* verb.

1. The stapler is on the desk. _____
2. My cat is a lover of tuna. _____
3. The music is extremely loud. _____
4. The graduation party is today. _____
5. That child is being unreasonable. _____
6. Her favorite picture from the vacation in Florida is a snapshot of a playful dolphin. _____
7. In her wallet are photos from the vacation in Florida. _____

see answer key, p. 377

Now let's consider how to diagram the first three sentence patterns. Every diagram begins with a base line, split in two, that contains the simple subject and verb of the sentence.

subject	verb

The complete subject (the subject and all of its modifiers) is then diagramed on the left side of the dividing line, while the complete predicate (the verb and all of its modifiers) is diagramed on the right.

Pattern 1 ● subject – be *verb* – adverb of time or place (s – be – adv/tp)

The adverb that completes the idea of the *be* verb is diagramed beneath the verb.

Pattern 2 ● subject – be *verb – subjective complement: predicate adjective*
(s – be – pa)

The predicate adjective is diagramed on the base line, with a diagonal or back slash line before it to indicate that the adjective points back to (modifies) the subject. It might help to think of this slash line as an arrow referring back to the subject, or as the curve of a circle showing the close relationship between the subject and the subjective complement. We can use this "circle test" to confirm that what follows the verb is a subjective complement.

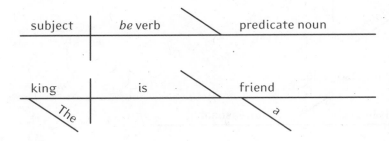

Pattern 3 ● subject – be *verb – subjective complement: predicate noun (s – be – pn)*

The predicate noun is also diagramed on the base line, with a diagonal or back slash line before it to indicate that the noun renames the subject. Again, think of the slash line as an arrow pointing back to the subject, or as the curve of a circle drawing together the predicate noun and the subject (the "circle test" once more).

Modifiers (adjectives, adverbs, prepositional phrases serving as adjectives and adverbs) are diagramed on diagonal lines beneath the words they modify. Remember that because adverbs are often movable, you must diagram them beneath the word(s) they modify, no matter where they appear in the sentence. If you can move an adverb without changing the meaning of the sentence, diagram the adverb beneath the verb. Prepositional phrases are diagramed as units in structures that place the preposition on a diagonal line, with the object of the preposition on an adjoining horizontal line and modifiers beneath the horizontal line. Frequently prepositional phrases occur in chains, with the result that one prepositional phrase may be diagramed beneath another. This happens when the second prepositional phrase modifies the object of the first prepositional phrase, as in the final sentence in this exercise ("the vacation in Florida"). Here are complete diagrams for the sentences above, in Exercise 2.2:

1. The stapler is on the desk.

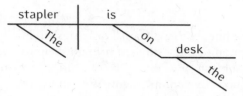

2. My cat is a lover of tuna.

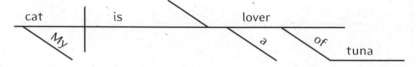

3. The music is extremely loud.

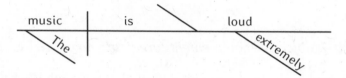

4. The graduation party is today.

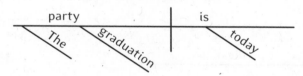

5. That child is being unreasonable.

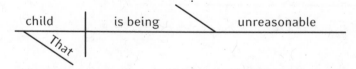

6. Her favorite picture from the vacation in Florida is a snapshot of a playful dolphin.

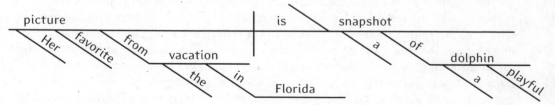

7. In her wallet are photos from the vacation in Florida.

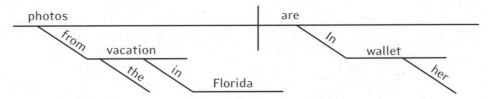

There is one problem. What happens when the predicate adjective is in the form of a prepositional phrase? How can a prepositional phrase fit on the base line? In this case, we use a "pedestal" or "tower" to accommodate the prepositional phrase structure. Let's compare the two sentences below, which have the same basic meaning but use two different structures. The first sentence is completed by a single-word adjective; the second sentence is completed by a prepositional phrase used as an adjective.

The king is *happy*.

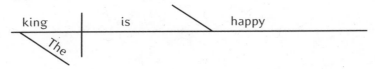

The king is *in a good mood*.

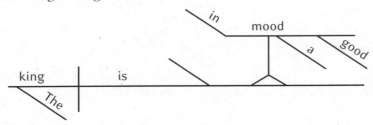

Remember that you will need a pedestal only when the prepositional phrase is the predicate adjective—in other words, when it is essential for the grammatical sense of the sentence—and when the prepositional phrase takes the place of what would normally be a single-word adjective on the base line of the diagram. If the prepositional phrase is an adverb, it is diagramed beneath the verb. If it is a non-essential adjective, one that can be omitted without harming sentence completeness, then diagram the prepositional phrase beneath the word it modifies.

The king is *on the throne*. (adverb in a Pattern 1 sentence)

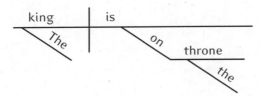

The king *on the throne* is Henry VIII. (non-essential modifier of "king" in a Pattern 3 sentence)

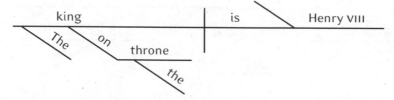

The king is *out of breath*. (predicate adjective in a Pattern 2 sentence because these words would not form a sentence without the prepositional phrase; also, "out of breath" can be replaced by the single-word predicate adjective "breathless")

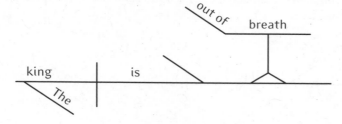

EXERCISE 2.3

For the sentences below, identify the sentence pattern as Pattern 1, 2, or 3, and then diagram each sentence.

1. The bread on the table is stale.

2. The officers at the academy should be strict.

3. The officers at the academy should be strict disciplinarians.

4. Our professor must have been a genius in her youth.

5. The car is in the garage.

6. The car is in good condition.

see answer key, p. 377

PATTERNS 4 AND 5 ● THE "LINKING VERB" PATTERNS

A linking verb is a verb that can be replaced by a *be* verb. Some textbooks subsume the *be* verb under the linking verb category because all of these verbs act in the same way, to join the subject to another element that follows the verb. Remember from Chapter 1 that linking verbs include verbs of sense (*look, sound, feel, taste, smell*) and verbs such as *become, appear, remain, grow, stay, seem*. Remember also that some of these verbs can function as action verbs, so you must determine if you can use *be* as a replacement before labeling a word as a linking verb.

> The king *looks* unhappy. (In this sentence, "looks" is a linking verb because no action is taking place and you can replace it with "is"—The king is unhappy.)

> The king *looks* with disdain at the court. (In this sentence, "looks" is an action verb and cannot be replaced with "is.")

The two linking verb patterns are identical, except that the form of the subjective complement differs. Pattern 4 ends with a predicate adjective, while Pattern 5 ends with a predicate noun. Remember that this was the only distinction between Patterns 2 and 3 also. Thus Pattern 2 and Pattern 4 are identical, except that Pattern 2 uses a *be* verb and Pattern 4 uses a linking verb. Pattern 3 and Pattern 5 are identical, except that Pattern 3 uses a *be* verb and Pattern 5 uses a linking verb. All of these patterns are diagramed identically, since in the diagram no distinction is made between an adjective or a noun used as a subjective complement:

$$\text{subject} \mid \textit{be} \text{ or linking verb} \diagdown \text{subjective complement}$$

(either a predicate adjective or predicate noun)

Pattern 4 ● subject – linking verb – predicate adjective/subjective complement (s – lv – pa)

The king seems unhappy.

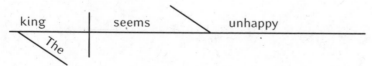

As in Pattern 2, a Pattern 4 sentence can end with a prepositional phrase that acts as the predicate adjective. When this happens, the predicate adjective must be diagramed on a pedestal. Remember that a pedestal is required only when the prepositional phrase is necessary to complete the sentence and that the prepositional phrase can usually be replaced by a single-word adjective modifying the subject.

The king seems *out of sorts*. (The prepositional phrase must be diagramed on a pedestal because it is essential to complete the sentence and can be replaced by a single-word adjective such as "upset" or "angry.")

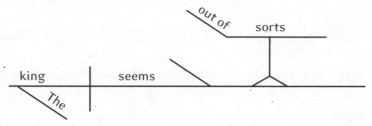

Pattern 5 ● subject – linking verb – predicate noun/subjective complement (s – lv – pn)

Pattern 5 is diagramed exactly as Patterns 2, 3, and 4.

The king became a tyrant.

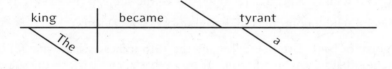

SUMMARY OF KEY CONCEPTS IN CHAPTER 2

1. Each sentence can be broken into two large components, the complete subject and the complete predicate.

2. The verb is the most important element of the sentence in terms of distinguishing its sentence pattern.

3. When a form of the *be* verb acts as the main verb of a sentence, three sentence patterns are possible:

  a. The sentence may end with an adverb of time or place. (PATTERN 1)

  b. The sentence may end with an adjective relating back to the subject. (PATTERN 2)

  c. The sentence may end with a noun renaming the subject. (PATTERN 3)

4. We can identify a linking verb by replacing it with a form of the *be* verb without substantially changing the sense of the sentence. When a linking verb acts as the main verb of a sentence, two sentence patterns are possible:

  a. The sentence may end with an adjective relating back to the subject. (PATTERN 4)

  b. The sentence may end with a noun renaming the subject. (PATTERN 5)

5. In the diagram, a diagonal or back slash line following the verb indicates that what follows is a subjective complement—that is, it is an adjective or noun that relates back to the subject. The diagonal line can be seen as an arrow pointing back to the subject or as the curve of a circle drawing the subject and subjective complement together.

6. In Patterns 2 and 4, use a pedestal when a prepositional phrase acts as the subjective complement (when it is necessary to complete the sentence and can be replaced by a single-word adjective that would ordinarily be placed on the base line).

CHAPTER 2 EXERCISE

I. Follow these steps for the sentences below:

[A] Circle all prepositional phrases.

[B] Underline the simple subject once and the verb twice.

[C] Identify the verb as a *be* verb or a linking verb.

[D] Determine the sentence pattern number of the sentence. If the sentence contains a *be* verb, it falls into a Pattern 1, 2, or 3 sentence; if it contains a linking verb, it must be a Pattern 4 or 5 sentence:

PATTERN 1: s – *be* – adv/tp	PATTERN 2: s – *be* – pa
PATTERN 3: s – *be* – pn	PATTERN 4: s – lv – pa
PATTERN 5: s – lv – pn	

[E] Diagram the sentence.

1. The party is here.

2. The computer on the desk was new.

3. The computer was on the desk.

4. The farewell present should have been John's idea.

5. The new perfume smelled delightful.

6. Flies are a nuisance during a picnic.

7. Candy can be harmful in large quantities.

8. Our business venture gradually became an embarrassment.

9. The pink slipper was under the bed.

10. After ten minutes, Theresa's face grew red with impatience.

II. Answer the questions below.

a. What is the only difference between a Pattern 2 and a Pattern 3 sentence?

_____

_____

_____

b. What is the only difference between a Pattern 2 and a Pattern 4 sentence, or between a Pattern 3 and a Pattern 5 sentence?

_____

_____

_____

c. What does the back slash mark in Patterns 2 through 5 indicate in the sentence diagram?

_____

_____

_____

d. How can you determine if a prepositional phrase should be diagramed on a pedestal? At this point, which two sentence patterns might have diagrams containing a pedestal?

_____

_____

_____

e. How can you test for a linking verb?

_____

_____

_____

see answer key, p. 378

Basic Sentence Patterns for Intransitive and Transitive Verbs

In Chapter 2 we discussed the basic sentence patterns built around state of being verbs and thus containing either a *be* or a linking verb. In this chapter we will examine the remaining five basic sentence patterns: those built around action verbs, both intransitive and transitive. Remember that an intransitive verb is *not* followed by an object (noun or pronoun) that "receives" the action of the subject. A transitive verb, on the other hand, *is* followed by an object. Observe the difference in the sentences below:

The baby *kicked*. (intransitive verb)

The baby *kicked* the blanket. (transitive verb because "blanket" is the object of the verb)

PATTERN 6 ◉ THE INTRANSITIVE VERB PATTERN

subject – intransitive verb (s – itv)

Pattern 6 provides us with a relatively simple diagram structure, since the only two essential elements in this pattern are the simple subject and the simple verb:

The king coughed.

Typically, of course, a Pattern 6 sentence will contain non-essential elements as well, as in the sentence below. Remember that it is helpful to circle prepositional phrases in order to clear away structures that obscure the simple subject and simple verb.

At the first mention of the scandal, the king coughed discreetly as a signal to his councilors.

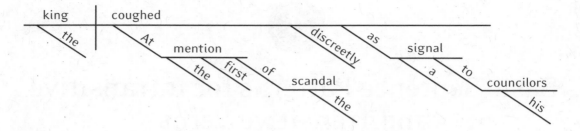

PATTERNS 7, 8, 9, AND 10 ● THE TRANSITIVE VERB PATTERNS

Pattern 7 ● subject – transitive verb – direct object (s – tv – do)

Pattern 7 constitutes the basic transitive verb pattern. Patterns 8, 9, and 10 are built from Pattern 7. In the following Pattern 7 sentence, notice that the verb is followed by an object, known as a **direct object** because it **answers the question "whom" or "what" after the verb.**

> The king proclaimed the *news* of his divorce.
> TEST: The king proclaimed what? He proclaimed "the news of his divorce," and so the direct object is "news." Notice that "divorce" is inside a prepositional phrase and therefore cannot be the direct object.

A Pattern 7 diagram looks like this:

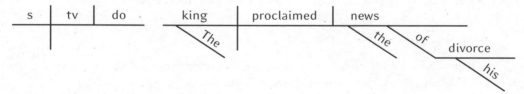

Notice that the straight line between the verb and direct object indicates that the subject and object have no direct relation but are two distinctly different entities. The back slash line that slants back to the subject in Patterns 2 to 5, on the other hand, indicates a relationship between the subject and the subjective complement (whether predicate adjective or predicate noun). The following sentences illustrate the differences between a predicate noun and a direct object. To make the comparison clearer, only the essential elements have been diagramed.

> Henry VIII became an enemy of Catholics.

Henry VIII	became \ enemy

Henry VIII banished Catholicism from England.

Henry VIII	banished	Catholicism

In the first sentence, "became" is a linking verb (it can be replaced by "was"), leading to the predicate nominative "enemy." Since "Henry VIII" and "enemy" are two terms that refer to the same person, we can visualize their relationship as a circular one. On the other hand, in the second sentence "banished" is an action verb because it cannot be replaced by "was." When we ask, "Henry VIII banished what?", we find the direct object, "Catholicism." If we apply the "circle test" as in the previous sentence, we find that it will not work here. "Henry VIII" and "Catholicism" are not two terms for the same person but two different entities altogether. Thus in the diagram, the vertical line between the verb and direct object shows that there is a wall, as it were, separating the subject from the object:

Henry VIII	Catholicism

Pattern 8 ● subject – transitive verb – indirect object – direct object (s – tv – io – do)

Pattern 8 is distinctive because it has two objects following the verb: s – tv – io – do. The first object, the indirect object, is followed by the direct object. Note that in Pattern 8, the subject, direct object, and indirect object are three separate, distinct entities.

The king gave *Anne Boleyn* his *love*.

When analyzing this sentence, remember to ask "whom" or "what" to find the direct object.

The king gave ____? He didn't give Anne Boleyn; he gave his love. "Love" is therefore the direct object.

The **indirect object answers one of six questions: to whom? for whom? of whom? to what? for what? of what?** For this sentence, we would ask the following: The king gave his love *to whom*? Since we find the answer "Anne Boleyn," this sentence contains an indirect object. The indirect object is a short way of expressing a prepositional phrase, and therefore the diagram treats the indirect object as a prepositional phrase that is always placed under the verb:

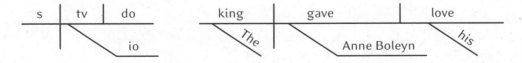

Notice the difference in the sentence pattern number for the following two sentences, then. Although the underlying meaning is the same, and the diagrams are almost identical, the surface grammatical structures are different:

The king gave *Anne Boleyn* his love. (PATTERN 8, with indirect object)

The king gave his love *to Anne Boleyn*. (PATTERN 7, with prepositional phrase)

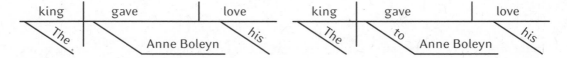

Many grammar texts would identify both sentences above as Pattern 8. This is a logical, accurate way of indicating that the sentences are identical in every way except for structure; the only difference is that in one sentence (PATTERN 8) the indirect object stands on its own, while in the other (PATTERN 7) the indirect object is contained within a prepositional phrase and therefore functions also as the object of the preposition. Not every prepositional phrase that begins with "to," "for," or "of" will function as an indirect object, however. To contain an indirect object, a sentence must express the notion of giving or offering something. Thus in both "The king gave Anne Boleyn his love" and "The king gave his love to Anne Boleyn," we can think of "Anne Boleyn" as an indirect object, while in "The king nodded his head to Anne Boleyn," there is no indirect object. This text makes an admittedly artificial distinction, labeling as Pattern 8 only those sentences with a freestanding indirect object, in an effort to avoid confusing those who may have difficulty recognizing indirect objects occurring within prepositional phrases.

EXERCISE 3.1

Determine the sentence pattern number (PATTERN 6–8) and diagram each sentence below.

1. We are studying.

2. We are studying grammar.

3. The energetic children ran around the block.

4. The manager handed everyone a cash bonus.

5. The nurse spilled the medicine.

6. Knowledge can give us power.

7. No one in that family can sit still for five minutes.

8. The reporter asked the politician many intrusive questions about her personal habits.

see answer key, p. 380

EXERCISE 3.2

A. This exercise will help you to understand how the first eight patterns compare with one another. The sentences below illustrate, in order, Patterns 1 through 8. Your job is to diagram the sentences and to observe the differences that make each one distinct. Note that in each case the subject is exactly the same; only the verb and what follows the verb will determine the basic pattern of any sentence.

1. Our walk on the beach was yesterday.

2. Our walk on the beach was short.

3. Our walk on the beach was an interesting experience.

4. Our walk on the beach seemed interminable.

5. Our walk on the beach became a comedy of errors.

6. Our walk on the beach ended abruptly with the onset of lightning.

7. Our walk on the beach saved us from boredom.

8. Our walk on the beach gave us a new sense of freedom.

B. Looking at these sentences and your diagrams, can you answer the following questions? Remember that the eight sentences above correspond in order to the eight sentence patterns.

1. Since the first three sentences contain the same simple subject and the same simple verb, what is the difference between Patterns 1, 2, and 3?

_____

_____

_____

2. What does the slanted line in the diagrams for Patterns 2, 3, 4, and 5 indicate?

_____

_____

_____

3. What is the only difference between Patterns 2 and 4, and Patterns 3 and 5?

_____

_____

_____

4. What is the only difference between Patterns 2 and 3?

_____

_____

_____

5. What is the only difference between Patterns 4 and 5?

_____

_____

_____

6. What is the test for a linking verb?

_____

_____

_____

7. What are the two possible categories of action verbs?

_____

_____

_____

8. How can you determine if a verb is intransitive or transitive?

_____

_____

_____

9. What is the basic difference between Patterns 6 and 7?

_____

_____

_____

10. What question is answered by a direct object? What question is answered by an indirect object?

_____

_____

_____

11. In Patterns 7 and 8, what is the significance of the vertical line between the verb and the direct object? What is the symbolic difference between a diagonal line and a vertical line after the verb in any sentence diagram?

_____

_____

_____

12. Where is the indirect object always diagramed?

_____

_____

_____

13. In English sentences that contain both a direct and an indirect object, which object occurs first in almost every instance?

_____

_____

_____

14. From Patterns 1–8, which two sentence patterns could possibly include a prepositional phrase placed on a pedestal? Why is there no need for a pedestal in the sentences given in this exercise?

_____

_____

_____

see answer key, p. 380

EXERCISE 3.3

As a final test of your understanding thus far, determine the sentence pattern (PATTERNS 1–8) and diagram each sentence below. This time the sentence patterns are in random order.

1. The music at the concert sounded too loud.

2. The karate students bowed respectfully to the sensei.

3. All of the teachers have submitted their lesson plans.

4. The mysterious stranger handed the young woman a large envelope.

5. A ferocious dog was in the yard.

6. Our visitor was a lecturer from Princeton University.

7. Nora has been angry with us for three days.

8. Your early childhood will seem a dim memory within twenty years.

9. The machine on the third floor is out of order.

10. Despite her misery, Santina maintained the appearance of a contented life.

see answer key, p. 382

Patterns 9 and 10 are comparatively rare in English and contain a sentence element known as an **objective complement—an adjective or a noun that modifies or renames, respectively, the direct object.** The objective complement is necessary in order to complete the idea of the sentence; in addition, a simple test to identify an objective complement is to insert "to be" between the direct object and the complement.

Pattern 9 ● subject - transitive verb - direct object - objective complement: adjective (s - tv - do - adj)

The following sentence illustrates Pattern 9:

The king considered Anne beautiful.

The king considered whom? "Anne" is the direct object. But if the sentence stopped here, it would sound as if the king were polite, not the same meaning as the original sentence intends. "Beautiful," the objective complement, is necessary in order to complete the intended meaning. In addition, "beautiful" modifies "Anne," and, as a final test, it is possible to read this sentence as "The king considered Anne [to be] beautiful." The diagram for this sentence indicates the importance of the objective complement and its relation to the direct object:

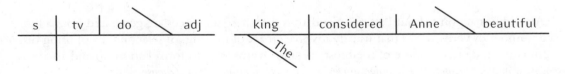

Notice that although "beautiful" is an adjective, it does not precede the noun it modifies as a normal adjective would. The fact that it follows the noun marks it as a special sentence element, and thus it is diagramed on the base line of the diagram rather than underneath as a normal modifier would be. In addition, note that the diagonal or back slash line between the direct object and the objective complement indicates the relationship between these two elements. **Just as the subjective complement in Patterns 2–5 points back to the subject, so the objective complement points back to the direct object.** The slanted line in the diagram acts as an arrow to indicate this relationship, or you might prefer to think of it as the curve of the circle unit-ing the direct object and its complement. The "circle test" we used earlier works with the objec-tive complement as well. It is clear that "the king" and "Anne" are two entirely different individuals; therefore, "king" cannot be included in this circle:

king   (Anne   beautiful)

Pattern 10: subject – transitive verb – direct object – objective complement: noun (s – tv – do – n)

Pattern 10, s – tv – do – n, is identical to Pattern 9 except that the objective complement is a noun that renames the direct object rather than an adjective as in Pattern 9:

> The king considered Anne a beauty.

Once again, "Anne" is the direct object, but the sentence cannot end here and still retain its intended meaning. "A beauty" is necessary to complete the idea of the sentence and is a noun that renames "Anne." In addition, it can be joined to the rest of the sentence by "to be":

> The king considered Anne [to be] a beauty.

"Beauty," therefore, is a noun used as an objective complement. Pattern 10 is diagramed just the same as Pattern 9, with the diagonal line indicating that the complement harks back to the direct object. As before, remember that you can think of the diagonal line as an arrow point-ing back to the object or as the curve of the circle uniting the objective complement and the direct object. "King" is clearly not part of this circle:

king   (Anne   beauty)

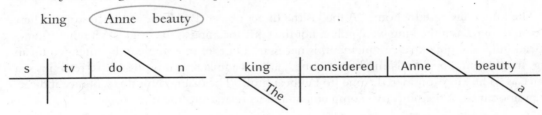

An additional point about Patterns 9 and 10 is that these sentences are generated from a lim-ited number of verbs, verbs that usually involve an act of making, of selecting, or of using dis-criminating judgment. Some of the most common verbs used to form Patterns 9 and 10 are as follows: *make, consider, think, judge, prefer, select, elect, nominate, vote, choose.*

You may be tempted to confuse Pattern 8 and Pattern 10 sentences because both patterns contain three noun slots. Both patterns contain a subject and a direct object; however, Pattern 8 contains an indirect object (different from the noun and direct object), whereas Pattern 10 contains an objective complement (a noun that renames the direct object). Note the difference in the sentences below.

PATTERN 8:   The king offered Anne Boleyn a crown.

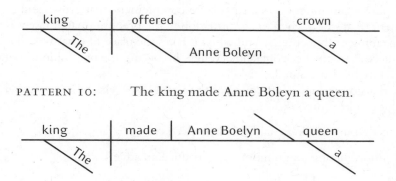

PATTERN 10:   The king made Anne Boleyn a queen.

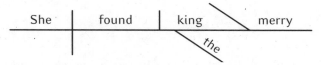

SPECIAL STRUCTURES

Now let's take a look at two structures that could arise in Patterns 9 and 10 to cause you some difficulty. **Remember that in Patterns 2 and 4, a prepositional phrase, rather than a single-word adjective, can function as a predicate adjective (or, to use the more general term, a subjective complement). In Pattern 9 as well, a prepositional phrase can function as an objective complement.** Let's look at two versions of the same sentence, the first with a single-word objective complement and the second with a prepositional phrase as an objective complement. Remember that the objective complement must meet two tests: it must complete the meaning of the sentence and must modify or rename the direct object. In addition, **we can normally insert "to be" between the direct object and the objective complement without changing the meaning of the sentence.**

> She found the king *merry*.
> ("Merry" modifies "king" and completes the sentence. Finally, we can insert "to be": "She found the king to be merry.")

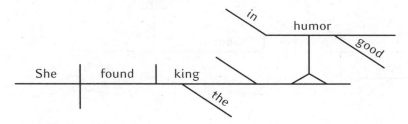

> She found the king in *good humor*.
> (Although it is a prepositional phrase, "in good humor" modifies "king" and completes the sentence, and "She found the king to be in good humor" confirms that the prepositional phrase is an objective complement.)

Thus a prepositional phrase can function as a subjective complement (Patterns 2 and 4) or as an objective complement (Pattern 9) when the information in the prepositional phrase is necessary to complete the meaning of the sentence and when it takes the place of what would normally be a single-word adjective on the horizontal line. When this occurs, the prepositional phrase is diagramed on the base line by using a pedestal.

The second difficulty that sometimes arises concerns the word "as," which has a number of functions. For example, it can be a preposition:

> *As* a tailor, he succeeded in building a faithful clientele.

"As" also functions as a subordinating conjunction to introduce an adverb clause:

> *As* the tailor steadily improved his skills, he built up a faithful clientele.

Finally, "as" can function in Pattern 10 (and, more rarely, in Pattern 9) as an **expletive**, a word that contributes nothing to the meaning or the required structure of the sentence but remains as an idiomatic expression:

> The citizens of our town elected Shannon *as* mayor.

In this sentence, "mayor" meets all the requirements for an objective complement. "Shannon" and "mayor" are two different words referring to the same person, and if we delete "as," we can insert "to be" for a logical sentence: The citizens of our town elected Shannon [to be] mayor. Thus this sentence meets the requirements for a Pattern 10 sentence, with "mayor" as the objective complement. To diagram this sentence, we place the expletive "as" above the base line, but connected to it by a dotted line, to show its basic irrelevance to the meaning and structure of the sentence:

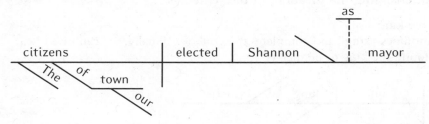

Note, though, that it is not always possible to delete "as" in a Pattern 10 sentence and retain an idiomatic flow. In "The citizens of our town accepted Shannon as mayor," the expletive cannot be omitted. Likewise, many Pattern 10 sentences cannot incorporate "as": "The citizens of our town thought Shannon an excellent candidate for mayor."

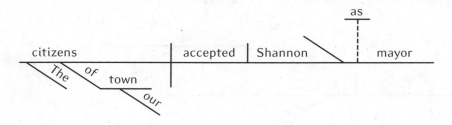

```
  citizens        |  thought | Shannon \ candidate
 The   of                                   an   excellent   for  mayor
          town
              our
```

EXERCISE 3.4

Write the sentence pattern numbers (PATTERNS 6–10) and diagram the following sentences.

1. Every neighbor on the block has been coming to our meetings.

2. The alumni group awarded Jason a plaque for his generous donation.

3. The committee selected the budget as its top priority for the year.

4. My family has always welcomed strangers.

5. Reporters consider accuracy essential.

6. Before her trip to the zoo, Paige had never seen a giraffe.

7. We found the bakery out of food.

8. The company's statistician blasted the report as faulty.

see answer key, p. 383

Now that we've seen the last five sentence patterns, those that contain an action verb, let's look at one more variation on the verb itself. We know already that a verb can be a single word or a verb phrase (a verb with helping or auxiliary verbs preceding it):

The king *slept*.

The king *has been sleeping* all day.

Occasionally, in English we encounter a structure known as a **phrasal verb**, an action verb followed by what appears to be a preposition (known as a particle). Together, the verb and particle constitute an **idiom**, a phrase that means something very different from what it would mean if the words were taken separately rather than as a unit. Consider the phrasal verb "turn on," for example. If you directed someone to "Turn on the television" and that person took you literally, he or she would climb on top of the television and begin to spin. Luckily, native speakers of English understand that "turn on" in this sentence means to manipulate the necessary knobs or buttons to generate electricity so that the TV will work. Those who are learning English as a foreign language, however, often have difficulty figuring out our idiomatic expressions, many of which involve the phrasal verb structure.

Let's look again at a single-word verb, verb phrase, and now a phrasal verb as well:

The king *turned*.

The king *has been turning* the pages of the book.

The king *turned in* late. (Here, "turned in" is a phrasal verb or idiom meaning "went to bed." Notice how "turn" can be used for many phrasal verbs, such as "The king turned out—or turned on, or turned off—the lights," "The king turned up at last," "The king turned down the offer.")

Sometimes what appears to be a phrasal verb is merely a verb followed by a prepositional phrase. Remember that, **to test for a phrasal verb, you must ascertain if the meaning of the phrase changes substantially compared to the meaning of the individual words taken separately. In addition, the verb and the particle of the phrasal verb can usually be separated by the direct object with no resulting change in meaning. Finally, phrasal verbs often have single-word equivalents.**

He *looked* up the alley. (verb + preposition)

*He looked the alley up. (Because "up" is a preposition, not a particle, it cannot be placed behind its object but must precede "the alley.")

He *looked up* the word. (phrasal verb; "looked up" = "researched")

He *looked* the word *up*. (Because "up" is a particle, it can be separated from the verb to follow the direct object. Note that, although it may appear that this sentence ends with a preposition, it actually ends with a particle.)

The teacher *passed* out of sight. (verb + preposition)

The teacher *passed out* our papers. (phrasal verb; "passed out" = "distributed"; sentence can be rephrased to "The teacher passed our papers out.")

The teacher *passed out*. (phrasal verb; "passed out" = "fainted")

Let's look at the difference in the way we would diagram the first pair of sentences. Notice that the particle is diagramed as part of the verb when the sentence contains a phrasal verb.

He looked up the alley.

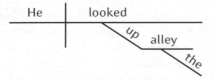

He looked up the word.   OR   He looked the word up.

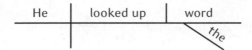

EXERCISE 3.5

Diagram each sentence below in order to demonstrate whether the verb is a verb phrase (one or more auxiliaries + main verb) or a phrasal verb (verb + particle). Indicate the pattern number of each sentence as well.

1. After three hours, they finally made up.

2. The students in the crafts class have made some impressive pieces.

3. The antique car drove up the alley.

4. Demand for housing has driven up the market value of homes.

5. The burglar kicked in the side door.

see answer key, p. 384

Another problem can arise if you encounter or write a sentence containing a **reflexive pronoun** (a pronoun that ends with the suffix "-self" or "-selves"). You might become confused about whether the reflexive pronoun is an object or a complement:

The king saw himself.

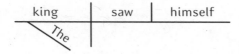

Here, the verb appears to be an action verb—a transitive verb because it is followed by a direct object—but the direct object refers back to the subject, as a subjective complement would do. Is "himself" a direct object or a subjective complement, then? The answer lies with the verb, the key element of any sentence. Since "saw" is not part of the *be* verb (and since, if you considered it a linking verb and tried to replace it with *be*, the meaning of the sentence would change), "himself" is a direct object. Reflexive pronouns that serve as objects might confuse you because they automatically refer back to the subject, but remember that a subjective complement can follow only the *be* verb or a linking verb. Thus the sentence would be diagramed as a Pattern 7, despite the fact that "king" and "himself" refer to the same individual.

For reflexive pronouns, then, we make an exception to the general rule that an object cannot refer back to the subject. The following two sentences illustrate that it is the category of the verb, not the nature of the direct object, that determines the sentence pattern.

She seems herself now.   She likes herself now.
(PATTERN 5)   (PATTERN 7)

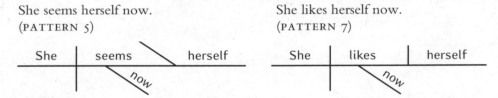

EXERCISE 3.6

Determine the pattern number and then diagram each sentence below.

1. Michael cut the bread with a sharp knife.

2. Michael cut himself with a sharp knife.

3. Michael is not himself in the morning.

see answer key, p. 384

Finally, let's consider two common diagraming situations that require a specialized structure. The first involves a word typically used as a noun but functioning within a sentence as an adverb. In this situation we label the noun an **adverbial objective**, a technical term that indicates its function (adverbial) but also its form (since "object" implies noun). Because in the traditional diagram nouns are placed on horizontal lines, the adverbial objective is also placed on a horizontal line, necessitating what looks like a prepositional phrase structure. Indeed, in many cases you can insert a preposition and the sentence will make perfect sense. When the prepositional phrase that you build functions as an adverb, you know that the noun on its own is an adverbial objective.

I am going to the zoo [on] Friday.

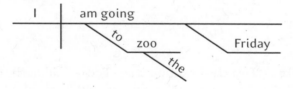

Corinne worked [for] three hours.

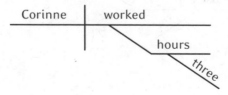

Consider the following sentence, however, which cannot make use of a preposition:

We walked home.

Although "home" looks like a direct object, it isn't. If we ask, "We walked what?" it becomes clear that "home" does not tell *what*, but *where* we walked. As an adverb, then, it should be diagramed beneath the base line, but it is not the usual adverb. Since "home" is typically a noun, but in this sentence functions as an adverb, it is an adverbial objective. Compare the difference between an adverbial objective, a prepositional phrase used as an adverb, and a single-word adverb in the sentences below.

We walked home. We walked out the door. We walked out.

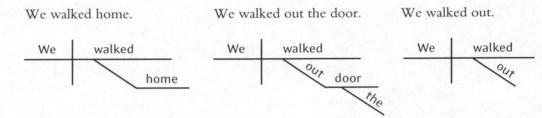

Here are a few other sentences to illustrate the adverbial objective:

Beth awakes at the same time every morning. ("Morning" explains *when*.)

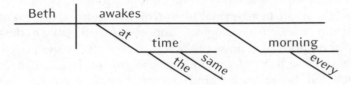

The turtle swam five miles. ("Miles" explains *where, how far.*)

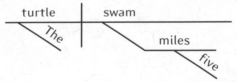

Today we mailed the package first class. ("First class" explains *how*. "Today," although it contains the noun "day" as a word part, is not an adverbial objective but an adverb.)

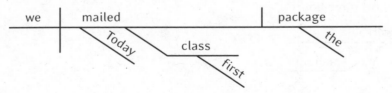

EXERCISE 3.7

In the sentences below, determine if the italicized words are being used as nouns or as adverbial objectives. Determine the pattern number and diagram each sentence.

1. *October* is my favorite month.

2. Last *October* I celebrated an important birthday.

3. Sheryl must visit the dentist three *times* next *year*.

4. An astrologer must know the *time* of your birth.

see answer key, p. 384

The second specialized structure you may need in diagraming occurs when one modifier is attached to another modifier, both diagramed below the base line on diagonal lines. This situation occurs when the second modifier is preceded by a possessive or by a qualifier, an adverb that qualifies an adjective or another adverb (as in "*somewhat* slow" or "*rather* quickly") or intensifies it (as in "*extremely* thin" or "*very* smoothly"). We use a "hook" in the diagram to show the exact relationship between the modifiers, as shown below.

My uncle's book made him a celebrity. (We cannot diagram "my" directly under "book" because the sentence is not about "*my* book" but "*my uncle's* book.")

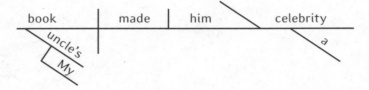

The team played very competitively. (We cannot diagram "very" under "played." The team did not play "*very*" but "*very competitively.*")

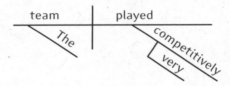

The surgeon performed the extremely delicate operation. (The operation is not "*extremely*" but "*extremely delicate.*")

EXERCISE 3.8

Identify the pattern number and diagram the sentences below, paying special attention to adverbial objectives and qualifiers.

1. Last night Sheena walked home quite rapidly in the rain.

2. A profusion of intensely bright flowers surrounds the cottage each spring.

3. A bad movie can seem excruciatingly slow.

4. His keenly insightful comments will influence our decisions next year.

see answer key, p. 385

SUMMARY OF KEY CONCEPTS IN CHAPTER 3

1. Action verbs fall into two categories, intransitive and transitive.

   a. INTRANSITIVE VERB = no direct object following the verb (PATTERN 6)

   b. TRANSITIVE VERB = direct object follows the verb (PATTERNS 7, 8, 9, and 10)

2. Three sentence patterns build on Pattern 7.

   a. PATTERN 8 = indirect object precedes the direct object
   (Note that Pattern 8 is the only pattern with three noun slots—subject, indirect object, and direct object, in that order—designating three separate entities. Remember to diagram the indirect object on a prepositional phrase structure beneath the verb.)

   b. PATTERNS 9 and 10 contain objective complements. Pattern 9 ends with an adjective that modifies the direct object; Pattern 10 ends with a noun that renames the direct object.
   Remember that only verbs of making, selecting, or using discriminating judgment can lead to objective complements.

3. An objective complement must pass at least the first two of the following three tests:

   a. It must be necessary to complete the intended meaning of the sentence.

   b. It must modify or rename the direct object. (Remember the "circle test.")

   c. In most cases you will be able to insert "to be" between the direct object and the objective complement without changing the sense of the sentence.

4. Distinguish between complements and objects.

   a. A subjective complement is an adjective or a noun (or pronoun) following a *be* or linking verb. Use a diagonal or back slash line in the diagram to indicate that the subjective complement relates back to the subject. (Think of the diagonal line as an arrow or as the curve of a circle.)

   b. An objective complement is an adjective or a noun (or pronoun) following a direct object. Use a diagonal or back slash line in the diagram to indicate that the objective complement relates back to the object. (Think of the diagonal line as an arrow or as the curve of a circle.)

   c. A direct object is a noun or pronoun following the action verb in a sentence. It answers the question "whom" or "what" after the verb. The straight line that separates the direct object from the verb is a wall indicating that there is no modifying or identifying relationship between the subject and the direct object; they are two entirely distinct entities.

   d. An indirect object is a noun or pronoun tucked between the transitive verb and the direct object. As a shortened form of a prepositional phrase, it answers one of the following questions: to whom? for whom? of whom? to what? for what? of what? The indirect object is diagramed beneath the verb on a prepositional phrase structure.

5. We have learned several specialized structures:

   a. The expletive "as" in a Pattern 10 (or, less frequently, a Pattern 9) sentence is diagramed above the base line with a dotted line extending to the spot before the objective complement.

   b. A qualifier is diagramed on a "hook" attached to the adjective or adverb it modifies when the adjective or adverb is diagramed on a diagonal line beneath the base line.

   c. The adverbial objective (a word that is typically a noun but functioning as an adverb in a particular sentence) is diagramed on a prepositional phrase structure beneath the verb.

   d. A phrasal verb consists of a verb and a particle (a preposition in appearance) that act as a unit to make up an idiomatic expression. Both the verb and the particle appear on the base line in the verb slot of the diagram.

   e. The pedestal can be used in Patterns 2, 4, and 9 when a prepositional phrase is taking the place of what would normally be a single-word adjective on the base line.

   f. Treat reflexive pronouns as objects, not complements, when they follow a transitive verb.

CHAPTER 3 EXERCISE

I. Write a sentence that conforms to each of the ten basic sentence patterns.

_____

_____

_____

_____

_____

_____

_____

_____

_____

_____

_____

_____

_____

_____

_____

_____

_____

_____

_____

_____

_____

_____

_____

_____

_____

_____

_____

II. Determine the sentence pattern number for each of the following sentences, and then diagram each sentence.

1. Shakespeare's early life is obscure.

2. Few documents with his name have turned up.

3. Biographers find his relationship with Anne Hathaway especially intriguing.

4. Shakespeare married Anne Hathaway in 1582.

5. Their first child arrived within six months.

6. Later Anne bore twins.

7. Anne never abandoned her domestic duties in Stratford.

8. Shakespeare spent most of his adult life in the theater world of London.

9. His contemporaries appreciated him as a brilliant playwright.

10. He probably considered himself a shrewd businessman.

11. Shakespeare's will left Anne nothing except their second-best bed.

12. Some biographers have interpreted the provision as sentimental in nature.

13. The reference has remained out of tune with other details of Shakespeare's life.

14. Shakespeare's will granted his elder daughter the bulk of his estate.

15. She seemed his favorite child.

16. Shakespeare's personal life still puzzles biographers.

17. The true nature of his domestic life is beyond our reach.

III. The sentences below contain special structures such as idiomatic subjective or objective complements, indirect objects, reflexive pronouns, phrasal verbs, adverbial objectives, and qualifiers. Determine the sentence pattern number for each sentence and then diagram the sentence.

1. Lily bought herself diamonds.

2. For the king's coronation, all of the citizens turned out in the streets.

3. Last year I received pearls for Valentine's Day.

4. Good manners are never out of fashion.

5. Her dog's dish is under the table.

6. We finally broke down the complex code this afternoon.

7. You should never give up.

8. With the arrival of our sales materials, we were finally in business.

9. New clues turned up every hour.

10. The majestically tall willow attracted many photographers.

see answer key, p. 385

Usage Problems Associated with Adjectives and Adverbs

WHAT IS USAGE?

Now that we have looked at the basic building blocks of the English language—the eight parts of speech and ten basic sentence patterns—we are ready to consider some of the usage problems that arise. We turn temporarily from **descriptive grammar** (how the elements of English work together to make meaning) to **prescriptive grammar, or usage** (how educated speakers of English pattern their sentences "correctly"). Of course, what is correct in any given situation depends on the context. In an informal setting, for example, among speakers of a particular dialect, you might choose to say "We might could handle this problem" (in certain areas of the American South), "He be looking for you" (with friends of color), "It don't matter" or "It ain't nothing" (in various areas throughout the United States). Although these sentences do not conform to what we call standard English, they may well be the most appropriate way to express yourself in a given situation or with a particular audience. "Correct" language is whatever communicates meaning most clearly in the context at hand. To become part of a specific language group, you must speak that language, even if it deviates from standard English. Standard English is itself a dialect, accepted as the norm for educated speakers but not inherently superior to any other dialect. Ideally each of us should be able to switch dialects as needed, in effect being bilingual or even multilingual.

Because English is such a rich, changing language—and because it varies among different regions of English-speaking countries as well as among the many countries that use English as an official language—I will not attempt here to discuss the peculiarities of dialect. Instead, we will focus on what is known as standard edited English, the so-called "correct" form. Keep in mind as we learn the following rules (or, more likely, review them, since no doubt you have encountered them before) that the most educated speakers are aware that different situations call for different uses of language. Ultimately, being versatile is more important than being "correct" all the time.

DISTINGUISHING ADJECTIVES AND ADVERBS

At the level of single-word modifiers, the greatest usage difficulty arises with adjectives and adverbs. What is the difference between the two, and what linguistic situations are likely to cause difficulties for even educated speakers? You'll remember from Chapter 1, of course, the basic differences between these two parts of speech:

ADJECTIVES	modify nouns
	typically appear before the noun being modified or after a *be* or linking verb
	answer the questions how many?, which one?, or what kind?
ADVERBS	modify verbs, adjectives, or other adverbs
	typically can move within a sentence (an independent clause) without changing meaning
	answer the questions when?, where?, why?, how?, for what purpose?, in what manner?, under what condition?

Ordinarily, adjectives and adverbs both look and function distinctively enough that little confusion occurs. However, certain irregularly formed adverbs can cause problems, in particular the combinations of **"good" and "well," "bad" and "badly."** When we take a look at how these words function, we see that one immediate difficulty is the fact that "well" can be used as both an adverb or an adjective (pertaining to health):

Good = adjective, as in "Have a *good* day" or "She is a *good* bowler."

Well = adverb, as in "Do *well* today" or "She bowls *well*."

Well = adjective when it refers strictly to health, as in "I feel *well* today after suffering from allergies for the past two weeks."

Thus our cliché greeting, "How are you?" would logically elicit either the response "I feel good" (speaking of overall well-being) or "I feel well" (speaking of physical health, with the implication that the person responding has *not* felt well recently). No wonder that most of us just reply, "Fine!" and skip the *good / well* dilemma entirely. If we remember Sentence Patterns 2 and 4, we will make the correct choice by knowing that an adjective must follow a *be* or linking verb. Although it is possible for an adverb to follow the *be* verb in Pattern 1 sentences, the adverb must refer to time or place. Let's first review Patterns 1, 2, and 4:

PATTERN 1:	subject - *be* verb - adverb of time or place
PATTERN 2:	subject - *be* verb - predicate adjective
PATTERN 4:	subject - linking verb - predicate adjective

With these sentence patterns in mind, consider the following usage examples:

INCORRECT	I did *good* on my driver's test yesterday. ("Did" is an action verb here, not a *be* or linking verb, and so the adjective "good" is incorrect.)
CORRECT	I did *well* on my driver's test yesterday. (The adverb "well" modifies the intransitive verb "did" in this Pattern 6 sentence.)

INCORRECT   We slept *good* in the tent.
("Slept" is an action verb, not a *be* or linking verb, and so the adjective "good" is incorrect.)

CORRECT   We slept *well* in the tent.
(The adverb "well" modifies the intransitive verb "slept" in this Pattern 6 sentence.)

INCORRECT   Margie can play guitar *good*.
("Play" is an action verb, and so the adjective "good" is incorrect.)

CORRECT   Margie is good at playing guitar.
("Good" serves as a predicate adjective in this Pattern 2 sentence.)

The same confusion reigns with "bad" and "badly." Although the adjective form is "bad," many people incorrectly use the adverb form "badly," especially after the linking verb *feel*.

INCORRECT   I feel *badly* about forgetting your birthday.
("Feel" is a linking verb here because no action is taking place; thus the adjective form, "bad," should follow the verb in this Pattern 4 sentence. In fact, the only situation in which "I feel badly" could be possible would involve an unlikely accident causing harm to the fingertips. "I feel badly" means, literally, that the speaker's sense of touch has been damaged.)

CORRECT   I feel *bad* about forgetting your birthday.
(Almost always, "bad" will be the correct choice in a sentence such as this, in which a *be* or linking verb requires a predicate adjective.)

INCORRECT   The sour cream tasted *badly* after sitting on the table for an hour.
(Because no action is taking place, "tasted" is a linking verb and should be followed by an adjective. You can also rephrase, replacing the linking verb with a *be* verb: "The sour cream was *bad* after sitting on the table for an hour.")

CORRECT   The sour cream tasted *bad* after sitting on the table for an hour.
(The predicate adjective "bad" refers back to the subject in this Pattern 4 sentence.)

INCORRECT	The stock market has done *bad* during this quarter. (Here the verb, "has done," expresses action and thus requires an adverb.)
CORRECT	The stock market has done *badly* during this quarter. (The adverb "badly" correctly modifies the intransitive verb in this Pattern 6 sentence.)

Another set of words frequently confused is "real" (actual, true) and **"really"** (usually employed as an intensifier meaning "truly" or "very"). In colloquial speech, "real" is often substituted for "really."

INCORRECT	I am *real* upset about what happened.
CORRECT	I am *really* upset about what happened.

INCORRECT	She is a *real* smart woman to have built her own business.
CORRECT	She is a *really* smart woman to have built her own business.
CORRECT	She is a *real* entrepreneur.

A final pair of confusing modifiers is **"sure"** (certain) and **"surely"** (certainly). You will rarely hear "surely" in spoken English, but you must keep the distinction in mind when writing.

INCORRECT	She is *sure* confident about her abilities. OR She *sure* is confident about her abilities.
CORRECT	She is *surely* confident about her abilities. OR She *surely* is confident about her abilities. OR She is *sure* about her abilities.

EXERCISE 4.1

Circle the correct choice in the sentences below.

1. The patient was feeling (GOOD, WELL) after receiving a blood transfusion.

2. Perry's new job pays (REAL, REALLY) (GOOD, WELL).

3. Everyone in the fraternity looked (BAD, BADLY) after a sleepless night of heavy drinking.

4. The news from the site of battle sounded (BAD, BADLY).

5. JoAnne has always fared (BAD, BADLY) in the practical details of managing her life.

6. This university needs student leaders who can handle themselves (GOOD, WELL) in the face of administrative pressure.

7. The director of the play was (SURE, SURELY) delighted by the audience's enthusiastic response.

8. The survey figures were (REAL, REALLY) out of line with what the researchers had expected to find.

9. Although her father plays bridge (BAD, BADLY), her mother plays exceptionally (GOOD, WELL).

10. Are you (SURE, SURELY) that I can dive into this pool? (SURE, SURELY) you can.

see answer key, p. 389

COMPARING ADJECTIVES AND ADVERBS

The *good/well* problem gets more complicated when we want to make comparisons. In English, we **use the comparative form (ending in "-er" or using "more") when we compare two entities and the superlative form (ending in "-est" or using "most") when we compare more than two.**

Let's take a look at some of the problems that arise in comparative situations, beginning with a simple chart listing the forms possible.

	Positive	Comparative	Superlative
1.	good	better	best
	well	better	best
2.	bad	worse	worst
	badly	worse	worst
3.	short	shorter	shortest
	jealous	more jealous	most jealous
4.	quick	quicker	quickest
	quickly	more quickly	most quickly

Now let's examine each pair listed on the previous page:

1. As we said before, "good" is the adjective form; "well" is the adverb form except when used to refer to health.

I am a *good* student. (adjective)

The nervous student performed *well* on the final exam. (adverb)

We ate *well* while we traveled through Italy. (adverb)

No one felt *well* after eating the soup. (adjective)

The comparative and superlative forms, though, are identical. Remember to use comparative when dealing with two entities, superlative when dealing with more than two.

Nancy is a *better* student than Carol. (adjective in comparative form)

Nancy did *better* than Carol on the test. (adverb in comparative form)

We felt *best* whenever we started the day with a hearty breakfast. (adjective in superlative form)

We ate *best* in Italy. (adverb in superlative form)

2. "Bad" is the adjective form and therefore precedes a noun or follows either a be or linking verb. "Badly" is the adverb form. As with "good" and "well," the comparative and superlative forms of "bad" and "badly" are identical. Again, keep in mind that comparative form signals two entities, while superlative form signals more than two.

I feel *worse* about forgetting your birthday than about forgetting our anniversary. (adjective in comparative form)

The stock market has done *worse* this year than ever before. (adverb in comparative form, comparing two time periods—then and now)

The *worst* experience of my life occurred in a college classroom. (adjective in superlative form)

Of all the contenders for the piano scholarship, Maya performed *worst*. (adverb in superlative form)

3. When a word consists of only one syllable, we usually form the comparative by adding "-er" and the superlative by adding "-est" (as in "shorter" and "shortest" in the preceding chart). This is also true of many two-syllable words, especially those ending in "-y" or "-ly" and some in "-le," "-ow," and "-er." All other words are usually formed by adding "more" or "most" (as in "more jealous" and "most jealous" in the preceding chart). Consider the adjective forms listed below:

tall	taller	tallest
friendly	friendlier	friendliest
simple	simpler	simplest

narrow	narrower	narrowest
tender	tenderer	tenderest
gorgeous	more gorgeous	most gorgeous

4. Adverb forms use "more" and "most" to form the comparative and superlative:

quickly	more quickly	most quickly
coldly	more coldly	most coldly
happily	more happily	most happily

An exception to this distinction between adjectives and adverbs occurs with the words "fast" and "slow," both of which may serve as either adjectives or adverbs, although "slowly" is the preferred adverb form for "slow."

fast	faster	fastest
slow	slower	slowest
OR (preferred forms)		
slowly	more slowly	most slowly

ADJECTIVE FORM: Ted drives a *fast* car. (*what kind* of car)

ADVERB FORM: Ted drives *fast*. (*how* he drives)

ADJECTIVE FORM: Julep is the *fastest* horse in the stable.

ADVERB FORM: Of all the horses in the stable, Julep runs the *fastest*.

ADJECTIVE FORM: Drive at a *slow* speed around this curve.

ADVERB FORM: Drive *slow* around this curve.
OR
Drive *slowly* around this curve.
("*Slowly*" is the preferred form.)

ADJECTIVE FORM: Martin is a *slower* learner than his brother.

ADVERB FORM: Martin learns *slower* than his brother does.
OR
Martin learns *more slowly* than his brother does.
(Again, "*more slowly*" is the preferred form.)

Except for rare cases such as "*fast*" and "*slow*," a word's adjective and adverb forms will be distinct. You may not have much difficulty determining whether to use an adjective or an adverb in the positive form, as in the example below:

She is a *quick* walker. (adjective)

She walks *quickly*. (adverb)

Be careful, however, not to confuse the comparative forms of adjectives and adverbs, especially when the adjective is a one-syllable word and therefore is not ordinarily preceded by "more" or "most."

INCORRECT   She walks *quicker* than I do.
                 (We cannot use the comparative form of the adjective when the sentence calls for an adverb to modify the action verb "walks.")

CORRECT   She walks *more quickly* than I do.

INCORRECT   She walks *quickest*.
                 (We cannot use the superlative form of the adjective when the verb makes an adverb necessary.)

CORRECT   She walks *most quickly*.

Finally, **be careful not to be redundant by using both "more" and "-er" or "most" and "-est."** Although this construction was at one time permissible in English (Shakespeare, for example, makes use of it in *Julius Caesar* 3.2.184, when Antony speaks of "the most unkind-est cut of all"), it is no longer acceptable in standard English.

INCORRECT   I am *more happier* than I've ever been.

CORRECT   I am *happier* than I've ever been.

EXERCISE 4.2

Correct the adjectives and adverbs in the following sentences as necessary.

1. All of the students felt badly after learning of the professor's illness.

2. Which of these two books did you enjoy most?

3. Patricia is the most youngest student in kindergarten.

4. Brenda always studied hard so that she could do good on the tests in her grammar class.

5. After my bout with the flu, I finally feel good again.

6. Who is more irresponsible—Ned, Tad, or Jason?

7. Mark's goal is to be handsomer than his father.

8. Jesse drives dangerous.

see answer key, p. 389

MISPLACING ADJECTIVES AND ADVERBS

Both prepositional phrases and certain commonly used adverbs can be misplaced. **It is especially important to place the word "only" (and such cousins as "just" and "even") in the exact spot where needed, before the word being modified.** Only when it modifies the last word in a sentence can "only" follow the word it modifies, as we see when we add "only" to the sentence below:

He said he loved her.

Only he said he loved her. (Although she is dating several other men, *only* he said he loved her.)

He *only* said he loved her. (She's in for a heartbreak; he didn't really mean it.)

He said *only* he loved her. (He knows about the other men and wants to make clear that he is the *only* sincere one.)

He said he *only* loved her. (He *only* loves; he has no plans for a long-term commitment because love is the extent of his capabilities.)

He said he loved *only* her. (He is dating several other women, but he insists that she is the *only* one he loves.)

He said he loved her *only*. (Because "only" ends the sentence, placing it either before or after the final word makes no difference in meaning.)

Let's look at a few more examples:

Misplaced "Only":	We *only* have two weeks left in this semester.
Corrected Version:	We have *only* two weeks left in this semester.
Misplaced "Almost":	We are *almost* spending half of our income on rent.
Corrected Version:	We are spending *almost* half of our income on rent.
Misplaced "Just":	The client *just* wants an hour of your time.
Corrected Version:	The client wants *just* an hour of your time.

Misplaced "Even":	I was even included.
Corrected Version:	Even I was included.
Misplaced Prepositional Phrase:	Don't give the medicine to the baby *in the bottle*.
Corrected Version:	Don't give the medicine *in the bottle* to the baby. OR Don't give the baby the medicine in the bottle.

Remember that prepositional phrases can serve as adjectives or adverbs. When you are composing sentences, then, make sure that you place a prepositional phrase used as an adjective behind the noun it modifies. Only the prepositional phrase used as an adverb can move freely within the sentence.

Prepositional Phrase as Adjective:	The diploma *on the wall* was hers. (*which* diploma)
Prepositional Phrase as Adverb:	The diploma was *on the wall*. (Pattern 1 sentence, s – *be* – adv)
	On the wall was a diploma. (also Pattern 1)
	She carefully placed the diploma *on the wall*. (*where* she placed it)
	On the wall she carefully placed the diploma. (also *where*)

EXERCISE 4.3

Rephrase the following sentences so that the modifiers are more appropriately placed.

1. The union negotiators are only asking for a small increase in salary.

   _____

   _____

2. Feed the fish to the cat with small bones in it.

   _____

   _____

3. The noise was tremendous from the planes overhead.

_____

_____

4. The child almost was in tears by the end of the first day of camp.

_____

_____

5. Good parents only want what is best for their children.

_____

_____

6. Just tell us the facts of this situation, not your opinion.

_____

_____

7. The picture caught everyone's attention above the fireplace.

_____

_____

8. The magician even has one more trick up his sleeve.

_____

_____

9. All items are not on sale.

_____

_____

10. We only have seven days left before graduation.

_____

_____

see answer key, p. 389

MODIFYING ADJECTIVES AND ADVERBS

Most adjectives can be modified by an adverb; most adverbs can be modified by another adverb (a qualifier or intensifier):

She is *extremely intelligent*.

She handled the situation *very intelligently*.

Two words in frequent use that *cannot* be modified, though, are "unique" (or "uniquely") and "favorite." Both "unique" and "favorite" imply an absolute state that cannot logically be broken down into degrees and therefore cannot be modified.

INCORRECT	This is a *very unique* situation.
CORRECT	This is a *unique* situation.
INCORRECT	Audrey Hepburn seemed *quite uniquely* suited for her role in *My Fair Lady*.
CORRECT	Audrey Hepburn seemed *uniquely* suited for her role in *My Fair Lady*.
INCORRECT	*My Fair Lady* is my *most favorite* musical.
CORRECT	*My Fair Lady* is my *favorite* musical.

SUMMARY OF KEY CONCEPTS IN CHAPTER 4

1. Do not confuse adjectives and adverbs, especially "good" and "well," "bad" and "badly," "real" and "really," "sure" and "surely."

ADJECTIVES		
	good	(We found a *good* deal.)
	well	(She looks *well* today.)
	bad	(Everyone feels *bad* about what happened.)
	real	(The *Oxford English Dictionary* is a *real* master work of scholarship.)
	sure	(No one can be *sure* about the future.)
ADVERBS		
	well	(James swims *well* enough to be a lifeguard.)
	badly	(Nola handled the situation *badly*.)
	really	(The *Oxford English Dictionary* is a really impressive work.)
	surely	(The jury was *surely* right to acquit the defendant.)

2. Remember that "fast" and "slow" can be either adjectives or adverbs in the positive, comparative, and superlative forms. As an adverb, though, "slowly" is preferred to "slow."

3. Use the comparative (-er or more) form when comparing two entities. Use the superlative (-est or most) form when comparing more than two entities.

4. Place modifiers carefully, especially words such as "only," "just," "almost," "even."

5. Do not modify "unique," "uniquely," or "favorite."

CHAPTER 4 EXERCISE

I. Correct all of the errors in the sentences below. Two of these sentences are correct!

1. Which one of the twins is the smartest?

   _____

2. Sarah only broke one of the rules, but it just was too much to forgive.

   _____

3. No one could hear the student who spoke the quietest.

   _____

4. The circumstances were worser than we had imagined.

   _____

5. The veterinarian felt badly about the animals that had to be euthanized.

   _____

6. The news about the flooding in Texas left us real worried about our friends there.

   _____

7. The piano sounded good even after it had been moved upstairs.

   _____

8. Margarine tastes better than butter if you eat it quick.

   _____

9. The technician explained that a computer mouse can perform badly if its inner mechanism gets dirty.

   _____

10. Kittens sure can be curious.

   _____

11. Once she felt well, the elderly widow resumed living in the mansion with her sister on the corner.

   _____

12. The artist's talent was quite unique, as recognized almost by all the spectators.

   _____

II. Write sentences of your own as directed below.

   1. Write a sentence that contains "good" used as a predicate adjective.

   _____

   _____

   2. Write a sentence that contains "badly."

   _____

   _____

   3. Write a sentence that contains both "surely" and "unique."

   _____

   _____

   4. Write a sentence that contains both "real" and "only."

   _____

   _____

   5. Write a sentence that correctly uses either the comparative or the superlative form of "bad."

   _____

   _____

see answer key, p. 389

COMBINING AND EXPANDING PATTERNS
Compound Structures

If we were confined to the ten basic sentence patterns, our speech would quickly become boring. The next few chapters will explain how we combine, expand, and transform the basic patterns in order to come up with a much richer variety of sentence possibilities. Along the way, we will also learn much about punctuation.

Before we proceed, we need to understand a few terms:

> **Clause** — a grammatical structure containing a subject and verb. **Clauses fall into one of two broad categories:**
>
> a. **independent (or main) clause** — a grammatical structure containing a subject and verb and expressing a complete idea. Another term for an independent clause, then, is a sentence.
>
> b. **dependent (or subordinate) clause** — a grammatical structure containing a subject and verb but not expressing a complete idea. We will learn about dependent clauses in more depth in the following chapters.

This chapter will discuss compound structures and the compound sentence. Chapters 6 and 7 will go on to discuss complex and compound–complex sentences, those that contain dependent clauses.

SIMPLE SENTENCES

A simple sentence consists of only one independent clause. All of the sentences we diagramed in Chapters 2 and 3, then, can be categorized as simple sentences. Occasionally, though, **a simple sentence may contain one or more compound structures**—a compound subject, compound verb, compound direct object, compound prepositional phrase, or some other grammatical structure. Let's take a look at how to build and diagram the most commonly used compound structures. Consider the sentences below:

> Mr. Brown owns a bookstore. His son manages it.

Both of these are simple sentences. Although we change the meaning, we can combine them into one sentence by using a compound subject.

Mr. Brown and his son own a bookstore.

Note that this sentence is simple because it retains the one-subject, one-verb structure of the simple sentence, even though the subject is now compound. We diagram the compound subject by using a "ticket" structure and joining the compound subjects with a coordinating conjunction:

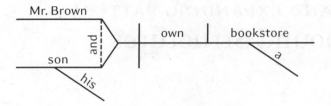

We can further build on this structure by incorporating a compound verb:

Mr. Brown and his son own and manage a bookstore.

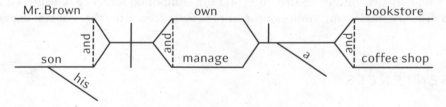

We can include a compound direct object as well. Notice that the article "a" is positioned in the diagram to indicate that it modifies both "bookstore" and "coffee shop."

Mr. Brown and his son own and manage a bookstore and coffee shop.

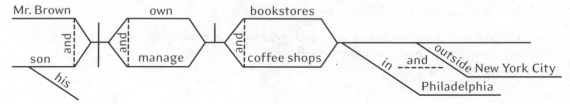

Finally, we can insert a compound prepositional phrase, in the form of either compound objects of one preposition or two prepositional phrases. Again notice the placement of the prepositional phrase (or phrases) to indicate modification of both direct objects.

Mr. Brown and his son own and manage bookstores and coffee shops in Philadelphia and outside New York City.

The final variation demonstrates how to illustrate compound structures that are separately modified:

> Mr. Brown and his son own and manage a large bookstore in Philadelphia and a popular coffee shop in New York City.

   Most likely you will seldom incorporate more than one or two compound structures within a sentence. What is most important to note in this section is that, regardless of how many compound structures the sentence can accommodate, it remains a simple sentence because it contains only one subject–verb unit. This will become clearer once you compare the compound *structure* with the compound *sentence* in the section that follows.

COMPOUND SENTENCES

The most basic way to combine two or more sentence patterns is the compound sentence structure. **A compound sentence is two (or more) independent clauses joined by a coordinating conjunction, by a semicolon, or by a semicolon and a conjunctive adverb.** Let's take a look at each variety.

1 ● Compound sentence joined by a coordinating conjunction

There are only **seven coordinating conjunctions**, and you can memorize them easily if you remember the acronym "**FANBOYS**." The coordinating conjunctions are as follows:

For
And
Nor
But
Or
Yet
So

Notice that the term itself, "coordinating conjunction," indicates by the "co–" prefix that the clauses joined together will be equal. In other words, they each remain an independent clause. The coordinating conjunction does not become part of either independent clause.
   Here are a few notes on the coordinating conjunctions:

   1. "For" can also be a preposition. It serves as a coordinating conjunction when it joins two independent clauses and means "because."

The Wife of Bath is a fascinating character, *for* she is not the typical medieval woman. (Here "for" is a coordinating conjunction.)

The pilgrims traveled *for* several days. (Here "for" is a preposition.)

2. Don't overwork "and." Sometimes another coordinating conjunction will express the relationship between the clauses more precisely.

3. "But" and "yet" are interchangeable, since they both show contrast between ideas.

4. "Nor" is the negative of "or."

5. "So" is different from "so that." "So" means "therefore" and is not considered part of either independent clause; "so that" means "in order to" and, as a subordinating conjunction, belongs to the dependent clause it introduces. Sometimes the "that" of "so that" is understood, creating even more opportunity for confusion. One test is to reverse the order of the clauses. If they can be switched, "so" (or "so that") is a subordinating conjunction. If they cannot be switched, "so" is a coordinating conjunction, and the sentence is compound.

Chaucer left *The Canterbury Tales* unfinished, *so* we will never know exactly how he intended the final work to appear. (Clauses cannot be reversed)

The pilgrims traveled to Canterbury *so that* [or *so*] they could visit the shrine of a martyr. (Clauses can be reversed—So that they could visit the shrine of a martyr, the pilgrims traveled to Canterbury.)

A compound sentence joined by a coordinating conjunction almost always needs a comma BEFORE the coordinating conjunction. The comma should be omitted only if both independent clauses are extremely short and the comma would unnecessarily slow down the flow of the sentence:

He *swept* and I *mopped.*

On the other hand, do NOT use a comma if the conjunction joins two subjects, two verbs, or two phrases rather than two clauses:

He and I swept. (compound subject, not a compound sentence)

He *swept* and *mopped.* (compound verb, not a compound sentence)

He *swept the garage* and *mopped the kitchen.* (compound verbs with direct objects, not a compound sentence)

To use a comma, you need two independent clauses:

He *swept the garage*, and I *mopped the kitchen.* (compound sentence)

Finally, although you should use this device sparingly, it *is* possible to begin a sentence with a coordinating conjunction, just for emphasis:

He swept the garage. But I mopped the kitchen, did the laundry, and washed the windows.

EXERCISE 5.1

Punctuate the following sentences.

1. Chaucer was not a nobleman nor was he a commoner.

2. Solitary travel was not safe in the fourteenth century so the pilgrims traveled together.

3. Chaucer and his contemporaries could write in Latin or English.

4. Chaucer could also write in French yet he chose English.

see answer key, p. 391

2 ● *Compound sentence joined by a semicolon*

Another way to construct a compound sentence is simply to place a semicolon between two independent clauses:

> Chaucer's Knight tells the first tale; it is a lengthy, slow-paced romance.

The semicolon alone will work when the relationship between the ideas of the clauses is immediately clear. If there is any delay in understanding the relationship, then the semicolon should be followed by a conjunctive adverb, as described next.

3 ● *Compound sentence joined by a semicolon and conjunctive adverb*

More often than not, the semicolon that joins two independent clauses is followed by a conjunctive adverb (sometimes called by an alternate label, an adverbial conjunction). The following is a partial list of conjunctive adverbs; you'll notice that in the context of a writing class you would probably label them "transitions."

accordingly	**instead**
additionally	**likewise**
also	**meanwhile**
consequently	**moreover**
finally	**nevertheless**
furthermore	**nonetheless**
hence	**on the contrary**
however	**on the other hand**
in addition	**otherwise**
in conclusion	**still**
in contrast	**then**
indeed	**therefore**
in fact	**thus**

Almost always, the conjunctive adverb is followed by a comma. The exception is that the comma is often omitted after a one-syllable conjunctive adverb, especially after "then." Use a comma, though, if you believe that the reader will or should pause after the one-syllable conjunctive adverb:

> Chaucer wanted to portray a spectrum of medieval social classes; *therefore*, he used the device of a pilgrimage.

> The pilgrims spent the night at the Tabard Inn; then they set off for Canterbury. (no comma necessary because no pause is necessary after the one-syllable "then")

> The pilgrims spent the night at the Tabard Inn; *then*, the next morning they selected Harry Bailly as their guide to Canterbury. (comma indicates the probable pause of most native speakers after the one-syllable "then")

Notice that, because these are conjunctive adverbs, many of these words and phrases can move (as adverbs do) within their own independent clause. In the first sentence above, we have a few options if we want to rearrange the wording:

> Chaucer wanted to portray a spectrum of medieval social classes; *therefore*, he used the device of a pilgrimage. (Here "therefore" is clearly a conjunctive adverb because it immediately follows the semicolon, thus joining the clauses together.)

> Chaucer wanted to portray a spectrum of medieval social classes; he used the device of a pilgrimage, *therefore*.

> Chaucer wanted to portray a spectrum of medieval social classes; he *therefore* used the device of a pilgrimage.

> Chaucer wanted to portray a spectrum of medieval social classes; he used, *therefore*, the device of a pilgrimage.

The fact that "therefore" can move helps us to identify it as a conjunctive adverb. Notice that when "therefore" does not immediately follow the semicolon, it is usually set off by two commas to mark it as a word that interrupts the flow of the sentence.

Diagraming Compound Sentences

One of the few areas where traditional diagraming falls short is the compound sentence. We can easily diagram two independent clauses joined by a coordinating conjunction or by a semicolon. There is no effective way, though, to demonstrate the function of a conjunctive adverb, since it serves simultaneously as an adverb for the second independent clause (where it is placed in the diagram) but also functions to join together the ideas of the two clauses. A possible solution is to extend the vertical line from the coordinating conjunction space so that the line reaches the conjunctive adverb. For purposes of illustration, let's take a look at the diagram for a compound sentence first joined by one of the FANBOYS, then joined by a semicolon, and finally joined by a semicolon and conjunctive adverb. Notice that the coordinating conjunction (or the "x" that takes its place) is on a horizontal line between the two independent clauses; think of this line as an "equals" sign symbolizing that both clauses are independent.

The Miller is tipsy, so he tells a bawdy tale.

The Miller is tipsy; he tells a bawdy tale.

The Miller is tipsy; therefore, he tells a bawdy tale.

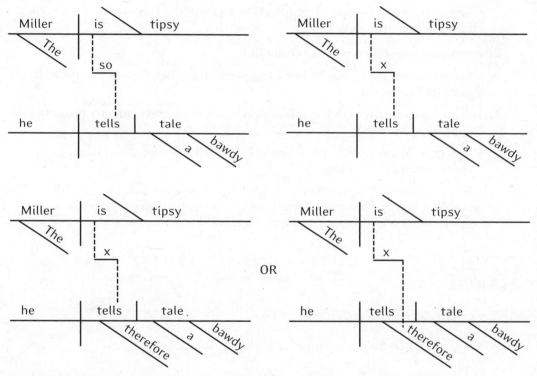

OR

You should also remember that since the compound sentence contains two independent clauses, you can now see two sentence patterns combined into one sentence:

The Miller is tipsy = Pattern 2 (s – *be* – adj)

He tells a bawdy tale = Pattern 7 (s – tv – do)

Using Compound Sentences to Repair Sentence Errors

Perhaps the most serious writing problem is the inability to recognize a complete sentence. You can use the compound sentence structure to help you avoid writing run-ons and comma splices.

Run-on (no punctuation between independent clauses):
Chaucer wrote in English he helped to establish the language as a respectable choice for literature.

Comma splice (using a comma between two independent clauses):
Chaucer wrote in English, he helped to establish the language as a respectable choice for literature.

Run-ons and comma splices are serious errors. To correct the problem, we now know three choices:

1. **compound sentence with coordinating conjunction**

   Chaucer wrote in English, *so* he helped to establish the language as a respectable choice for literature.

2. **compound sentence with a semicolon**

   Chaucer wrote in English; he helped to establish the language as a respectable choice for literature.

3. **compound sentence with a semicolon and conjunctive adverb (usually followed by a comma)**

   Chaucer wrote in English; *consequently*, he helped to establish the language as a respectable choice for literature.

   Chaucer wrote in English; *thus* he helped to establish the language as a respectable choice for literature. (one-syllable conjunctive adverb does not require comma; however, a comma to indicate a pause after "thus" is also acceptable)

EXERCISE 5.2

Punctuate and diagram the following sentences.

1. Mary is my best friend so I must remember her birthday.

2. The friends were quietly conversing meanwhile a burglary was going on in the next room.

3. I am not athletic I can however play tennis and golf.

4. The door opened then a mysterious figure stepped inside.

5. We waited for hours but the bus did not appear finally we walked into town.

6. Husbands and wives should not reveal their personal lives or their fantasies to strangers.

7. Vegetarianism is admirable nevertheless it is not an easy choice.

see answer key, p. 391

SUMMARY OF KEY CONCEPTS IN CHAPTER 5

1. A simple sentence consists of one independent clause, although that clause may include compound elements.

2. A compound sentence consists of two independent clauses joined by

    a. a coordinating conjunction (for, and, nor, but, or, yet, so—FANBOYS)

    b. a semicolon

    c. a semicolon followed by a conjunctive adverb (such as "therefore," "however," "meanwhile," "thus," "then") and a comma; the comma is optional after one-syllable conjunctive adverbs but should be used to indicate a pause.

3. The compound sentence structure is an effective way to correct run-on and comma splice errors.

CHAPTER 5 EXERCISE

I. Identify the following as simple (s) or compound (CD) sentences. Diagram each sentence.

1. The young journalist turned on her computer and immediately experienced writer's block.

2. She had faith in the power of the unconscious, so she took a nap.

3. She dreamed images of dragons, mice, and castles.

4. After her nap, she wrote a short children's story; she illustrated the story with watercolor pictures.

5. The news editor did not appreciate her efforts, but in her children's stories the journalist eventually found a new career and immense satisfaction.

II. Punctuate the following sentences, making sure to avoid creating run-on or comma splice errors. Not all sentences will need punctuation.

1. Natasha was frightened of flying for she had once seen a plane crash.

2. Her entire family was planning a trip overseas Natasha however was reluctant to go.

3. Her mother arranged for her to see a special counselor so Natasha began working on a series of exercises designed to reduce her fear.

4. After a few months of therapy, Natasha thought that she had overcome her fear she believed she was cured.

5. She even sat on an empty plane and imagined herself feeling relaxed in the sky.

6. Natasha had done all she could yet she was not completely prepared for the actual experience of flying.

7. As the jet's engines revved up on the runway, Natasha closed her eyes and breathed deeply then she fainted.

8. When she regained consciousness, she found herself looking out at wispy clouds of white and at last enjoying the wonder of air travel.

9. Natasha had finally conquered her fear so she began flying frequently.

10. Family members now refer to Natasha as a professional traveler moreover she is happy to share her story with others who are still wrestling with their fear of flying.

III. Combine the sentences in each item below into one smooth compound sentence. Add coordinating conjunctions or conjunctive adverbs as necessary, with correct punctuation.

1. The dog was whining at the door. It was wet and cold outside.

   _____

   _____

   _____

2. Daisy had saved her allowance for months. She bought the bicycle she wanted.

   _____

   _____

   _____

3. The restaurant has an excellent reputation. Our meals were not quite as good as we had expected.

   _____

   _____

   _____

4. Nicole was certain that she had seen a ghost. Her roommate agreed with her.

   _____

   _____

   _____

5. Most people believe that wealth will bring them happiness. The story of Midas proves that this is not necessarily true.

   _____

   _____

   _____

IV. Write sentences of your own as directed below.

1. Combine two Pattern 7 sentences into one compound sentence joined by a semi-colon.

———————————————————————————————

———————————————————————————————

———————————————————————————————

2. Combine a Pattern 2 sentence and a Pattern 6 sentence into one compound sentence joined by a semicolon and a conjunctive adverb.

———————————————————————————————

———————————————————————————————

———————————————————————————————

3. Combine two Pattern 1 sentences into one compound sentence joined by a coordinating conjunction.

———————————————————————————————

———————————————————————————————

———————————————————————————————

see answer key, p. 392

COMBINING AND EXPANDING PATTERNS
Complex Sentences with Noun Clauses

So far we have learned that a simple sentence consists of one independent clause, while a compound sentence consists of two or more independent clauses. We move on now to the complex and the compound-complex sentence structure. **A complex sentence contains one independent clause plus one or more dependent clauses. There are three types of dependent clauses:**

a. **noun clause**—a dependent clause that takes the place of a noun in a sentence (that is, it can serve as subject, object, complement, or appositive)

b. **adverb clause**—a dependent clause that takes the place of an adverb in a sentence (that is, it answers one of the following questions: when, where, why, how, for what purpose, under what condition?)

c. **relative clause (or adjective clause)**—a dependent clause that takes the place of an adjective in a sentence (that is, it answers one of the following questions: which one? what kind?)

We will examine each type of dependent clause in detail. Chapter 6 will deal with the noun clause, while Chapter 7 will take up the adverb clause and the adjective clause.

CHARACTERISTICS OF THE NOUN CLAUSE

By its nature, the noun clause contradicts the basic definition of a complex sentence as an independent clause joined to one or more dependent clauses. Although adverb and adjective (relative) clauses are grammatically optional structures, just as adverbs and adjectives are, most nouns are essential to the grammatical integrity of a sentence. If we remove the noun structure that is a subject, for example, how can we possibly have an independent clause left? Noun clauses, then, are different in kind from adverb and relative clauses, as we will see even more clearly once we can compare the sentence diagrams for all three varieties of the dependent clause. The noun clause is almost always embedded within the independent clause rather than being an adjunct to it, as is the case with the adverb and relative clause.

Keeping in mind that we cannot detach the noun clause from the rest of the sentence, consider the following example:

What Sheila wanted most was a cup of tea with honey.

The italicized portion of this sentence is a noun clause; it contains a subject and verb, but does not express a complete idea. We know it is a noun clause, not an adverb or relative clause, because it serves as the subject of the sentence. One easy way to test for a noun clause is to replace it with a pronoun; in this case "it" will work to make a complete sentence: It was a cup of tea with honey. "Something" or "someone" will usually work with a noun clause as well.

Now let's look at a list of all the characteristics of noun clauses:

1. **A noun clause must contain a subject and a verb.**

2. **A noun clause will take the place of a noun, meaning that you can test for a noun clause by replacing it with a pronoun (usually "it," "someone," or "something").**

3. **A noun clause is introduced by a limited number of words that fall into two categories:**

    a. interrogatives   **who, whoever, whom, whomever, what, whatever (diagramed as nouns)**
    which, whose (diagramed as adjectives)
    when, where, why, how (diagramed as adverbs)

    b. expletives   **if, that, whether, whether or not (diagramed above the verb of the noun clause, with a dotted line drawn to that verb)**

4. **A noun clause performs the usual function of a noun.** Let's look at an example for each of these functions.

    subject   Whoever rang the doorbell has disappeared.

    subjective complement   The question was whether or not we should arrive early.

    object of preposition   I asked for help from whoever could afford a donation. (Note that the preposition itself is not part of the noun clause.)

    direct object   We wondered if the train had arrived.

    indirect object   You should give whoever buys the painting a certificate of value.

    objective complement   Sherry considered the bribe as what was necessary.

    appositive   Your decision, when you should apply to graduate school, is an important one.

The only noun function we have not yet discussed is the last one, the appositive. Basically, **an appositive is a noun or noun structure that stands in apposition to (next to) the noun it renames or identifies. It usually follows the noun it renames, usually is surrounded by commas, and can be omitted without changing the meaning of the sentence.**

one-word appositive   My cat, Max, suffers from arthritis.

appositive phrase	Max, *my cat*, suffers from arthritis.
appositive (noun) clause	The answer to her question, *if Max suffers from arthritis*, seems obvious.

Notice that **only when the noun clause is used as an appositive does it need punctuation.** When we diagram an appositive, we place it next to the noun it renames and place it within parentheses, with modifiers beneath the headword of the appositive. The first two sentences above would look like this in diagram form:

My cat, Max, suffers from arthritis.

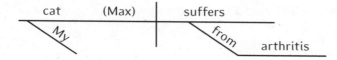

Max, my cat, suffers from arthritis.

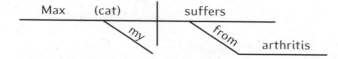

EXERCISE 6.1

Underline the noun clauses in the sentences below and identify their function as subject (s), subjective complement (sc), object of preposition (op), direct object (do), indirect object (io), objective complement (oc), or appositive (app).

1. What is unusual about the Navajo culture is its respect for all living things.

2. Navajos see how all inhabitants of the natural world are related.

3. They offer whoever can grasp this concept a sense of unity and connection.

4. Their explanation of this unity is that the same Supreme Being created all

   living things.

5. One of their beliefs, that the Navajo were once victims of a great flood, appears in other cultures as well.

6. They also believe that the number four is sacred.

7. With four seasons, four directions, four winds, four sacred mountains, and four sacred colors, the Navajo relate this number to why the universe operates smoothly.

8. They find progress through four worlds as what is necessary for spiritual growth.

9. I often wonder when other cultures will discover the wisdom of the Navajo.

10. Our reaction to their concept of oneness may determine whether humans will survive in the centuries to come.

see answer key, p. 394

DIAGRAMING THE NOUN CLAUSE

More often than not, the noun clause is embedded within an independent clause. Thus **to diagram a noun clause, we need a tower or pedestal**, a structure that will allow us to raise the subject and verb of the dependent clause so that it will be separate from the subject and verb of the independent clause. Before we can diagram, though, we need to analyze how the noun clause relates to the sentence as a whole. One way to do this is to refer to the ten basic sentence patterns we have already learned.

In every complex sentence, we can determine the sentence pattern for each of the clauses, whether independent or dependent. Because the noun clause is essential to the sentence, our first step will be to replace the noun clause with a pronoun or a single-word noun to determine the pattern number of the sentence as a whole. Next we focus on just the noun clause to determine its sentence pattern. Once we understand the sentence pattern of the entire sentence and of the noun clause, we are ready to diagram. Put the pedestal for the noun clause in the same place you would diagram a single-word noun. (It does not matter where the pedestal attaches to the base line of the noun clause.) We will use the example sentences from the beginning of this chapter once more for illustration:

Noun clause as subject
Whoever rang the doorbell has disappeared.

First, replace the noun clause with a pronoun in order to determine the overall sentence pattern:

Someone has disappeared. (sentence is a Pattern 6 = s – itv)

Next, isolate the noun clause to determine its sentence pattern:

Whoever rang the doorbell (noun clause is a Pattern 7 = s – tv – do)

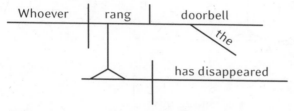

Noun clause as Subjective Complement
The question was *whether or not we should arrive early*.

The question was *something*. (sentence is a Pattern 3 = s – *be* – pn)

whether or not we should arrive early (noun clause is a Pattern 6 = s – itv; remember that "whether or not" is an expletive)

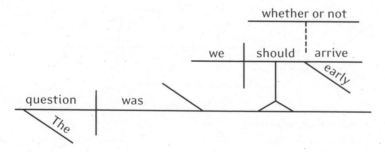

Noun Clause as Object of Preposition
I asked for help from *whoever could afford a donation*.

I asked for help from *someone*. (sentence is a Pattern 6 = s – itv)

whoever could afford a donation (noun clause is a Pattern 7 = s – tv – do)

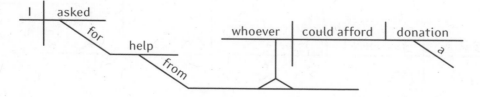

Noun Clause as Direct Object

We wondered *if the train had arrived.*

We wondered *something.* (sentence is a Pattern 7 = s – tv – do)

if the train had arrived (noun clause is a Pattern 6 = s – itv)

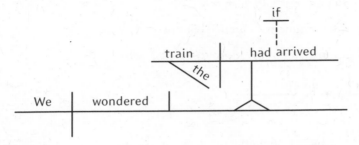

Noun Clause as Indirect Object

You should give *whoever buys the painting* a certificate of value.

You should give *someone* a certificate of value. (sentence is a Pattern 8 = s – tv – io – do)

whoever buys the painting (noun clause is a Pattern 7 = s – tv – do)

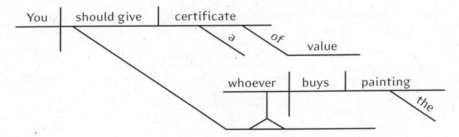

Noun Clause as Objective Complement

Sherry considered the bribe as *what was necessary.*

Sherry considered the bribe as *a necessity.* (sentence is a Pattern 10 = s – tv – do – n; remember that "as" is an expletive)

what was necessary (noun clause is a Pattern 2 = s – *be* – pa)

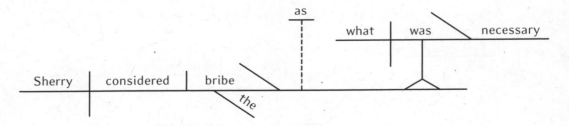

Noun Clause as Appositive

Your decision, *when you should apply to graduate school*, is an important one.

Your decision is an important one. (sentence is a Pattern 3 = s – *be* – pn; note that the appositive is ignored when determining the sentence pattern because it simply restates a noun, in this case the subject)

when you should apply to graduate school (noun clause is a Pattern 6 = s – itv)

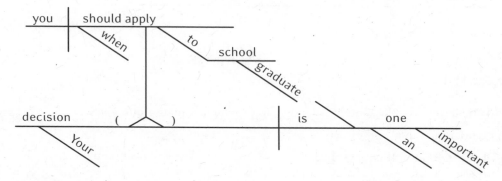

One peculiarity of this type of clause is that you may come upon a noun clause apparently lacking an introductory expletive:

The professor indicated *she was pleased with the class's progress.*

When the noun clause is in object position and would ordinarily begin with "that," as in the sentence above, the expletive can be omitted from the sentence, although it is still understood to be operative. In this case, insert "that" as an expletive in the diagram and surround it with square brackets to indicate that it did not appear in the original sentence.

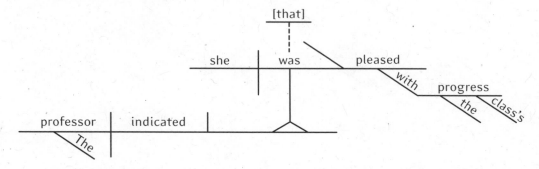

Another peculiarity is that the typical order of sentence elements within the dependent clause may be rearranged:

The professor asked *which text the students preferred.*

In this noun clause, the direct object ("text") precedes the subject and verb ("students preferred"). In the diagram, though, you will sort the elements of the clause into their normal syntactic order:

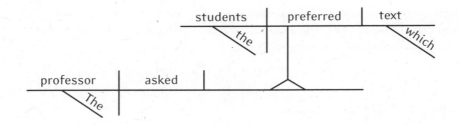

EXERCISE 6.2

Follow these steps for the sentences below, all of which contain noun clauses:

[A] Underline the noun clause.

[B] Label the noun function of each noun clause and double-check your accuracy by replacing each noun clause with a pronoun ("it," "someone," or "something").

[C] Determine the sentence pattern number for the sentence as a whole and for the noun clause.

[D] Diagram each sentence, remembering to place each noun clause on a pedestal in the same location you would place a pronoun or a single-word noun that could replace the noun clause.

1. The messenger asked who was at home.

2. What will happen at the party is a secret.

3. Jay wondered whose advice he should accept.

4. Last week the students in the advanced class debated which novel they should read.

5. No one knew whether the performance would continue.

6. How Erica would handle her new fortune was what all of us wondered.

7. Your announcement about where we could find half-price theater tickets helped us immensely.

8. Nancy's claim, that she did not love him, baffled Sam.

9. Nancy claimed she did not love Sam.

10. We asked when the membership drive would begin.

see answer key, p. 394

SUMMARY OF KEY CONCEPTS IN CHAPTER 6

1. Because a noun clause can function in the same way as a noun, it is often essential to the structure and meaning of a sentence. A noun clause can serve as subject, subjective complement, object of preposition, direct object, indirect object, objective complement, or appositive.

2. You can identify a noun clause by replacing it with a pronoun (usually "it," "something," or "someone").

3. A noun clause is introduced by an interrogative (who, whoever, whom, whomever, what, whatever, which, whose, when, where, why, how) or by an expletive (if, that, whether, whether or not). When the noun clause is a direct object and would ordinarily begin with "that," the expletive may be understood rather than actually appearing in the sentence.

4. A noun clause is diagramed on a tower or pedestal.

CHAPTER 6 EXERCISE

I. Follow these steps for the sentences below:

[A] Underline the noun clause and circle the interrogative or expletive that introduces it. If the expletive does not appear in the sentence but is understood, write it in and then circle it.

[B] Determine the sentence pattern number for the sentence as a whole and for the noun clause.

[C] Diagram the sentence.

1. No one has asked if the university can afford twenty new professors.

2. The question in the minds of many citizens is whether or not terrorism can stop.

3. The burglar thought he could easily escape detection.

4. Which job was most desirable was the foremost question in Ellen's mind.

5. The children discovered where their parents had been hiding the presents.

6. Your concern, why this office has never returned your call, is important.

7. The reporter interviewed all of the neighbors about what had happened.

8. We debated whose situation seemed worse.

9. The expert salesperson gave whoever would listen to her spiel a bonus gift.

10. The ancient Greeks considered poetry what made life worthwhile.

II. Write sentences of your own containing a noun clause as specified below. Underline the noun clause in each sentence and, for the last two sentences, identify the function of the noun clause.

a. noun clause functioning as a direct object and beginning with "what"

_____

_____

b. noun clause functioning as a subject and beginning with "why"

_____

_____

c. noun clause functioning as a subjective complement

_____

_____

d. noun clause functioning as the object of a preposition

_____

_____

e. noun clause beginning with "whose"

_____

_____

f. noun clause beginning with an expletive

_____

_____

see answer key, p. 396

COMBINING AND EXPANDING PATTERNS

Complex Sentences with Adverb and Relative Clauses, and the Compound-Complex Sentence

We have learned that the complex sentence contains an independent clause plus one or more dependent clauses. When the dependent clause serves as a noun, it usually cannot be detached from the sentence. If the noun clause is a subject, direct object, or subjective complement, for example, removing it leaves us with a fragment.

Because adverbs and adjectives are usually optional elements in a sentence, though, sentences containing adverb or adjective (relative) clauses more clearly fit the definition of a complex sentence. If we remove the adverb or adjective (relative) clause from a sentence, a complete thought—an independent clause—remains. This chapter will first examine adverb clauses and relative clauses and then move on to a brief consideration of the most complicated sentence structure of all, the compound-complex sentence.

ADVERB CLAUSE

Unlike the noun clause, the adverb clause can be detached from the rest of the sentence to leave a grammatically complete structure:

> *After Erin read the book*, she saw the movie.

The italicized portion of this sentence is an adverb clause. It contains a subject and verb but does not express a complete thought, and it answers one of the questions an adverb would: *when* did she see the movie? In addition, the adverb clause can be moved: Erin saw the movie *after she read the book*.

Let's list all of the characteristics of an adverb clause:

1. **An adverb clause contains a subject and a verb.**

2. **An adverb clause answers an adverb question: when? where? why? how?** Sometimes related questions, such as "in what way?" or "under what condition?"or "for what purpose?", may be more appropriate than "how?" or "why?"

3. **An adverb clause can usually be moved—as a whole—to another location in the sentence without changing the meaning of the sentence.**

4. **An adverb clause begins with a subordinating conjunction.** Although not

complete, the following list contains **the most common subordinating conjunctions**:

after	so that
although, though	unless
as	until
because	when, whenever
before	where, wherever
even though	whereas
if	whether or not
once	while
since	

Don't confuse the coordinating and subordinating conjunctions. Remember that a *coordinating* conjunction (one of the FANBOYS) signals a compound sentence, in which the clauses are both independent and therefore equal; a *sub*ordinating conjunction signals a complex sentence because the conjunction "subordinates" or lowers an independent clause by transforming it into a dependent one.

> Independent clause: the rooster crowed

> Dependent (adverb) or subordinate clause: when the rooster crowed

Also remember that "so" and "so that" may cause confusion. When used as a coordinating conjunction, "so" means "therefore"; "so that" (even if it appears as "so," with "that" understood) is a subordinating conjunction that means "in order to," "for the purpose of."

> Chuck has a degree from Oxford University, *so* he considers himself well-educated. (compound sentence because "so" joins two independent clauses and means "therefore," marking it as one of the FANBOYS)

> Chuck received his degree from Oxford University *so that* he could impress his friends. (complex sentence because "so that" introduces an adverb clause answering the question of *why* Chuck received his degree from Oxford; "so that" means "in order to," marking it as a subordinating conjunction; the clauses can be reversed without changing the meaning of the sentence)

Likewise, don't confuse subordinating conjunctions with the interrogatives and expletives used to begin noun clauses, although a few words appear on both lists: "when," "where," "if," "whether or not." **When trying to determine what type of clause you have before you, remember that a noun clause can be replaced by a single-word noun or a pronoun and that an adverb clause can move.**

> *Whether or not you like it,* I plan to resign. (adverb clause because it describes "under what condition" and can move: "I plan to resign whether or not you like it")

> *Whether or not you like it* is an important factor in our choice of advertising slogan. (noun clause because it is the subject of the sentence and can be replaced by "something" or "it")

Punctuating an Adverb Clause

There are two basic rules about punctuating an adverb clause:

1. **When the adverb clause begins the sentence, always set it off with a comma.**

   Because Erin read the book, she wanted to see the movie.

2. **When the adverb clause ends the sentence, eliminate the comma— UNLESS the subordinating conjunction shows contrast.**

   Erin wanted to see the movie *because she had read the book*.
   BUT
   Erin wanted to see the movie, *although she had read the book*.

   Here a comma precedes the subordinating conjunction to emphasize the contrast. **Only five subordinating conjunctions show contrast: although, even though, though, whereas, and while.** Note that "while" can also indicate simultaneous action and then does not require a comma:

   Erin read *while Mindy jogged*. (no comma ← simultaneous action)
   BUT
   Erin likes to read, *while Mindy prefers to jog*. (comma — contrast)

Diagraming an Adverb Clause

As with a sentence containing a noun clause, a sentence containing an adverb clause introduces another subject and verb. Somehow the diagram must indicate that there are now two subject-verb units, one independent and one dependent. **Because the noun clause took the place of a single-word noun, we merely inserted a pedestal at the appropriate spot in the main diagram. To diagram an adverb clause, though, we use two layers or tiers of diagrams. The diagram always begins with the independent clause. Then, underneath the independent clause, we diagram the adverb clause.** Since an adverb clause can move, this means that sometimes you will diagram the adverb clause last even though it appears first in the sentence.

Note that once again the ten basic sentence patterns can help you determine how to diagram each clause. If you analyze each clause separately, rather than attacking the sentence as a whole, your task will be lighter.

The final step in diagraming an adverb clause is to join the two tiers together. When dealing with an adverb clause, **always join the verbs of the two clauses together with a dotted line; then, on the dotted line, write the subordinating conjunction.** Let's look at an example, using the same sentence but reversing the order of the clauses to illustrate how the adverb clause can move:

She drank coffee *because she was sleepy*.

Independent clause = She drank coffee (Pattern 7 = s - tv - do)

Adverb clause = because she was sleepy (Pattern 3 = s – *be* – pa)

```
  She    |  drank   |  coffee
_____|_____|_____

              :
            because
              :
         she  |  was  \  sleepy
        _____|_____
              |
```

Because she was sleepy, she drank coffee.
(Despite the reversal in order, the independent clause and dependent clause remain exactly the same.)

```
  she    |  drank   |  coffee
_____|_____|_____

              :
            Because
              :
         she  |  was  \  sleepy
        _____|_____
              |
```

Because the independent clause is always diagramed first, no matter where it appears in the sentence, these sentences have identical diagrams. If you retain in your diagram the capital letter in the first word of the sentence, though, you will be able to distinguish the sentence beginning with the independent clause from the sentence beginning with the adverb clause.

EXERCISE 7.1

All of the following sentences contain adverb clauses.

[A] Underline the adverb clause and then punctuate the sentence if necessary.

[B] Determine the sentence pattern of both the independent clause and the adverb clause.

[C] Diagram each sentence.

1. After the party ended we could not find the keys to our hotel room.

2. Bonnie's father bought her a new car for graduation even though she could not drive.

3. The children held their complaints about the school until the new principal arrived.

4. Dogs are sociable creatures whereas cats are usually solitary.

5. Wanda will ask me twenty questions unless I can avoid her.

6. Wherever Lucy goes Charlie Brown follows her.

7. Everyone will suffer if civility vanishes from our social interactions.

8. If civility vanishes from our social interactions everyone will suffer.

see answer key, p. 398

EXERCISE 7.2

The following sentences contain both noun clauses and adverb clauses.

[A] Underline the adverb clauses and circle the noun clauses.

[B] Punctuate each sentence as necessary.

[C] Determine the sentence pattern number for each independent clause and each dependent clause.

[D] Diagram each sentence.

1. If we are grateful for small things we understand their importance in our lives.

2. I wondered if the bus would ever arrive.

3. Since their relationship began both of them have been extremely jealous.

4. Bob's dilemma where he should invest his inheritance is an enviable one.

5. Bob asked where he should invest his inheritance.

6. Wherever Bob invests his inheritance he wants a good return on his capital.

7. While the thunder roared the dog cowered beneath the bed.

8. People learn lessons about life from whomever they admire during their child-hood.

9. What our schools need now is leadership although I am not advocating more government intervention.

10. Once we reconcile ourselves to Dean's resignation we will give assistance to whoever assumes his duties.

see answer key, p. 399

RELATIVE OR ADJECTIVE CLAUSE

Like the adverb clause, the relative clause can be detached from the rest of the sentence, leaving behind an independent clause. Let's consider additional qualities of the relative clause:

1. **A relative clause contains a subject and a verb.**

2. **A relative clause is an adjective clause that relates to, or modifies, the noun that it follows.** (Note that although the single-word adjective usually precedes the noun it modifies, as in "the *red* dress," the adjective clause follows the noun, as in "the dress *that is red*.")

3. **A relative clause can be introduced by a relative pronoun (who, whom, whose, which, that) or a relative adverb (when, where, why).** Here are a few pointers on how to choose the correct relative:

   a. Use a form of "who" when referring to people.

   b. Use "which" when referring to things.

   c. Use "that" when referring to things or people, although careful writers tend to restrict "that" to things and to use "who" exclusively for people.

   d. As the possessive form, "whose" can refer to people or things, although many writers rephrase in order to relate "whose" only to people:

   I asked the man whose car was in the driveway for help.

   The car whose tire had been damaged was in the driveway. (This sentence could easily be rephrased to read "The car with the damaged tire was in the driveway.")

   e. As a relative adverb, "when" will always follow a unit of time. Remember, though, that "when" can also be a subordinating conjunction to introduce an adverb clause or an interrogative to introduce a noun clause:

   I will always treasure the moment *when we met*. (Here, "when we met" is a relative clause and modifies the direct object, "moment." *Which* moment will I always treasure? The moment "when we met.")

   When we met, the war had just ended. ("When we met" is an adverb clause in this sentence, indicating *when* something happened. We also know it is an adverb clause because we can move it within the sentence without changing the meaning: The war had just ended *when we met*.)

   I remember *when we met*. ("When we met" here serves as a noun clause because it is the direct object—I remember *what*?—and also because we can easily replace it with a pronoun: I remember *something*.)

   f. "Where" is another versatile word that can introduce a relative, adverb, or noun clause. As a relative adverb, it always follows a noun that indicates a place:

   The places *where I go* are my private retreats. (relative clause)

   Where I go, you must follow. (adverb clause)

   Where I go is none of your business. (noun clause, subject)

   g. "Why" can introduce a relative or a noun clause. As a relative adverb, it almost always follows the word "reason" or a synonym:

   I refuse to discuss the reason *why I left*. (relative clause)

   The manager asked *why I left*. (noun clause, direct object)

One more complexity of the relative clause is that, once you have memorized all of the relative pronouns and relative adverbs, you may find yourself faced with a relative clause that appears to have no introductory word at all. In a situation like this, the relative clause begins with an understood relative pronoun or an understood relative adverb.

The guide *we met at the aquarium* was knowledgeable.

The guide [*that*] OR [*whom*] *we met at the aquarium* was knowledgeable.

Kerry's grandmother recalled the year *World War II began.*

Kerry's grandmother recalled the year [*in which*] OR [*when*] *World War II began.*

EXERCISE 7.3

Underline the relative clauses in the following sentences. Notice that when you remove the relative clause, an independent clause (grammatically complete sentence) remains.

1. The town where I grew up is extremely small.

2. People who have extensive classroom experience are valuable resources for beginning teachers.

3. The printer which we hooked up to the computer is not working properly.

4. The year when they eloped was a difficult one for her parents.

5. I do not understand the reason why we must negotiate secretly.

6. A person whose will is strong can live through bad times.

7. The swimmers saw a turtle that was injured.

8. The manager fired the worker whom she did not like.

9. The table we found at the yard sale is actually a valuable antique.

10. The car that we bought last year is very reliable.

see answer key, p. 400

Punctuating Relative Clauses

It is sometimes difficult to determine whether commas are necessary to set off a relative clause. In general, there are **two rules for punctuating relative clauses:**

1. **Use commas to set off a nonrestrictive relative clause.** A nonrestrictive relative clause is one that does not at all restrict the meaning of the noun it modifies (in other words, the noun it follows). Another way to think of the nonrestrictive relative clause is to consider it a "commenting" clause; that is, it comments upon the noun it follows rather than identifying it or narrowing it in some way. This is always true when the noun being modified by the relative clause is a proper noun and usually true when it is preceded by a possessive form or by a demonstrative pronoun ("this," "that," "these," "those"). A simpler way to remember this concept is to memorize the following all-purpose rule, one which applies to many comma situations:

> *extra* **information** = *extra* **commas**

You can even visualize the commas as "hooks" holding information that can be lifted out of the sentence without substantially changing the meaning of the independent clause.

> Mary, *who studied her comma rules*, passed the exam.

"Who studied her comma rules" is a nonrestrictive relative clause because it modifies a proper noun (which therefore needs no further identification). Thus the relative clause provides extra information, and the extra commas can be thought of as hooks used to detach the extra information provided by the clause.

2. **Do not use commas to set off a restrictive relative clause.** A restrictive relative clause is one that *does* restrict the meaning of the noun it modifies. This is true when the noun being modified is identified only in general terms:

> A student *who knows the comma rules* should pass the exam.

A simpler way to remember this rule is to memorize the following, which again applies to many comma situations:

> *necessary* **information** = *no* **commas**

One of the most difficult times to determine whether or not commas are necessary arises when the noun being modified is preceded by the definite article, "the." You may need more context than an isolated sentence can provide in order to make the best decision:

> The student *who knew her comma rules* passed the exam.

Are we referring here to a specific student, already identified? If so, the relative clause provides extra information and should have extra commas. If, however, the relative clause "who knew her comma rules" is used to identify the student, then no commas are needed.

Take special note of two situations that indicate restrictive relative clauses. First, when the relative clause begins with "that," do not use commas. Second, when the relative clause begins with a relative adverb (when, where, why), you normally do not need commas.

Finally, as a general rule use "which" as the relative pronoun for nonrestrictive relative clauses (with commas) describing a thing and use "that" as the relative pronoun for restrictive relative clauses (without commas) describing a thing. (To help you remember the distinction, here is a mnemonic device: "which" and "comma" both contain five letters.) Notice that although the sentences below have the same subject, the meaning of the relative clause determines the punctuation and therefore also indicates the use of "which" or "that" as the relative pronoun:

A bouquet of flowers, *which can express many thoughts*, speaks eloquently.

("Which can express many thoughts" is a nonrestrictive relative clause because it comments upon, rather than narrowing, the subject. *All* bouquets of flowers can express many thoughts.)

A bouquet of flowers *that arrives on time* can prevent an argument.

(Here, "that arrives on time" is a restrictive relative clause because only bouquets of flowers that arrive in a timely fashion—not all bouquets of flowers—can prevent an argument.)

Let's look at one more example to demonstrate how to differentiate between a restrictive and a nonrestrictive clause:

A man *who owns a bookstore* is lucky.

STEP 1	**Which noun does the relative clause modify?** Since a properly placed relative clause modifies the noun it follows, "who owns a bookstore" modifies "a man."
STEP 2	**Is the noun being modified a proper noun or specifically identified in some other way?** Since the answer is "no," we appear to be dealing with a restrictive clause here, one that is necessary to identify the noun. Proper nouns, those preceded by possessive forms or demonstrative pronouns, and often those preceded by the definite article, "the," need no further identification.
STEP 3	**Does the relative clause give us extra or necessary information? If you use extra commas and "unhook" the relative clause, does the sentence retain its basic meaning?** If we unhook "who owns a bookstore," we are left with "A man is lucky." Although this sentence is grammatically complete (a Pattern 2 sentence), its meaning is very different from the intended meaning of the original sentence. It seems clear, then, that "who owns a bookstore" is a necessary, or restrictive, relative clause that accordingly does not need to be set off by commas.

Occasionally it is possible to change the meaning of a sentence by choosing whether or not to set off the relative clause with commas. Consider the meaning of the following sentences:

Pain, *which is debilitating*, can lead to depression. (*All* pain is debilitating.)

Pain *which is debilitating* can lead to depression. (Only severe pain, not all pain, can lead to depression.)

Pain *that is debilitating* can lead to depression. (If the writer means that only severe pain can lead to depression, then both omitting the commas and choosing "that" as the relative pronoun will emphasize the intended sense of the sentence.)

EXERCISE 7.4

Underline the relative clauses in the following sentences and then punctuate the sentences correctly. For extra practice, diagram them as well once you have read the section that follows on diagraming.

1. Simon who had just started his diet woke up at midnight because he was hungry.

2. This old doll which has been in the closet for years might be extremely valuable.

3. Wanda framed the first check that she received from her publisher.

4. Many elderly people nostalgically recall their youth as a time when life was simpler.

5. The children who were playing at the end of the block could not hear the shouts of their parents.

6. Stamp collecting which can consume much time and money is an educational hobby.

7. The fugitive concealed the reason why he had no identification.

see answer key, p. 401

Diagraming the Relative Clause

As with the noun and adverb clauses, the relative clause also introduces another subject and verb into the sentence that must be accommodated somehow in the diagraming structure. As with the adverb clause, we **place the relative clause on a second tier below the independent clause**.

We now need to tie the two clauses together in some way. **Since the relative pronoun or relative adverb refers back to the noun it follows, we draw a dotted line between these two words. And since the relative pronoun or the relative adverb is diagramed within the relative clause itself, nothing is written on the dotted line.** If you are not sure that you have connected the right words, one test is to substitute the noun for the relative pronoun in the relative clause.

Finally, remember that in some sentences the relative pronoun or relative adverb will not actually appear in the sentence but is understood. When you diagram such a sentence, insert the appropriate relative pronoun or relative adverb in the diagram (usually "that" will work) and surround it with square brackets to indicate it did not appear in the original sentence.

Let's look at a few examples of sentences containing relative clauses:

The person *who bought the chair* paid by check.

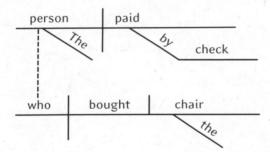

This diagram illustrates that the relative pronoun can serve as the subject of its own clause. If you have any doubt about connecting "person" and "who" in the diagram, substitute the noun for the relative pronoun: "The person bought the chair." This confirms your accuracy.

The chair *that he bought* was an antique.

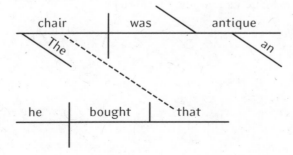

In this example, "that" serves as the direct object in the relative clause. As above, a way of checking to make sure you are right is to substitute the relative pronoun with the noun it modifies. When we rearrange the relative clause a bit, we find "he bought that"—or, in other words, "he bought the chair."

The day *when he bought the chair* was his birthday.

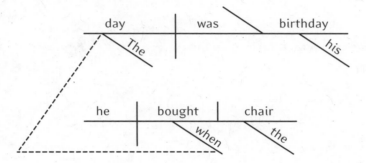

The relative clause, "when he bought the chair," begins with a relative adverb. We cannot perform the same test here, since we cannot replace an adverb with a noun. It should be clear, though, that "when" refers back to the unit of time "day." Remember that each of the relative adverbs ("when," "where," "why") is diagramed on a diagonal line beneath the verb of the relative clause.

The computer Mike bought yesterday has already crashed.

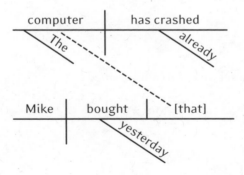

In this sentence the relative clause begins with an understood relative pronoun: The computer [*that*] Mike bought yesterday has already crashed.

EXERCISE 7.5

a. Underline the relative clauses in the sentences below.
b. Determine the sentence pattern of the independent clause and the relative clause.
c. Diagram each sentence.

1. Juliet, who has been my friend for ten years, now lives in France.

2. This young woman, whom many of us admired for her multiple talents, has become a well-known photographer.

3. She published the first photograph that she submitted to a magazine.

4. The explanatory letter she wrote caught the attention of the editor.

5. Juliet still remembers the desolate place where she took the photo.

6. Photography, which requires intelligence and creativity, is a perfect match for Juliet's natural gifts.

7. I understand the reasons why Juliet has been so tremendously successful in this field.

see answer key, p. 402

Relative Clause or Appositive?

The nonrestrictive relative clause (the one that comments upon or provides extra information about the noun it follows) has much in common with the appositive. These two structures can cause confusion unless you remember a key difference. The relative clause begins with a relative pronoun or a relative adverb and performs the function of an adjective; the appositive consists of a noun and its modifiers and renames the noun it follows. **Because it renames the noun, you can substitute the appositive for the noun it modifies. You *cannot* substitute the relative clause for the noun it modifies.**

Professor Mitchell, *who was my first English teacher,* is my mentor. (relative clause)

Professor Mitchell, *my first English teacher*, is my mentor. (appositive)

Notice that in the first sentence the italicized portion begins with the relative pronoun "who," whereas in the second sentence we have a noun, "teacher," preceded by modifiers. The final test to determine which is the relative clause and which is the appositive is to substitute the italicized portion for the noun being modified.

⋆*Who was my English teacher* is my mentor. (not a sentence and therefore the italicized words are not an appositive but a relative clause)

My first English teacher is my mentor. (a sentence and therefore the italicized words are an appositive)

EXERCISE 7.6

Mark the italicized portion of each sentence below as either a relative clause or an appositive. For extra practice, diagram each sentence as well.

1. Mom's china, *which she inherited from her grandmother*, is a family treasure.

2. Mom's china, *an inheritance from her grandmother*, is a family treasure.

3. The day *when Susan arrived from Peru* was my birthday.

4. Brad is dating Merissa, *who has an unusual outlook on life*.

5. Toby, *the dog that lives down the street*, visits our house frequently.

see answer key, p. 403

COMPOUND-COMPLEX SENTENCES

The most complicated sentence structure in English combines the compound and the complex structures we have already seen. **The compound-complex sentence, then, consists of two (or more) independent clauses as well as one (or more) dependent clauses.** Let's take a look at a couple of examples:

Anna, who is my neighbor, works in Philadelphia, but her husband works in Denver.

We can isolate two independent clauses: *Anna works in Philadelphia*
her husband works in Denver

Since these clauses are joined by the coordinating conjunction "but," this sentence contains a compound structure. We can also isolate a dependent (relative) clause:

who is my neighbor

The relative clause gives us a complex sentence structure, which, combined with the compound structure, yields a compound-complex sentence. The following diagram visually illustrates the compound and complex nature of this structure:

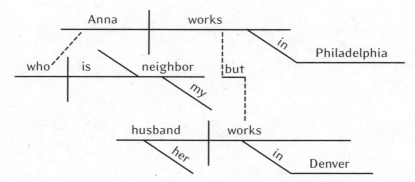

As the wind howled, we huddled in our makeshift shelter; then our fire went out.

independent clauses: *we huddled in our makeshift shelter*
                         our fire went out

dependent (adverb) clause: *as the wind howled*

Because the independent clauses are joined by a semicolon and a conjunctive adverb, we have a compound structure; the adverb clause adds the element of complex structure. Overall, then, the sentence is compound-complex, as illustrated by the following diagram as well. (Note that the conjunctive adverb "then" is diagramed as an adverb within the second independent clause but also connected to the horizontal line where a coordinating conjunction would appear. This indicates that "then" functions here as a conjunctive adverb.)

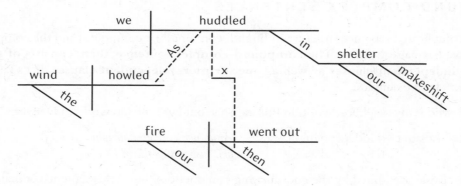

COMPLETE SENTENCES

The most basic, and most important, grammar essential is the ability to recognize and write a complete sentence. Now that we have examined the ten basic sentence patterns and learned how to distinguish among simple, compound, complex, and compound-complex sentence structures, we should be able to avoid writing fragments, run-ons, and comma splices.

FRAGMENT:	My neighbor plays tennis every day. *Although he is seventy-five years old.*
RUN-ON:	My neighbor is seventy-five years old he plays tennis every day.
COMMA SPLICE:	My neighbor is seventy-five years old, he plays tennis every day.

Perhaps the most common variety of fragment is the one listed above, a dependent clause (in this case an adverb clause) that follows an independent clause rather than being attached to it. The solution, then, is to join the two together: My neighbor plays tennis every day, although he is seventy-five years old.

To correct the run-on or comma splice error, we have five options:

1. Use two separate sentences.	My neighbor is seventy-five years old. He plays tennis every day.
2. Use a coordinating conjunction.	My neighbor is seventy-five years old, *but* he plays tennis every day.
3. Use a subordinating conjunction.	*Although* my neighbor is seventy-five years old, he plays tennis every day.
4. Use a semicolon.	My neighbor is seventy-five years old; he plays tennis every day.
5. Use a semicolon and conjunctive adverb.	My neighbor is seventy-five years old; *however*, he plays tennis every day.

The following chart will help you review ways to combine sentences and to avoid fragments, run-ons, and comma splices:

Sentence Options

COORDINATING CONJUNCTIONS

for	but
and	or
nor	yet
	so

Use a comma with these conjunctions *only* when the conjunction separates two complete sentences.

Mary is a child, *but* she is very wise.

CONJUNCTIVE ADVERBS

accordingly	instead
additionally	likewise
also	meanwhile
consequently	moreover
finally	nevertheless
furthermore	nonetheless
hence	on the contrary
however	on the other hand
in addition	otherwise
in conclusion	still
in contrast	then
indeed	therefore
in fact	thus

Before you use a semicolon, make sure you have two complete sentences.

Mary is a child; *nonetheless*, she is wise.
OR
Mary is a child; she is wise.

SUBORDINATING CONJUNCTIONS

after	so that
although, though	unless
as	until
because	when, whenever
before	where, wherever
even though	whereas
if	whether or not
once	while
since	

Use a comma when an adverb clause begins the sentence or when the subordinating conjunction shows contrast.

Even though Mary is a child, she is wise.

Mary is wise, *even though* she is a child.

Mary is wise *because* she is a child.

RELATIVE PRONOUNS

who, whom (to refer to people)
which (to refer to things)
that (to refer to people or things)

Use extra commas for extra information in a relative clause; use no commas for necessary information.

Mary, *who is a child*, is wise.

A child *who is wise* commands attention.

SUMMARY OF KEY CONCEPTS IN CHAPTER 7

1. A complex sentence consists of one independent clause and one or more dependent clauses.

2. Dependent clauses perform three functions:

    a. The noun clause takes the place of a noun (acts as subject, object, complement, or appositive) and can therefore be replaced by a pronoun ("it," "someone," or "something"). The noun clause is diagramed on a pedestal in the same place that a one-word noun would be diagramed.

    b. The adverb clause answers an adverb question (when? where? how? why? for what purpose? in what manner? under what condition?) and is introduced by a subordinating conjunction (such as "when," "although," "if," or any other word that will turn a complete sentence into a dependent clause). Always place a comma after an introductory adverb clause; otherwise, use a comma only when the adverb clause at a later point in the sentence begins with a subordinating conjunction showing contrast ("although," "though," "even though," "whereas," "while"). The adverb clause is diagramed beneath the independent clause, with a dotted line joining the verbs of the two clauses and the subordinating conjunction written on the dotted line.

    c. The relative or adjective clause modifies the noun it follows and is introduced by a relative pronoun ("who," "whoever," "whom," "whomever," "whose," "which," "that") or by a relative adverb ("when," "where," "why"). Set off a relative clause with commas when it provides extra information—usually, that is, when the noun it modifies is a proper noun or a noun preceded by a possessive form or a demonstrative pronoun used as a determiner. Diagram the relative clause beneath the independent clause, including the relative pronoun or relative adverb as part of the relative clause. Draw a dotted line between the relative pronoun or relative adverb and the noun it modifies in the independent clause.

3. The compound-complex sentence consists of two or more independent clauses and one or more dependent clauses.

4. What we have discussed so far can help you avoid writing fragments, run-ons, and comma splices.

CHAPTER 7 EXERCISE

I. The sentences below contain adverb or relative clauses.

[A] Underline each dependent clause and label it as an adverb clause (A) or a relative clause (R).

[B] Punctuate each sentence.

[C] Diagram each sentence.

1. After we found the puppy we took it to the animal shelter.

2. The puppy that we found was friendly and playful.

3. Helen's computer which was quite old remained reliable.

4. Helen's computer remained reliable although it was quite old.

5. Everyone who was on the team appreciated Coach Tina.

6. Bethany who was on the team appreciated Coach Tina.

7. Coach Tina complimented the team because each player had worked hard during the season.

II. The sentences below contain all three types of clauses.

[A] Underline each dependent clause and label it as a noun clause (N), an adverb clause (A), or a relative clause (R).

[B] Punctuate each sentence.

[C] Diagram each sentence.

1. Princess Lila who had slept for a century suddenly awakened.

2. The evil fairy whom the queen had employed as a guardian had finally died.

3. The princess thought that she had slept for a short time.

4. The first conversation that she held confused her.

5. When she heard an unfamiliar language she grew frightened.

6. She grew even more frightened until she looked in a mirror.

7. The sight of her own face reassured her at the moment when she needed a friend.

8. Although most princesses depend on handsome princes Lila took matters into her own hands.

9. She took responsibility for what happened from that moment.

10. Soon Lila wondered if her memories of an earlier lifetime were real.

III. The following set of sentences will be harder because each one contains at least two dependent clauses. This exercise will be a challenge!

[A] Underline each dependent clause and label it as a noun clause (N), an adverb clause (A), or a relative clause (R).

[B] Punctuate each sentence.

[C] Diagram each sentence.

1. Because I am allergic to dogs we must find a new home where our collie will be happy.

2. After the lawyer read the will I realized I would be responsible for the locked chest that had always remained in my grandmother's bedroom.

3. Seth Brown whom everyone respected as a fine pianist lost all memory of the tune that had been in his head.

4. Idealistic people who fight for their dreams usually receive several disappointments in life whereas cynics usually receive what they expect.

5. While he was researching the history of a particularly obscure word the scholar
irritated the librarians who were in the reference area.

6. As she efficiently handled her duties the waitress demanded an apology from the
rude customer even though he protested his innocence.

7. The note the child handed to his mother brought tears to her eyes after she read it.

8. Whatever you decide will be acceptable to the people who support you because they trust your judgment.

IV. Use the following base sentence to create sentences of your own as specified.

The governess frightened the children.

a. Write a compound sentence using a coordinating conjunction.

_____

_____

_____

b. Write a compound sentence using a semicolon and a conjunctive adverb.

_____

_____

_____

c. Write a complex sentence containing a noun clause.

_____

_____

_____

d. Write a complex sentence containing an adverb clause.

_____

_____

_____

e. Write a complex sentence containing a nonrestrictive (extra information) relative clause.

_____

_____

_____

f. Write a complex sentence containing a restrictive (necessary information) relative clause.

_____

_____

_____

g. Write a simple sentence containing an appositive.

_____

_____

_____

h. Write a compound–complex sentence.

_____

_____

_____

V. The passage below consists of simple sentences. Rewrite the passage to make it smoother by incorporating compound structures, appositives, and compound and complex sentences. Make sure that you are writing complete sentences and avoiding fragments, run-ons, and comma splices.

Great Expectations is a novel by Charles Dickens. It tells the story of Pip. Pip is a young orphan. He lives with his rather cruel, cold sister. She has a good-hearted husband. Eventually Pip attracts the attention of a wealthy woman named Miss Havisham. Years ago, she was jilted on her wedding day. She still wears her wedding dress. She still has the wedding cake. Nothing has changed since the day of the jilting. Even the clock has been stopped. She has taken in a young girl named Estella. Pip falls in love with Estella. Miss Havisham has trained Estella to break the hearts of young men. This allows Miss Havisham some measure of satisfaction. It is a way of imposing vengeance upon men in return for her own jilting. Pip, Estella, and Miss Havisham are three of the most memorable characters created by Charles Dickens. Dickens is an author famous for distinctive characters.

_____

_____

_____

_____

_____

_____

_____

_____

_____

_____

_____

_____

_____

_____

_____

_____

_____

_____

_____

_____

_____

_____

_____

see answer key, p. 403

Usage Problems of Case, Agreement, and Consistency

Now that we understand how independent and dependent clauses work together, we are ready to tackle some of the more sophisticated usage problems that arise in English. Both within sentences and within paragraphs (as well as even larger units of writing), one mark of excellence is consistency, a broad term that we will use to encompass several usage issues addressed in this chapter: (1) agreement between subjects and verbs; (2) agreement between pronouns and antecedents; and (3) consistency of pronoun case, number, and person.

SUBJECT-VERB AGREEMENT

Everyone understands the basic principle that a singular subject needs a singular verb, while a plural subject needs a plural verb. Until you think about it, though, you may not realize the inherent difficulty in this. For example, how can you distinguish a singular from a plural verb? The answer is that we can't, except in third person singular, present tense, the verb form that ends in "-s." Consider the following sentences.

The ducks *walk* around the pond every day. (plural subject + plural verb)

The duck *walks* around the pond every day. (singular subject + singular verb)

If you are not careful, you are likely to say that "walk" is a singular verb because it doesn't end in "-s." If you are tempted to make such a statement, remember that subjects and verbs are different. A regular noun forms its *plural* by adding "-s"; a present tense verb forms its *singular* in third person by adding "-s." This brings us to **"the rule of one –s": In present tense, if the subject ends in "-s," the verb cannot also end in "-s."** (Of course, if the subject is an irregular plural, this rule does not apply literally. A plural subject, no matter what its form, requires a verb that does *not* end in "-s.")

Most native speakers of English, though, have no difficulty with this aspect of subject–verb agreement. Instead, problems result from a few specialized grammatical structures—compound structures, indefinite pronouns, relative clauses, collective nouns, and a sentence structure involving the expletive "there."

I ● *Compound Structures*

In the sentences below, circle the verb that sounds correct to you:

1. The words and the music of that song (IS, ARE) familiar.

2. Either the words or the music (IS, ARE) familiar.

3. Neither the music nor the words (IS, ARE) familiar.

4. The words, as well as the music, (IS, ARE) familiar.

5. The words, in addition to the music, (IS, ARE) familiar.

6. The music, along with the words, (IS, ARE) familiar.

Let's look at the correct answers now and an explanation for each of these situations.

1. The words *and* the music of that song *are* familiar.

When two subjects are joined by *and*, the subject is almost always plural and therefore requires a plural verb (that is, a verb that does not end in "-s"). The only exception occurs when "and" joins two words that actually make up one unit, as in the following sentence: The macaroni and cheese is on the table.

2. Either the words *or* the music *is* familiar.

3. Neither the music *nor* the words *are* familiar.

Both of these subjects are compound because they are joined by "or" or its negative variant, "nor." If both subjects are plural, you need a plural verb; if both subjects are singular, you need a singular verb. The hardest case occurs when, as in our examples, one subject is singular and one is plural. What do we do then? Because it is more pleasing to the ears of native speakers of English, we ignore the subject farther away from the verb and have the verb agree with the subject that is closer. In 2, then, we think "the music *is* familiar"; in 3, we think "the words *are* familiar."

4. The words, *as well as* the music, *are* familiar.

5. The words, *in addition to* the music, *are* familiar.

6. The music, *along with* the words, *is* familiar.

In all three of these sentences, the subject precedes a prepositional phrase. Remember that we will not find a subject inside a prepositional phrase; therefore, if you eliminate the intervening prepositional phrases, you'll have no difficulty making the subjects and verbs agree. The only exception to this rule occurs when the subject is an indefinite pronoun, as we'll see below.

2 ● Indefinite Pronouns

Because indefinite pronouns are just that—indefinite—it is often difficult to determine whether they should be treated as singular or plural. From the point of view of subject-verb agreement, we have two categories of indefinite pronouns.

A. the "any-," "some-," "every-," and "no-" pronouns = singular:

anyone	someone	everyone	no one
anybody	somebody	everybody	nobody
anything	something	everything	nothing

All of the above pronouns are grammatically singular. Logically speaking, all of these pronouns (except for "everyone," "everybody," and "everything") clearly fall into the singular category:

No one *wants* to play with me.

Something always *goes* bump in the night.

Do you know if anybody *lives* here?

The "every-" pronouns, although logically plural, are also treated as grammatically singular in terms of subject-verb agreement. In addition, the word "every" as a pre-noun modifier automatically indicates the singular. Observe that in each sentence below, the word part or word "every" is followed by a singular form ("every*one*," "every*body*," "every*thing*," "every *experience*").

Everyone *enjoys* an intriguing story.

Everybody at the office *is* being unreasonable today.

I am elated when everything *runs* smoothly in the computer lab.

Every experience *teaches* us something valuable.

Like "every," "each" also requires a singular verb.

Each day *brings* surprises.

Each of the employees *was* on time.

B. words that specify a number or amount, such as "enough," "many," "none," "some," and "much" = singular or plural

The indefinite pronouns in this category are not as clear-cut. More often than not, **we need the information contained in an attached prepositional phrase in order to determine if the pronoun is singular or plural**. (Ordinarily, prepositional phrases do not contain any significant grammatical information; this is an important exception.) Notice how **the same indefinite pronoun can be either singular or plural, depending on whether the object of the preposition is a mass or count noun**:

Some of the cookies *are* left. (Because "cookies" is a count noun, and also plural in form here, we use the plural verb.)

Some of the coffee *is* left. (Because "coffee" is a mass noun, singular in form, we use the singular verb in this sentence.)

None of the newspaper accounts *were* accurate. (We can count the number of newspaper reports, and so "were" agrees with "accounts." Although you may hear the rule that "none" is always singular because it means "not one," follow the general rule and treat "none" as you would any other indefinite pronoun.)

None of the speculation *was* accurate. (We cannot count speculation, and so it is a mass noun requiring the singular verb "was.")

Native speakers of English rarely have difficulty with this situation, except in one instance. The indefinite pronoun "a number" (as in "a number of people") is frequently confused with the phrase "the number."

A number of people *were* planning to see the show.

The number of people *was* too large for the concert hall to accommodate.

"A number" requires a plural verb, since a plural count noun will always follow; "the number" requires a singular verb, since it always refers to a specific, single number.

3 ● *Relative Clauses*

Relative clauses can cause difficulty in terms of subject-verb agreement because we must determine the antecedent of the relative pronoun in order to decide on a singular or plural verb. If a relative clause begins with "who," for example, we cannot tell whether the word is singular or plural unless we find the word that it modifies, or relates back to. This problem is especially tangled in a sentence such as this one:

Jim is one of those people who *are* unaccountably moody.
(Although the independent clause is about a single individual, the relative pronoun "who" refers back to the plural "people." Within the relative clause, then, we need a plural verb, "are": "people are moody.")

Jim is the only one of the employees who *is* on the job at 7 a.m.
(In this sentence, although "who" refers back to the plural "employees," the meaning of the relative clause is affected by the word "only" earlier in the sentence. "Only" makes it clear that we are speaking of Jim, not of employees in general, and therefore the singular verb, "is," is correct.)

In most cases, though, the relative clause will not create difficulties:

San Francisco is a *city* that *has* character.

Large *cities*, which *are* sometimes overwhelming, can also be exciting.

Julia was amazed by the *drivers* who *were* flagrantly breaking the speed limit.

4 ● Collective Nouns

A collective noun is a word that "collects" together a few or many members of a group to signify that all the members comprise a single unit. We use collective nouns frequently, without thinking much about the actual concept; for example, "audience," "jury," "team," "company," "class," "group" all serve as collective nouns. A collective noun is singular when all the members in the unit are acting in concert. In this situation (which almost always holds true), the collective noun requires a singular verb. Which sentence below sounds correct to you?

The jury *were* asked for a decision.

The jury *was* asked for a decision.

Most likely, you chose the second version of this sentence. Besides sounding more natural, the second option is correct because "the jury" is a collective noun. In the situational context of the sentence, the members of the jury would be treated as a single unit. All would have been included in the asking process. You could also, of course, avoid possible difficulties by rephrasing to "The *members* of the jury *were* asked for a decision."

On rare occasions a collective noun does require a plural verb, when it is clear that the members in the unit are not acting in unison but individually. Can you determine the difference between these two sentences? Why does "cast" in the first sentence act as a collective noun, while "cast" in the second sentence does not?

The cast *was* engaged in a dress rehearsal.

In small groups scattered throughout the theater, the cast *were* rehearsing several scenes to prepare for the performance that evening.

5 ● "There" as Expletive

One idiomatic sentence structure in English involves moving the subject in a Pattern 1 sentence to the end of the sentence and beginning with "there," an expletive because it carries no semantic weight. "There" is almost always followed by some form of *be*. Examine the sentences below and the differences in the way they are diagrammed.

A face was in the mirror. PATTERN 1 (subject – *be* – adverb of time or place)

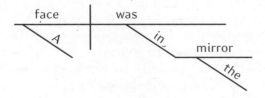

There was a face in the mirror. (PATTERN I rearranged because of expletive "there")

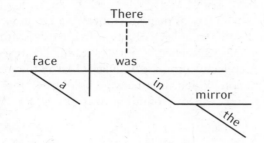

A face was *there*. ("there" as adverb, explaining "where")

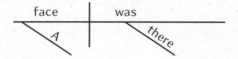

Notice how the expletive "there" carries a different intonation, a different emphasis, as compared with the adverb "there." The adverb carries more weight, since it provides information within the sentence, whereas the expletive is a word empty of meaning. The diagram also indicates the difference between an adverb, located within the diagram as a modifier, and the expletive, floating above the diagram as a grammatically unnecessary element.

Although "there" as expletive usually occurs first in the sentence, the adverb "there" can also occupy this position. When it does appear at the beginning of a sentence, the adverb "there" occurs with the definite article ("the") rather than the indefinite ("a" or "an") when the noun in question is singular. Say these sentences out loud to hear the difference in emphasis when "there" functions as an adverb:

> *There* was *a* face in the mirror.   (expletive)

> *There* was *the* face in the mirror.   (adverb)

The use of the expletive "there" often leads to problems of subject-verb agreement. When speaking, we almost always use the singular *be* verb in contracted form: "There's a hole in my sock," or "There's been an accident." Because we hear this form so frequently, many people automatically use the singular even when the plural is called for: "There's three reasons to work hard," or "There's a man and a woman in the driveway."

Basically, when a sentence begins with the expletive *there*, you must remember that the subject follows the verb. Although it is permissible to use the singular verb in speaking, in a formal written situation you must make sure that the verb agrees with the subject that follows. You might also choose to avoid the situation altogether by rephrasing the sentence; in fact, a sentence beginning with "there" is automatically a weak construction—as close to passive as a sentence in active voice can be—and therefore would be stronger if reworded.

INCORRECT:	There's three reasons to work hard.
CORRECT:	There are three reasons to work hard.
BETTER:	Three reasons to work hard are . . . .
INCORRECT :	There's a man and a woman in the driveway.
CORRECT :	There are a man and a woman in the driveway.
BETTER :	A man and a woman are in the driveway.

As mentioned above, "there" can also be used as an adverb when it indicates location. In addition, "there" can serve as an interjection when it expresses emotion. These situations, of course, do not affect subject-verb agreement, although confusion may arise when the adverb comes first in the sentence and the subject follows the verb.

There *is* the book that I was searching for. ("There" is an adverb here, indicating "where"; "is" agrees with the singular subject "book.")

There *are* the books that I was searching for. (Again, "there" is an adverb; "are" agrees with the plural subject "books.")

The books that I was searching for *are* there. (Because the adverb "there" has been moved to the end of the sentence, it is clear that the verb "are" agrees with "books.")

There! I found the books! (Here we see "there" as an interjection.)

There *is* a book on the shelf. In fact, there *are* at least twenty books on the shelf. ("There" serves as an expletive in both of these sentences; it does not indicate location and is therefore not an adverb.)

EXERCISE 8.1

Circle the correct choice in the sentences below.

1. There (WAS, WERE) shiny bits of glass on the counter.

2. Either the secretaries or the manager (WAS, WERE) responsible for the snafu.

3. The committee that evaluates scholarship winners (IS, ARE) meeting this week.

4. Both the secretary and the treasurer (WAS, WERE) expected to give reports.

5. A doctor, along with three nurses, (WAS, WERE) on call the night of the disaster.

6. A number of the cities involved (IS, ARE) talking about a class-action lawsuit.

7. This breed of cat is the only one that (HAS, HAVE) extra toes on each paw.

8. New Orleans is one of those cities that (HAS, HAVE) distinct neighborhoods.

9. (DOES, DO) either of the coaches expect the team to win? (Hint: Before making a choice, rearrange the words of this question to form a statement.)

10. A box of apples, oranges, and pears (WAS, WERE) delivered yesterday.

11. Everyone in both classes (WANTS, WANT) to perform in the talent show.

12. None of the answers in the teacher's manual (WAS, WERE) correct.

13. There (WAS, WERE) a few pink spots on the toddler's tongue.

14. Neither the books nor the movies in my childhood home (WAS, WERE) able to surpass my own imagination.

15. A hamster, as well as a guinea pig, (HAS, HAVE) a high metabolic rate.

see answer key, p. 410

PRONOUN AGREEMENT

In addition to ensuring that subjects and verbs agree, we must make sure that each pronoun agrees with the noun or the pronoun it refers back to, known as its **antecedent**. In many cases, the decision is easy:

Marla enjoyed her experience at the game.

But if we change the subject, the pronoun choice becomes more difficult:

Everyone enjoyed their experience at the game.

In this sentence, "their" is technically incorrect because it is plural, while the indefinite pronoun "everyone" is singular. The pronoun "their" seems logical in a sentence such as this, yet to be grammatically correct, we would have to write "Everyone enjoyed his or her experience at the game." Some would argue that we could shorten this to "Everyone enjoyed his experience at the game." This version of the sentence, although grammatically correct, is likely to offend many people because it implies that only males enjoyed the game. What is the best version, then? In speaking situations, almost everyone nowadays will use "their" in a sentence like this one. In a written situation, though, a writer must weigh the options. Is it preferable to use perfect grammar or to use the more natural-sounding alternative, even if it is grammatically incorrect? One solution is to reword the sentence entirely: "All of them enjoyed their experience at the game."

Indefinite pronouns, as we see in the example above, cause difficulty because many of them are singular in grammatical number although often plural in logical meaning. "Everyone," "everybody," "everything," "every," and "each" are singular in number but imply the plural, thereby creating agreement problems for the unwary writer. Substituting "all," as we did in the example above, will work in many cases. The important issue here, though, is to be aware of the agreement problems so that, if you decide to use "their," you have made a deliberate choice and not an automatic, unrealized error.

The example above raises another concern, that of **sexist language**. This problem arises when we use the generic "he" to refer to both genders, as in "*Everyone* enjoyed *his* experience at the game." The problem also occurs when we use occupational titles that seem to exclude one gender, as in "The mailmen appreciated the free tickets to the game." "Mailmen" might be correct if only men received the tickets, but more likely the sentence would be better worded as "The mail carriers appreciated the free tickets to the game."

Books have been written debating the philosophical and practical issues of what has come to be known as sexist language. Some argue that language should *reflect* reality; for example, if most people who fight fires are men, why not call them "firemen"? Others argue that language helps to *shape* reality, so that using the label "firemen" insinuates to young girls, as they grow up within our culture, that only men can perform the duties associated with firefighting, whereas the gender-neutral term "firefighter" allows for the possibility that both men and women can choose this career. We will leave aside the philosophical issues and focus instead on the pragmatic. On a practical level, you should be aware that all professional publications insist on nonsexist language. To write professionally—or to teach others to write professionally—you must be aware of what sexist language is and how to avoid it.

Let's look at another example, again with an indefinite pronoun (used here as an adjective) causing the problem.

Every student in this class must complete _____ homework.

The easy solution, and the one we probably all would use when speaking, is to insert "their." Since "every" is singular, though, this solution is grammatically incorrect. Let's look at the possible solutions, in the order of desirability:

1. **Make the antecedent plural**, especially if several sentences will be affected and the pronoun agreement problem will recur.

All of the students in this class must complete *their* homework.

2. **Change the wording of the sentence** to avoid the pronoun problem altogether.

Every student in this class must complete *the* homework.

3. **When absolutely necessary, use "his or her" or "he or she."** You should not use this alternative more than once or twice within the work you are writing because it is a distraction for the reader. For the same reason, avoid using the "s/he" solution. In a longer work, though, you might consider alternating between "he" and "she"; for example, if you are writing a textbook involving case studies, you might alternate gender as you progress through the case studies or through chapters. In most cases, "one" is not a viable alternative to "he or she" because it sounds

rather stilted and requires the repeated use of "one" to ensure pronoun agreement. "He," "she," or "they" cannot refer back to "one":

INCORRECT:	*One* must complete *his or her* homework.
INCORRECT:	*One* must complete *their* homework.
CORRECT:	*One* must complete *one's* homework.

A final area of difficulty involving pronoun agreement arises with **collective nouns**. (We have already seen that collective nouns cause difficulty with subject-verb agreement as well.) As long as the entities constituting the collective noun are acting together as a single unit, these nouns are grammatically singular. Confusion arises because, like many of the indefinite pronouns, collective nouns seem logically plural. For example, consider the following sentences:

The *team* celebrated *their* victory.
(This is technically incorrect, since "team" is singular and "their" is plural; however, it sounds logical and is probably phrased the way that most people would say it, at least in a relatively informal speech context.)

The *team* celebrated *its* victory.
(This is grammatically correct but may sound peculiar to you. Remember that you have the option of rephrasing: The *members* of the team celebrated *their* victory.)

Some other commonly used collective nouns include "jury," "class," "company," "committee," "herd," "family," "group," and "audience." Keep in mind that these nouns are used collectively when all of the members making up the unit are acting in concert; if the members are acting as individuals, then the noun is not collective and a plural pronoun would be appropriate. Almost always, though, the collective noun is used to signal joint action.

The *herd* followed *its* usual direction.
(Here the herd is acting collectively, as a unit.)

The *herd* straggled off in various directions as *they* searched for food.
(Here the sentence makes clear that the herd is not acting collectively, and so "they" is the appropriate pronoun. To make the sentence sound more natural, though, rephrase: "The herd straggled off in various directions as the animals searched for food.")

EXERCISE 8.2

Write in the correct or best pronoun choice in the sentences below. If necessary, reword the sentence.

1. Someone left _____ keys on the table.

_____

2. Each person who saw the film said that _____ disliked the ending.

_____

3. The Spanish Club decided to revamp _____ constitution.

_____

4. It took several days before the jury returned with _____ verdict.

_____

5. Anyone who lived through the 1960s can tell you about _____ memories of the era.

_____

see answer key, p. 410

PRONOUN CASE

Another category of "agreement" involves choosing the appropriate pronoun case. The two cases that are sometimes confused are the nominative (or subjective) and the objective.

Nominative		*Objective*	
I	we	me	us
you	you	you	you
he, she, it	they	him, her, it	them

We use the nominative form when we need a subject or when the pronoun follows the *be* verb, as in "*He* found the stray kitten" or "It was *he* who found the stray kitten." We use the objective form when we need an object for a verb or for a preposition, as in "The kitten saw *him*" or "The kitten ran to *him*." Normally, choosing the correct case of a pronoun is not difficult, except in the following circumstances.

1. The correct case of pronouns in compound structures can be difficult to determine.

Jim and (I, me) wanted Marty and (she, her) to join us.

In the sentence above, there are two ways to determine the correct pronoun choice. First, analyze the function of the pronoun in the sentence. Since the first pronoun is part of the subject, you would choose the nominative or subjective form, "I." Since the second pronoun is part of the direct object, you would choose the objective form, "her."

A second, easier way to determine the correct pronoun choice is to eliminate the other element in the compound structure. The sentence would then read, "I wanted her to join us."

When you eliminate the proper nouns, the correct pronouns become obvious, at least to a native speaker of English. However, two prepositions—"between" and "among"—may cause some trouble because, by virtue of their meaning, we cannot eliminate part of the compound structure. Note that careful writers tend to distinguish between these prepositions, using "between" to indicate the involvement of two entities and "among" to indicate more than two.

> Between you and (I, me), who did it?
>
> Among the Smiths, the Browns, and (we, us), we had a total of five dollars for the rest of the day.

Just remember that, because "between" and "among" are prepositions, an objective pronoun will always follow, no matter how strange that pronoun may sound to you.

> Between *you* and *me*, who did it?
>
> Among the Smiths, the Browns, and *us*, we had a total of five dollars for the rest of the day.
>
> Surviving the hurricane became a contest between *it* and *them*.
>
> The secret was kept between the family and *her*.
>
> The message circulated among *them* and *us*.

A variation on compound structure occurs when a pronoun directly precedes the noun, usually for emphasis:

> All of (we, us) workers united.

As with the compound structure, you can choose correctly if you determine the function of the pronoun (here, the object of a preposition) or if you eliminate the distracting noun, so that the sentence reads "All of us united."

2. Determining whether to use "who" or "whom," especially in a dependent clause, can be difficult. In many situations, especially spoken contexts as opposed to formal writing, "whom" has become practically obsolete. When you need the correct form, though, there are two basic rules to follow:

> a. Use "who" (which you can think of as correlating with the subjective form "he") when you need a subject or a subjective complement following a *be* or linking verb.
>
> b. Use "whom" (which you can think of as correlating with "him" because both pronouns end with *m*) when you need the objective form following a verb or a preposition.

Because the "who/whom" choice is usually more difficult in complex sentences, let's begin with independent clauses:

> (Who, Whom) is to blame?
> Since you need a subject form, and since you could say "He is to blame," the correct choice is "who."

To (who, whom) is this envelope addressed?
Since you need an object of a preposition, and since you could rewrite the sentence
as "This envelope is addressed to him," the correct choice is "whom."

Making the correct choice gets more complicated when the sentence structure is complex
rather than simple. Remember that both noun and relative clauses can begin with "who" or
"whom." In this case we must first isolate the noun or relative clause and then determine
whether we need a subject ("who") or object ("whom") within the bounds of the dependent
clause. Diagraming can help us see what happens in these sentences.

We received sympathy from (whoever, whomever) listened to us.

At first glance, it would appear that "whomever" should be the correct choice because it follows a preposition. However, the object of the preposition is actually the entire noun clause,
not just a word. And inside the noun clause, a subject—"whoever"—is necessary. The diagram
below may help to clarify this situation.

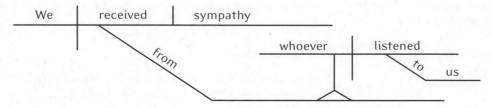

Now let's look at a similar sentence:

We received sympathy from (whoever, whomever) we saw.

Again, at first glance it may seem that "whomever" is the correct choice because it follows a
preposition. Once more, though, closer analysis reveals that the object of the preposition is the
entire noun clause. Inside the clause, we already have a subject-verb combination: we saw. Since
we could say "we saw him," we know that we should choose the object form, "whomever."
Notice where it fits in the diagram below.

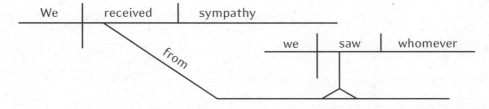

Finally, consider the following:

We asked (who, whom) the special guest was.

Within the noun clause we find "guest" as a subject, but the *be* verb indicates that we need
the nominative form, "who," as subjective complement. The subject and subjective complement are interchangeable:

"He was the special guest" or "The special guest was he."

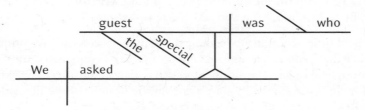

3. **A final area of difficulty with pronoun case arises in elliptical clauses of comparison, clauses beginning with "than" or "as."** An elliptical clause, as its name implies, includes an ellipsis; in other words, important words have been omitted so that it is not a complete but an understood clause. Because words have been omitted, even careful users of English often make the wrong pronoun choice in an elliptical clause. Although the incorrect pronoun is often acceptable and sounds more natural in spoken English, we must exercise greater care in written form. Frequently the best solution is to add the missing words so that the clause is no longer elliptical.

INCORRECT:	Sam is taller than *her*.
CORRECT:	Sam is taller than *she*. (If written in its entirety, this sentence would read, "Sam is taller than *she is*.")
INCORRECT:	I wish I could be as relaxed as *them* about this matter.
CORRECT:	I wish I could be as relaxed as *they* [are] about this matter.

In some sentences, the choice of pronoun in an elliptical clause affects meaning. When this situation occurs, it is probably better to rephrase to avoid a possible misunderstanding.

Bill likes her better than *me*. (Bill likes her better than *he likes me*.)

Bill likes her better than *I*. (Bill likes her better than *I do*.)

EXERCISE 8.3

Circle the correct pronoun in the sentences below.

1. The dog will bite any intruder (WHO, WHOM) walks through the door.

2. (WHO, WHOM) are the geniuses in charge here?

3. You should mail this chain letter to (WHOEVER, WHOMEVER) is gullible enough to believe that it will bring good luck.

4. The shirts will be delivered by the person (WHO, WHOM) we hired yesterday.

5. There was tension between Brandon and (THEY, THEM).

6. (WE, US) students should protest the next tuition hike.

7. During the twenty years of their marriage, Betty has never been as devoted as (HE, HIM).

8. No one wanted to interfere in the argument that Pete started with Ritchie and (HE, HIM).

9. (Whoever, Whomever) sold the raffle tickets is a good salesperson.

10. The executives fired everyone (WHO, WHOM) the consultant advised them to reassign.

11. After the explorers found aliens on the faraway planet, they discovered that the aliens could communicate much more quickly than (THEY, THEM).

12. (JILL AND I, JILL AND ME, ME AND JILL) decided to order pizza for the party.

see answer key, p. 410

PRONOUN FORM

Although choosing the correct form of pronouns is not actually related to pronoun case or to the overall topic of agreement, this seems a logical place to discuss this difficulty. Two categories of pronouns cause usage problems because many people do not use the correct forms of the pronouns. This typically occurs with reflexive pronouns and reciprocal pronouns.

Reflexive pronouns are those that end in "-self" or "-selves." They are called reflexive because they *must* reflect back to an antecedent within the same sentence. Examine the difference in how the reflexive pronoun "myself" is used in the following two sentences.

INCORRECT: Carol and *myself* went to the museum.

CORRECT: I went by *myself* to the museum.

Reflexive pronouns can also be used for emphasis; when they serve this function, they immediately follow the antecedent and are often labeled as intensive or emphatic pronouns.

Ken *himself* must deal with this problem.

What creates even more difficulty than determining when to use reflexive pronouns is determining which forms to use. Below are the only acceptable forms for reflexive pronouns in standard English:

myself	ourselves
yourself	yourselves
himself, herself, itself	themselves

You have probably heard "hisself," "ourself," "themself," or "theirselves." Although these pronouns do not conform to standard English, many people use them. The nonstandard forms probably result from the fact that in first and second person we attach the suffix "self" or "selves" to the possessive form of the pronoun, while in the third person we attach the suffix to the objective pronoun form. Notice also from the chart above that only in the reflexive pronoun can we clearly distinguish between singular and plural "you." "Yourself" (singular) becomes "yourselves" (plural). An urge to distinguish between singular and plural "you" accounts for such dialect forms as "y'all," "youse," or "you guys." However, only the reflexive form makes the singular/plural distinction in standard English.

The second type of pronoun that causes difficulty is the reciprocal pronoun. **Reciprocal pronouns** have only two forms, "each other" and "one another." When you are referring to only two people or things, use "each other." When referring to more than two, use "one another."

A husband and wife should love *each other*.

In our family, everyone respects *one another*.

EXERCISE 8.4

Circle the correct pronoun in each sentence below.

1. The students all evaluated (EACH OTHER'S, ONE ANOTHER'S) projects at the end of the semester.

2. The children exhausted (THEMSELF, THEMSELVES, THEIRSELF, THEIRSELVES) at the playground.

3. John excused Michelle and (I, ME, MYSELF) from further duties.

4. Paul and Gloria looked at (EACH OTHER, ONE ANOTHER) in dismay.

5. The wedding date was kept a secret between the rabbi and (THEY, THEM, THEMSELVES).

see answer key, p. 410

PRONOUN CONSISTENCY PROBLEMS

One problem that recurs in writing is inconsistency in choice of pronouns. **Pronouns should be consistent in person and number.** The following chart labels person (first, second, or third) and number (singular or plural) for each pronoun form.

first person singular	I
second person singular	you
third person singular	he, she, it
first person plural	we
second person plural	you
third person plural	they

Now, in the following short passage, notice the shifts in pronouns:

> A student should keep a pen in hand while reading. If *you* take notes, underline important words or passages, and use symbols in margins, a student can remember the key points of *their* reading.

This passage begins in third person singular ("a student"), switches to second person ("you") in the second sentence, and then ends in third person singular ("a student") with a pronoun agreement error, a switch to third person plural, at the end of the sentence ("their reading").

The most important issue here is consistency. If you decide to use third person, remember that third person plural is usually best, in order to avoid pronoun problems later:

> Students should keep *their* pens in hand while reading. If *they* take notes, underline important words or passages, and use symbols in margins, students can remember the key points of *their* reading.

Third person singular is possible if sentences can be reworded to avoid sexist language:

> A student should keep pen in hand while reading. Taking notes, underlining important words or passages, and using symbols in margins will help a student remember the key points of a reading assignment.

Finally, since this passage gives instructions, second person is also appropriate if used consistently:

> *You* should keep a pen in hand while reading. If *you* take notes, underline important words or passages, and use symbols in margins, *you* can remember the key points of *your* reading.

As mentioned earlier, avoiding the use of "one" is often advisable, since it sounds a bit stilted and requires "one" as the pronoun to agree with it. In other words, rather than saying "One must prove himself in the Boy Scouts," you would have to say, "One must prove oneself in the Boy Scouts" to be technically correct. Also, "one" frequently results in the later use of "their," a pronoun shift that is incorrect in person and in number: "One should mind their manners in a formal setting" would be correct if written "One should mind one's manners in a formal setting."

EXERCISE 8.5

Rewrite the following passage so that the pronouns are consistent in person and number.

For many people, being the perfect host is not as easy as it seems. While one is cooking, he is simultaneously supposed to be engaging in witty conversation. And how do you check the toilet paper supply or change the bed sheets without feeling as if you are invading the guest's privacy? The perfect host is just a myth; he never really existed.

_____

_____

_____

_____

_____

_____

_____

see answer key, p. 411

Another problem with pronoun consistency may arise with relative clauses beginning with "which." We learned in Chapter 5 that "which," as a relative pronoun, can introduce a relative clause. English speakers and writers often overextend the "which," trying to make it refer to an entire clause rather than simply the word before it.

INCORRECT:　　　　We found a locked chest in the *basement, which* made us shout with excitement.
(Although logically we know that it was finding the locked chest that caused the excitement, the sentence's grammatical structure indicates that the basement made us shout with excitement.)

We can correct this use of "which," known as broad-reference "which," in a couple of ways. For example, we can reword the sentence:

Finding the locked chest in the basement made us shout with excitement.

When we found a locked chest in the basement, we shouted with excitement.

If we want to retain the "which," we should ensure that it relates back to the noun preceding it. Since clearly "basement" will not work, we must add another noun, one that will sum up the preceding main idea.

> We found a locked chest in the basement, a *discovery which* [or, even better, *that*] made us shout with excitement.

Although the broad-reference "which" rarely leads to a confusion of meaning, and is frequently overlooked by both readers and writers, correcting this error results in stronger, more direct sentences.

EXERCISE 8.6

Revise the following sentences to eliminate the broad-reference "which."

1. Hemingway's trademark is to use short sentences, which makes his style the antithesis of Faulkner's.

   _____

   _____

   _____

2. All of my money was spent on graduate school, which depressed me.

   _____

   _____

   _____

3. He hated classical music, which made him incompatible with Rhonda.

   _____

   _____

   _____

see answer key, p. 411

SUMMARY OF KEY CONCEPTS IN CHAPTER 8

1. Subject and verb must agree.

    a. Rule of "one –s"

    b. Compound structures: subject *and* subject = plural verb

                                    subject *or* subject = verb agrees with closer subject

    c. Distracting elements: unless the subject is an indefinite pronoun, ignore a prepositional phrase between subject and verb; also ignore any other grammatical structures that separate the subject and verb or that cause the subject to follow the verb

    d. Indefinite pronouns: singular if the indefinite pronoun begins with "any," "every," "some," or "no"; otherwise, may need to determine whether singular or plural depending on the prepositional phrase that follows the indefinite pronoun

    e. Collective nouns: use singular verb if members of the collective noun are acting in unison

    f. Expletive "there":   verb agrees with the subject, which follows the verb in this structure

    g. Relative clauses: verb agrees with the relative pronoun; relative pronoun can be singular or plural, depending on the noun it follows, except when the modifier "only" is involved

2. A pronoun must agree with its antecedent in person (first, second, or third person) and number (singular or plural). Because English has no graceful alternative to "he or she," avoid sexist language (using "he" to include both genders) by rephrasing in third-person plural whenever possible.

3. Use nominative case pronouns as subjects and subjective complements; use objective case pronouns as direct objects, indirect objects, objects of prepositions, and objective complements. When deciding between "who" and "whom," remember that "who" = "he" (nominative case), "whom" = "him" (objective case). To determine which case is correct within a noun or relative clause, ignore the independent clause and consider the function of "who" or "whom" within the dependent clause only.

CHAPTER 8 EXERCISE

1. Rewrite the passage below in order to correct all errors of case, agreement, and consistency. In addition, correct any fragments, run-ons, or comma splices. Make sure that each period marks the end of a complete sentence.

Students must know how to study effectively and efficiently. You can study with another student, for example, and help one another. The "buddy method," as it is called, usually is more effective than having a student working by hisself. Studying in pairs or groups are especially helpful for those whom are in need of motivation and discipline, it also helps if students compare notes to see if they agree on the key concepts to be learned. A student can usually improve his grade substantially. Just by being able to distinguish major points from minor ones. An entire class can improve their average if everyone studies together. The "buddy method" is such an effective tool that it should not be kept a secret. Between you and I, we can spread the word to many other students, which might lead to widespread scholastic success.

_____

_____

_____

_____

_____

_____

_____

_____

_____

_____

_____

_____

_____

_____

_____

see answer key, p. 411

Verbs

Verbs are usually the richest—and the most complicated—aspect of any language. English is no exception, although our verb system is simpler than that of many other languages. A good place to begin our study of verbs is with an outline of the **five main forms of English verbs**, the forms upon which all of our verbs are built:

1. **infinitive, root, or base (the dictionary form)**
2. **third person singular, present tense (always ends in –s)**
3. **simple past (the "yesterday" form)**
4. **past participle (the form that follows auxiliary *have*)**
5. **present participle (the form that follows auxiliary *be* and always ends in –ing)**

The next step is to recognize that **English verbs fall into two categories:**

1. **weak or regular (simple past and past participle end in –ed)**
2. **strong or irregular (simple past and past participle do not end in –ed;** instead, these forms must be memorized by both native and foreign speakers)

Let's take a look at the five basic forms of verbs by using both a regular and an irregular verb as examples. Note that the irregular verb varies from the regular only in the past tense and past participle. Appendix 2 lists the majority of irregular verb forms in English.

	Regular	*Irregular*
Infinitive, base, or root form	walk	break
Third person singular, present tense	walks	breaks
Past tense	walked	broke
Past participle	walked	broken
Present participle	walking	breaking

Once we understand this much about verbs, we are ready to go on to tenses and aspects of verbs. **Verbs have two basic tenses, present (as indicated by the base form and the third person singular –s form) and past.** If you're wondering what happened to the future tense, we'll get to it eventually. We can identify the present and the past tenses without adding auxiliaries, and so in the purest terms only present and past verbs exist in English. To express the notion of future action, we must rely on auxiliaries.

Verbs also possess what grammarians call "aspects"—perfect and progressive modes. A perfect verb uses a form of *have* (has, have, had) as an auxiliary, followed by the past participle form of the verb, in order to express a completed action. A progressive verb uses a form of *be* (am, is, are, was, were) as an auxiliary, followed by the present participle form of the verb, to express an action that is or was in progress.

Present perfect	(*has* or *have* + *past participle of main verb*): action that began in the past and still continues, or recently completed action
	She *has walked* to class every day. (past but ongoing action)
	She *has broken* the record. (completed action)
Past perfect	(*had* + *past participle of main verb*): action already completed at the time of another past action
	She *had walked* into class before the bell rang.
	When the coach realized that she *had broken* the school record, he was ecstatic.
Present progressive	(*am, is, are, be* + *present participle of main verb*): action currently in progress
	She *is walking*.
	She *is breaking* the school record.
Past progressive	(was, were, been + *present participle of main verb*): action in progress when another action in the past occurred
	She *was walking* when the accident happened.
	She *was breaking* the school record as we watched in disbelief.
Present perfect progressive	(*has been, have been* + *present participle of main verb*): action currently in progress but begun in the past
	She *has been walking* for three hours.
	She *has been breaking* records since her debut in track events.
Past perfect progressive	(*had* + *been* + *present participle of main verb*): action in progress in the past, prior to another past action
	She *had been walking* for hours before she found the camp.
	She *had been breaking* the record when the coach stopped her for a violation.

To express the sense of future action, we add one of the modal auxiliaries before the base form of the verb. Remember that the modals are limited in number: shall, should, will, would, can, could, may, might, must, have to, had to, ought to. From this group, "shall" or "will" can express the future tense. Although years ago students were instructed to use "shall" with first person ("I shall" or "we shall"), nowadays "shall" is reserved almost exclusively for emphasis, as in "That child shall come to no good if he doesn't learn better manners." Since future action is almost always expressed by "will," that is the modal used below for additional variations on the perfect and progressive aspects of the verb.

Future progressive

(*will + be + present participle of main verb*): action that will be in progress in the future

She *will be walking* to class at 8:00.

She *will be breaking* few records now.

Future perfect

(*will + have + past participle of main verb*): action that will be completed in the future

She *will have walked* for hours by the time she reaches us.

She *will have broken* another record before she graduates.

Future perfect progressive

(*will + have + been + present participle of main verb*): action that will be in progress in the future at the same time as another future action

She *will have been walking* for hours when we meet her tomorrow.

She *will have been breaking* records all her life by the time she writes her memoirs as a senior citizen.

"Shall" and "will" express future time, but we can place other modals before the main verb or verb phrase in order to fill in shades of meaning. These meanings are often difficult to artic-ulate, even though native speakers of English understand perfectly the nuances associated with modals. Native speakers also understand how to put together verb phrases, but they may seem a mystery to someone just beginning to learn the language. Let's first take a look at how the verb phrase develops in English:

one-word verb

she *walks* (present tense)

he *walked* (past tense)

two-word verbs

modal + base form of verb (he *should walk*)

have + past participle (he *has walked*, he *had walked*) = perfect aspect

be + present participle (he *is walking*, he *was walking*) = progressive aspect

three-word verbs	modal + have + past participle (he *should have walked*) = modal + perfect aspect
	modal + be + present participle (he *should be walking*) = modal + progressive aspect
four-word verbs	modal + have + been + present participle (he *should have been walking*) = modal + present perfect progressive aspect

Here is another way of thinking about the order of verbs in a verb phrase:

1. **Modals do not change the form of the verb that follows. A modal is always followed by the base form of a verb.**

2. **The auxiliary *have* (has, have, had) is followed by the past participle form of a verb, forming the perfect aspect of the verb.**

3. **The auxiliary *be* (am, is, are, was, were, be, been) is followed by the present participle form of a verb, forming the progressive aspect of the verb.**

If you look again at the four-word verb formula above, you can see this more clearly. Think of it as a domino effect. The modal means that the next verb ("have") is in base form; "have" as an auxiliary means that the next verb ("been") is in past participle form; "been" as an auxiliary means that the next verb ("walking") is in present participle form. In addition, "have" is in present tense, so that "have been" is a present perfect form. The verb "been" necessitates the present participle form, the progressive aspect of the main verb. Thus we label the verb phrase as present ("have") perfect ("been") progressive ("walking").

Besides modals, *have*, and *be*, an additional auxiliary sometimes appears. We use *do* in order to transform a sentence with no auxiliaries into interrogative, negative, or emphatic form.

Octavia *drives* her parents crazy by spending money foolishly. (present tense)

Octavia *drove* her parents crazy by spending money foolishly. (past tense)

INTERROGATIVE:	*Does* Octavia drive her parents crazy by spending money foolishly?
	Did Octavia drive her parents crazy by spending money foolishly?
NEGATIVE:	Octavia *does* not drive her parents crazy by spending money foolishly.
	Octavia *did* not drive her parents crazy by spending money foolishly.
EMPHATIC:	Octavia *does* drive her parents crazy by spending money foolishly.
	Octavia *did* drive her parents crazy by spending money foolishly.

EXERCISE 9.1

Identify the tense (past, present, future) and aspect (perfect, progressive) of the verbs below.

1. had been going _____

2. will have been _____

3. is driving _____

4. was _____

5. has seen _____

6. had been happening _____

7. will be studying _____

8. will have been studying _____

see answer key, p. 413

EXERCISE 9.2

Write the verb represented by the verb strings below.

1. could + have + past participle of *find* _____

2. am + present participle of *look* _____

3. had + past participle of *be* + present participle of *skate* _____

see answer key, p. 413

Once we understand that verb phrases are not arbitrary but follow an invariable order, we are ready to look more closely at the modals themselves. Notice that a modal, unlike all other verbs, cannot serve as a main verb in a sentence and cannot be inflected in any way, unless we consider that pairs such as can/could, will/would, shall/should express present and past tense. Because the meanings of the words in each pair are slightly different, though, even this concept is misleading. With a modal, what you see is what you get—at least in terms of form. Without modals, we would have much difficulty expressing fine differences of meaning, so fine that those learning English as a foreign language can only gradually grasp, through exposure to the language and inductive reasoning, when to employ which modal in a given situation. It is almost impossible to capture the essence of the modals in a denotative way, employing dictionary definitions. Nevertheless, we will take an admittedly sketchy look at the meaning of modals:

I *should walk* home. (a moral imperative, identical to "I *ought to* walk home")

I *can walk* home. (a statement of ability)

I *might walk* home. (a statement of possibility, tentative in nature)

I *must walk* home. (an imperative or necessity, identical to "I *have to* walk home" or, in past tense, "I *had to* walk home")

I *may walk* home. (a statement of permission or of possibility)

I *could walk* home (a statement of possibility, usually associated with a particular circumstance or condition, as in "I could walk home if I had to")

If I did not have a car, I *would walk* home. (a statement expressing a course of action given a particular circumstance or condition)

The final two examples above lead us into a slight detour because they introduce the concept of the conditional mood of the verb. **English verbs have four moods:**

1. **indicative**—sentences that make a statement or ask a question.

2. **imperative**—sentences that issue commands or demands, usually dropping the subject so that "you" is understood, as in "Close the door" or "Please hand me that notebook."

3. **conditional**—sentences that set up conditions under which certain attitudes or actions will occur. Modals that signal the conditional mood are "could," "may," "might," "would," and "should." The conditional mood often causes verb tense problems that do not arise in the other moods. As you will see in the sentences below, the tense and aspect of the verb in the adverb clause (the "if" clause that sets up the condition) directly affect the form of the verb in the independent clause.

If I *know* you *are coming*, I *will bake* a cake. (future tense, not conditional mood)

If I *knew* you *were coming*, I *would bake* a cake. ("would bake" expresses conditional mood)

If I *had known* you *were coming*, I *would have baked* a cake. ("would have baked" expresses conditional mood)

Although the "if" clause determines the appropriate tense of the verb in the main clause, the adverb clause is not necessary. Verbs in simple sentences such as "I might bake a cake," "I could bake a cake," "I would bake a cake" also express the conditional mood.

4. **subjunctive**—sentences that express a condition contrary to fact or that make a demand or strong recommendation in a noun clause beginning with "that." The subjunctive survives as a vestige of Anglo-Saxon, the earliest form of the English language. See Chapter 11 for a full discussion of the subjunctive.

Jamie wishes that she *were* somewhere else. (contrary to fact)

Jamie demanded that she *be* allowed to leave. (demand expressed in noun clause)

Once you have a grasp of the various forms, tenses, aspects, and moods of the English verb, you are ready to tackle the concept of voice as well. **English verbs have two voices, active and passive.** Although "active" and "passive" refer to the voice of the verb, we often generalize and refer to sentences themselves as active or passive. This generalization is logical because the overall sentence structure changes when we transform a verb from active to passive or vice versa. The active voice indicates that the grammatical subject of the verb is performing the action of the clause or sentence. The passive voice indicates that the grammatical subject of the verb is not performing the action of the clause or sentence but instead is being acted upon (and thus the term "passive"). **Only sentences with transitive verbs can be transformed into passive voice.** Let's see how this happens:

1. **The object that follows the transitive verb in the original sentence becomes the subject of the passive sentence.** The original subject is either omitted or becomes part of a prepositional phrase.

2. The verb form changes. **Every passive verb consists of at least two parts, a form of *be* followed by the past participle of the main verb.**

ACTIVE: The inept burglar *left* the diamonds in the safe. (Pattern 7)

PASSIVE: The diamonds *were left* in the safe by the inept burglar.

ACTIVE: The owner of the restaurant *has given* us free meals. (Pattern 8)

PASSIVE: We *were given* free meals by the owner of the restaurant.

Almost all passive sentences, when diagramed, will look like a Pattern 6 or a Pattern 7 sentence. Instead of an active verb, though, a passive verb appears on the base line.

The diamonds were left in the safe by the inept burglar.

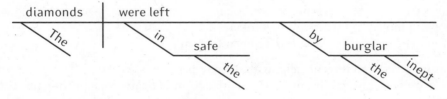

We were given free meals by the owner of the restaurant.

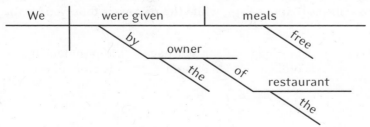

Don't be fooled by the diagrams into believing that these actually are Pattern 6 or Pattern 7 sentences. If pressed to determine the sentence pattern of a passive sentence, you must first change it into its active form and then determine whether it is a Pattern 7, 8, 9, or 10 sentence. Consider the diagram of the passive sentence below and its sentence pattern number:

The teacher was asked for an explanation of his grading policy.

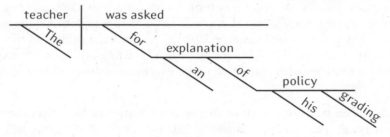

Although the diagram makes this sentence appear to be a Pattern 6 sentence, because it is passive we must first rewrite the sentence into its active voice, in this case providing a subject that does not appear in the original sentence:

The students asked the teacher for an explanation of his grading policy.

Once this sentence has been rephrased into active voice, we can see that it is a Pattern 7 (s – tv – do) sentence. With passive sentences, then, the sentence pattern number will not agree with the appearance of the sentence diagram.

Using third person singular, here is a quick rundown of the most common passive verb forms, using the irregular verb *break*:

PRESENT	it is broken
PAST	it was broken
PRESENT PROGRESSIVE	it is being broken
PAST PROGRESSIVE	it was being broken
PRESENT PERFECT	it has been broken
PAST PERFECT	it had been broken
FUTURE (with modal "will")	it will be broken
FUTURE PERFECT	it will have been broken

Each of these passive verbs ends identically, with the past participle "broken." Tense and aspect of the verb are expressed through the auxiliaries, with a form of *be* always appearing just before the past participle.

Note that the progressive form of the verb also uses *be* as a helping verb, but the **progressive is followed by the present participle (–ing), while the passive is followed by the past participle.**

PRESENT PROGRESSIVE:	is breaking	is burning	is pronouncing
PRESENT PASSIVE:	is broken	is burnt	is pronounced

EXERCISE 9.3

First identify the verbs below as either active or passive. Then identify the tense (past, present, future) and aspect (perfect or progressive) of each verb.

1. had been speaking

   _____

2. had been spoken

   _____

3. was looking

   _____

4. will have been hurt

   _____

5. will be hurting

   _____

6. has found

   _____

7. was found

   _____

8. will have been eating

   _____

9. has been eating

   _____

10. has been eaten

   _____

see answer key, p. 413

EXERCISE 9.4

Write the verb represented by the verb strings below. Identify each verb as either active or passive voice.

1. may + be + present participle of *sell*   _____

2. may + be + past participle of *sell*   _____

3. will + have + been + past participle of *take*   _____

4. ought to + be + present participle of *go*   _____

5. should + have + past participle of *go*   _____

see answer key, p. 413

EXERCISE 9.5

a. Determine whether each sentence below is written in active or passive voice. Rewrite each sentence so that those in active voice become passive and those in passive voice become active.

b. Write the sentence pattern number for each sentence. Remember that if the sentence is in passive voice, you must rephrase it in active voice to determine its sentence pattern.

c. Diagram the active-voice version of each sentence.

1. The child placed the blocks in a tall column.

2. The actor named his poodle Hollywood.

3. Your medicine should be given to you by a nurse.

4. Lola's ears were damaged by the painfully loud noise of the machinery.

5. The newspaper omitted any mention of the violent incident on campus.

6. My research paper was finished in an hour.

7. The wreath on the door was made by my best friend.

see answer key, p. 414

Now let's go on to consider *when* to use the passive voice. Since in a passive sentence the subject receives the action, rather than initiating it, **the passive construction is preferable for indicating passivity, helplessness, or victimization**:

He *was thrown* from the car by the force of the crash.

The flowers *were wilted* from the long drought.

In addition, the passive voice is necessary whenever we don't know the initiator of the action or don't wish to highlight that information by putting it first in the sentence. Politicians can be especially astute at using passive to make it seem that sometimes things just happen, with no one (least of all themselves) to blame. Journalists in particular should avoid using passive voice, since their job is to root out the facts of who did what—a task that only the active voice can accomplish. Note the strategic use of passive voice in the sentences below, especially the last two; an alert journalist reporting on the occurrences in these sentences would definitely search for the appropriate subject in order to rewrite these sentences in active voice.

The bank *was robbed* of all its cash. (The speaker does not know who did the robbing.)

The document *was* accidentally *shredded*. (The speaker either does not know or does not want to admit who did the shredding.)

Taxes *were increased* in order to cover the local budget deficit. (The speaker may be attempting to evade responsibility for having a hand in increasing taxes.)

Finally, you may find it necessary to make frequent use of the passive voice when writing scientific or technical reports and legal documents. Although active voice is preferable even here, the customary mode for many scientific, technical, and legal writers is passive, often because naming the agent of the action seems pointless or redundant.

The temperature *was decreased* over a period of ten days.

Tab A *should be inserted* into Tab B.

The custodial parent's income *will* not *be considered* for the purposes of this agreement.

Almost certainly, at some point in your formal writing instruction you have been advised *not* to use passive verbs. (Notice the passive voice here to avoid pinpointing anyone!) In general, the dictum to avoid passive and use active voice in your own writing is good advice. When the subject performs the action of the sentence, the effect is one of vigor and energy, positive qualities that will enhance the effect of your writing. Keep in mind, though, that there are occasions when passive voice is actually preferable to active. Be alert for the use of passive voice by others, since it is often a manipulative ploy, and be savvy enough to know how and when to use it yourself.

SUMMARY OF KEY CONCEPTS IN CHAPTER 9

1. English verbs have *five main forms*:

   a. infinitive, root, or base form

   b. third person singular, present tense (ending in –s)

   c. past (no auxiliary)

   d. past participle (the form that follows auxiliary *have*)

   e. present participle (the form that follows auxiliary *be* and always ends in –ing)

2. English verbs are classified as either *regular* (past and past participle forms end in –ed) or *irregular* (past and past participle forms must be memorized).

3. As expressed by their single-word forms, English verbs have *two tenses*: present and past. Future tense requires an auxiliary.

4. English verbs possess *two aspects*:

   a. perfect (a form of *have* followed by the past participle verb form);

   b. progressive (a form of *be* followed by the present participle verb form).

5. Modal auxiliaries (shall, should, will, would, can, could, may, might, must, have to, had to, ought to) influence the meaning of the verb.

6. Insert a form of *do* when you need to insert an auxiliary to form a question, to make a negative statement, or to indicate emphasis.

7. English verbs have *four moods*:

   a. indicative (statement)

   b. imperative (command, with "you" usually serving as the understood subject)

   c. conditional (signaled by the modals "could," "may," "might," "would," and "should")

   d. subjunctive (expressing a condition contrary to fact or making a demand in a noun clause beginning with the expletive "that")

8. English verbs have *two voices*: active or passive.

   a. With an active verb, the subject performs the action of the verb; with a passive verb, the subject does not perform the action of the verb but is instead acted upon.

   b. The essential form of the passive verb is *be* + past participle. (Keep the passive form distinct from the present progressive, *be* + present participle.)

   c. Use the passive voice when you wish to emphasize the weakness or victimization of the subject, when you wish to avoid placing blame, when you do not know the performer of the action or when that information is not pertinent, or when it seems appropriate in scientific, technical, or legal documents. Otherwise, use the active voice.

The following chart may help you better understand tense, aspect, and voice. The last row of this chart includes verb forms that you will seldom if ever use, but they are included for purposes of illustration.

	Present Tense	Past Tense	Future Tense	Voice
	He bites.	He bit.	He will bite.	Active
	He is bitten.	He was bitten.	He will be bitten.	Passive
Progressive Aspect	He is biting.	He was biting.	He will be biting.	Active
	He is being bitten.	He was being bitten.	He will be being bitten.	Passive
Perfect Aspect	He has bitten.	He had bitten.	He will have bitten.	Active
	He has been bitten.	He had been bitten.	He will have been bitten.	Passive
Perfect Progressive	He has been biting.	He had been biting.	He will have been biting.	Active
	He has been being bitten.	He had been being bitten.	He will have been being bitten.	Passive

CHAPTER 9 EXERCISE

I. Change the verb "give" as directed below. Assume that the subject for the verb is "she."

    1. present progressive   _____

    2. past perfect   _____

    3. future   _____

    4. future progressive   _____

II. Change the sentence below as directed.

    The choir sang an uplifting melody.

    1. passive voice

    _____

    2. interrogative

    _____

    3. conditional mood

    _____

III. Write sentences of your own that include verb forms as specified below.

    1. present perfect aspect of *go*

    _____

    _____

    2. modal "should"

    _____

    _____

    3. emphatic *do*

    _____

4. active voice, Pattern 7 sentence

_____

_____

5. transform your active voice, Pattern 7 sentence into passive voice

_____

_____

6. past perfect progressive aspect of _read_

_____

_____

7. present progressive aspect of _close_

_____

_____

8. modal "may"

_____

_____

9. modal "can"

_____

_____

10. past perfect aspect of _swim_

_____

_____

11. past tense of _drink_

_____

_____

12. subjunctive mood of _be_

_____

_____

IV. Identify the verb forms below in terms of tense, aspect (if applicable), and voice:

1. was seeing

   _____

2. was seen

   _____

3. will have been shopping

   _____

4. had been

   _____

5. is being

   _____

6. have found

   _____

7. have been found

   _____

see answer key, p. 415

Verbals

Besides giving us a variety of verb forms, English allows us to use some of those forms in specialized structures (usually phrases) known as verbals. Frequently verbals act as shortened forms of clauses. They lend the language further versatility and richness.

Basically, there are **three categories of verbals: infinitives, gerunds, and participles**. In form, all of the verbals look like verbs. In function, though, they act as different parts of speech. **An infinitive can be used as a noun, an adverb, or an adjective; a gerund is always used as a noun; and a participle is always used as an adjective.** Besides using function to distinguish verbs from verbals, you should be able to tell the difference between finite and nonfinite verb forms. **Verbs are finite—that is, they can be inflected according to person and number, and they are able to make an assertion. Verbals, though, are nonfinite. They cannot be inflected and are unable to make an assertion.**

FINITE: The cup *overflows* with milk.
The cup *overflowed* with milk.
The cups *overflow* with milk.

The verbs in all three of these sentences make an assertion and change form depending on the number (singular or plural) of the subject and the desired tense (present or past in this case).

NONFINITE: the cup *overflowing* with milk
the cups *overflowing* with milk

The nonfinite form "overflowing" is incapable of making an assertion (resulting in fragments rather than sentences) and is not inflected. It is a verbal (an adjective describing "cup"), not a verb.

INFINITIVES (NOUNS, ADVERBS, OR ADJECTIVES)

Whether it functions as a noun, as an adverb, or as an adjective, the infinitive always appears in the same form: *to* followed by a verb. The only difficulty is that since *to* can also be used as a preposition, you must be careful to distinguish infinitives from prepositional phrases. Can you distinguish between the two in the phrases below?

to move   to dance
to be   to a dance
to the end   to feel

Notice that all types of verbs—*be*, linking, intransitive, and transitive—can be used to form an infinitive.

One other characteristic of the infinitive (in fact, of all the verbals) is that, because it is formed from a verb, it can be followed by either an object or a complement.

> She wanted *to see* the exotic flower. ("To see" is the infinitive, but the entire infinitive phrase is "to see the exotic flower"; "flower" is the object of the infinitive because "see" is an action verb.)

> Everyone wants *to be* happy. ("To be" is the infinitive, but the entire infinitive phrase is "to be happy"; "happy" is the complement of the infinitive because "be" is a *be* verb.)

Infinitives as Nouns

Like the noun clause, the infinitive used as a noun can be identified quite easily. **It takes the place of a noun, so we can replace the infinitive with "it" or with "something." We can label its function as subject, object, complement, or appositive. Also, as with a noun clause, the infinitive used as a noun does not require punctuation unless used as an appositive.**

> *To sound intelligent on political issues* was Wayne's goal during his date with the senator. (Here, even though the infinitive is long, no comma is necessary because the infinitive is the subject of the sentence. Because it is the subject, and because we could replace the infinitive phrase with a pronoun—"It was Wayne's goal during his date with the senator"—this infinitive is definitely a noun.)

> Wayne's goal during his date with the senator, *to sound intelligent on political issues*, seemed impossible to those of us who knew him well.
> (Because the infinitive is serving as an appositive for "goal," it is set off by commas and is unquestionably a noun.)

Again like the noun clause, the infinitive used as a noun is diagramed on a pedestal. Because the infinitive has the same structure as a prepositional phrase, it is diagramed on a prepositional phrase structure on the pedestal. Note that if there is an object or complement that follows the infinitive, it is included with the infinitive, with the appropriate line preceding it (a vertical line to indicate an object, a diagonal or slash line to indicate a complement.)

> *To sound intelligent on political issues* was Wayne's goal. (*It* was Wayne's goal.)

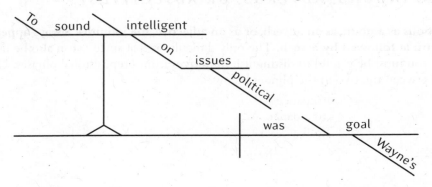

The boy learned *to play the piano beautifully*. (The boy learned *something*.)

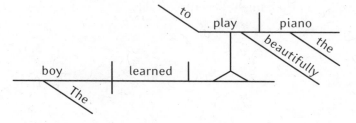

Sally tried *to sprint to third base*. (Sally tried *it*.)

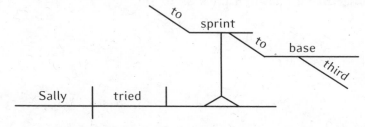

EXERCISE 10.1

In the following sentences, underline infinitive phrases used as nouns. Then diagram each sentence.

   1. No one wanted to accept Dracula's invitation to the castle.

   2. To become wealthy is not the primary objective in life.

3. Elizabeth's dream, to live in England, might become a reality.

4. To be healthy is to possess the first key to happiness.

5. The rabbits wanted to eat the lettuce in our garden.

see answer key, p. 416

Infinitives as Adverbs

Infinitives used as adverbs fall into two categories: (1) those that modify a verb; (2) those that modify an adjective.

1. An infinitive used as an adverb to modify a verb

Like other adverbs, these infinitives can usually change position in the sentence. When an infinitive used as an adverb begins the sentence, it is followed by a comma (just as an introductory adverb clause is followed by a comma). These infinitives answer the typical adverb questions of when, where, why, how. Because they are adverbs that can move, they are diagramed on a prepositional phrase structure under the verb.

To make money for summer camp, Joe washed cars. (Here "to make money for summer camp" answers the question of why Joe washed cars.)

Notice that no comma is necessary when we move the infinitive to the end of the sentence:

Joe washed cars *to make money for summer camp*.

Both of these sentences would be diagramed the same way:

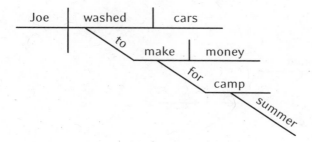

Here's one other tip: **If you can insert the words "in order to" before the verb, the infinitive is definitely an adverb modifying the verb.**

Joe washed cars *in order to* make money for summer camp. (Since this test works, "to make" is definitely an infinitive used as an adverb modifying the verb.)

Now suppose that rather than mentally inserting the words "in order to," you actually see those words in the written sentence. Here is what the diagram would look like:

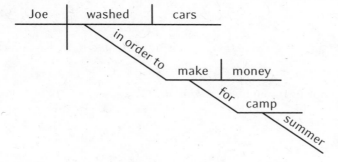

2. An infinitive used as an adverb to modify an adjective

The second category of infinitives used as adverbs is not as easy to identify as the first. These adverbs are not movable, do not readily answer the typical adverb questions, and do not pass the "in order to" test. Instead, they are adverbs by virtue of the fact that they follow and modify an adjective. (Remember that only an adverb is capable of modifying an adjective.) These adverbs are diagramed on a prepositional phrase structure under the adjective, not under the verb.

Crossword puzzles can be hard *to do.*

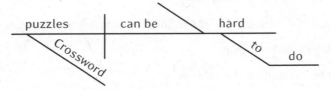

Terry will be able *to visit us tonight.*

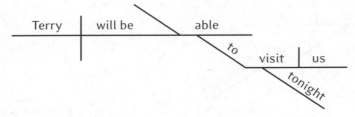

Phyllis is eager *to be helpful.*

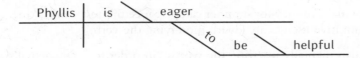

EXERCISE 10.2

In the sentences below, underline the infinitive phrases used as adverbs, and then diagram each sentence.

1. To be friendly, we invited our new neighbors to dinner.

2. Sarah enrolled in a review course to increase her chances of a high score on the SAT.

3. The cat was ready to pounce on the unsuspecting mouse.

4. To find your soulmate, you must be open to all possibilities.

5. Some people are unable to smile at adversity.

see answer key, p. 416

EXERCISE 10.3

In the following sentences, underline the infinitive phrases used as adverbs and circle the infinitive phrases used as nouns. Then diagram each sentence.

1. To learn his multiplication tables, Mark decided to construct a math game.

2. Everyone was eager to hear about the new coach in order to determine the team's chances of success.

3. To be responsible for a pet is to demonstrate maturity.

4. To be responsible for a pet, you must volunteer to make a few personal sacrifices.

see answer key, p. 417

Infinitives as Adjectives

Infinitives used as adjectives do not occur as frequently as infinitives used as nouns or adverbs. The primary way to identify them is to look for an infinitive that immediately follows a noun and modifies it. In the diagram, the infinitive is placed on a prepositional phrase structure underneath the noun it modifies.

We must find a way *to be successful*. (*What kind* of way? "To be successful" is an adjective because it answers this question, modifying the noun.)

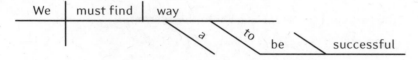

The name *to use* is the one on your passport. (*Which* name? "To use" is an adjective modifying the noun "name.")

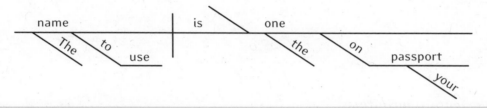

EXERCISE 10.4

In the sentences below, underline the infinitive phrases used as adjectives, and then diagram the sentences.

  1. The best coffee to drink is this blend of two flavors.

2. Sheila asked a question about which letter to type first.

3. No one told us the password to use for entry into the chatroom.

see answer key, p. 418

Complementary Infinitives

English occasionally uses the infinitive idiomatically to complete the meaning of the verb rather than to act as a noun, adverb, or adjective. **An infinitive used to complete the verb is a complementary infinitive.** To identify it, you can first run the usual tests to confirm that the infinitive is *not* fulfilling one of its more typical functions:

1. Can you replace it with a pronoun? If not, it cannot be an infinitive used as a noun.

2. Can you move it or insert "in order to" before the infinitive? Alternatively, does it follow and modify an adjective? If not, then it cannot be an infinitive used as an adverb.

3. Does it follow and modify a noun? If not, then it cannot be an infinitive used as an adjective.

If the infinitive is not serving as a noun, adverb, or adjective, then it is a complementary infinitive, attached to the verb in order to form an idiomatic expression. In all cases where the infinitive is actually attached to the verb, diagram the infinitive on the base line as part of the verb.

The party *is going to start* in a few minutes. (**going to + verb = future tense**)

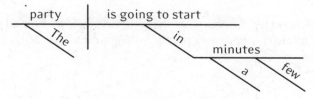

The party *has to start* in a few minutes. (**has to, have to, or had to + verb = obligation; the forms of *have to* act as a modal, a synonym for the modal "must"**)

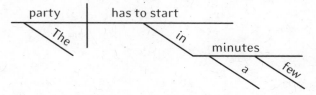

The party *is to start* in a few minutes. (***be* + infinitive = imminent future action, or a mild obligation**, as in "You *are to leave* for the party now.")

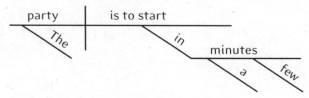

The party *ought to be* fun. (**ought to + verb acts as a modal, a synonym for the modal "should"**)

```
party        | ought to be        fun
   The
```

The party *used to begin* at midnight. (**used to + verb = repetitive past action**)

```
party        | used to begin
   The              at
                        midnight
```

EXERCISE 10.5

Underline the phrases used as complementary infinitives in the sentences below. Not all sentences will contain complementary infinitives. For extra practice, diagram each sentence.

1. No one was going to ask for a favor.

2. No one was going to the concert.

3. Your attitude has to change.

4. Their goal is to increase sales by the end of the month.

5. The salespeople are to increase their quotas in order to receive a bonus.

see answer key, p. 419

EXERCISE 10.6

In the sentences that follow, underline the infinitive phrases used as nouns, circle the infinitive phrases used as adverbs, place a square box around the infinitive phrases used as adjectives, and double underline phrases used as complementary infinitives. Then diagram each sentence.

1. Many executives would like to have more free time.

2. Josh wears boots to appear taller.

3. The best time to study is now.

4. Will was happy to find his sister.

5. The best way to eat pancakes is to smother them with syrup.

6. To stay young, you have to maintain an optimistic outlook.

see answer key, p. 419

EXERCISE 10.7

In the sentences that follow, underline the infinitive phrases used as nouns, circle the infinitive phrases used as adverbs, place a square box around the infinitive phrases used as adjectives, and double underline phrases used as complementary infinitives. Then diagram each sentence. Warning: You will find a few dependent clauses to diagram as well as infinitives!

1. To escape from the maze, Tina decided to mark her path with bits of paper.

2. The last day to withdraw from this course is Friday.

3. When she arrived in the United States to help her sister, Maria's primary objective was to establish permanent residency.

4. Whoever has to know this information must prove security clearance to see it.

5. A gardener who waters faithfully will be able to display beautiful flowers.

6. The refrigerator that Jim bought was too big to fit into the kitchen.

7. If you try to complete this crossword puzzle, you will probably fail.

8. My mother read novels to learn about places that she could never visit.

9. Many scholars believe that children read fairy tales to cope with their fears about adult culture.

10. If you are afraid to travel by plane, you should cancel your trip to Europe.

see answer key, p. 420

GERUNDS (NOUNS)

Like the infinitive, the gerund is formed from a verb. **A gerund always ends in -ing and is always used as a noun.** This means that, as with the other noun structures (the noun clause and the infinitive used as a noun), you can replace a gerund with "it" or "something" and you can identify it as a subject, object, complement, or appositive.

In addition, as with the other noun structures, the gerund is diagramed on a pedestal. The only difference is that, as you can see below, we place the gerund on a "step" structure on top of the pedestal.

Shouting at your teacher is disrespectful. (*It* is disrespectful.)

Here the gerund is "shouting," identifiable as a gerund because it ends in –ing and serves as the subject of the sentence. You can also replace the entire gerund phrase, "shouting at your teacher," with the pronoun "something" or "it."

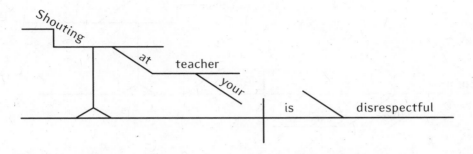

One possible source of confusion is that **gerunds are not the only structure to end in –ing. A progressive verb also ends in –ing, as does a present participle.** Can you see the difference in the way that "playing" is used in the sentences below?

She is *playing* tennis.

Her favorite form of exercise is *playing* tennis.

In the first sentence, we recognize a progressive verb because "playing" follows a form of the *be* verb and together these verbs tell us the action of the sentence. In the second sentence, "playing" is a gerund because, even though it follows a form of the *be* verb, it does not indicate action. In other words, "her favorite form of exercise," the subject, is not performing the action of playing tennis. Instead, "is" acts as the verb of the sentence, and "playing tennis" is the predicate nominative (or subjective complement) that renames the subject. We can easily see these differences by looking at sentence diagrams:

She is playing tennis.

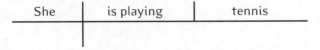

Her favorite form of exercise is playing tennis.

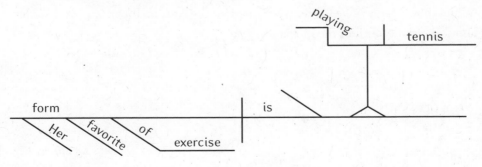

The second sentence also shows us that, like the infinitive, a gerund can be followed by an object or a complement. Let's change the sentence slightly in order to insert a complement:

Her favorite form of exercise is being lazy.

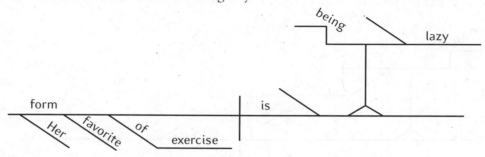

EXERCISE 10.8

Identify the italicized words, all of which end in –ing, as progressive verbs or gerunds. For extra practice, diagram each sentence.

1. *Knowing* the alphabet is essential for a child who is *learning* to read.

2. The *dripping* of the faucet was *making* too much noise.

3. While they were *visiting* Coventry Cathedral, the tour members enjoyed *hearing* about the symbolism of reconciliation.

see answer key, p. 422

EXERCISE 10.9

In the sentences below, underline the gerund phrases and then diagram each sentence.

1. Giving her parents headaches is Alison's pastime.

2. His occupation, transcribing medical records, demands special skills.

3. The children were enthusiastic about experimenting with hydrogen.

4. The ancient Romans enjoyed building structures to improve the comforts of everyday life.

5. Tony has been searching for help in tracing his ancestry.

see answer key, p. 423

PARTICIPLES (ADJECTIVES)

Like the infinitive and the gerund, the participle is a verb form, in this case acting as an adjective to modify a noun or pronoun. Participles appear as either the present participle form of the verb (ending in –ing) or the past participle form (typically ending in -ed, -en, -n, or -t, or in some cases simply the form that an irregular verb changes to when preceded by the auxiliary "have"). Here are a few examples:

Present participles	Past participles
walking	walked
eating	eaten
taking	taken
burning	burnt
singing	sung

As with the gerund, then, we must be careful to distinguish actual verbs—used to indicate action—from participles, which are used as adjectives.

Until now, we've assumed that only adverbs can move within a sentence without changing meaning. A participle, though, can also move within a sentence without changing meaning as long as it modifies the subject and is punctuated correctly. Let's see how this works by looking at variations on the following sentence.

Dropping her suitcases, Susan ran toward us.

This is the most common structure of a sentence containing a participial phrase. First we see the participial phrase, set off by a comma, then the subject (which the participial phrase modifies) and the rest of the sentence. If something goes wrong with this sentence structure and the participial phrase does NOT modify the subject, we have what is known as a **dangling participle:**

★*Dropping her suitcases*, we saw Susan run toward us.

In this version, it sounds as if "we," not Susan, are dropping the suitcases—an unlikely situation. Often, dangling participles of this variety are comic:

★*Hanging from his drawer*, Ralph found his underwear. (It sounds as if Ralph has had a tough night!)

★*Driving home*, a deer ran into the road. (What a smart deer to have a driver's license!)

Here are ways to fix these dangling participles:

Ralph found his underwear *hanging from his drawer*.

As we were driving home, a deer ran into the road. / *Driving home*, we saw a deer run into the road.

Now let's return to our original sentence:

Dropping her suitcases, Susan ran toward us.

Because the participial phrase modifies the subject, we can move it to the end of the sentence as long as we set it off with a comma:

Susan ran toward us, *dropping her suitcases.*

Punctuation can sometimes be crucial in determining the meaning of a sentence with a participial phrase:

Kristin watered the sunflower, *standing in the garden.* (In this sentence, Kristin is the one standing in the garden because the comma before the participial phrase indicates that "standing in the garden" modifies the subject.)

Kristin watered the sunflower standing in the garden. (In this sentence, since there is no comma before the participial phrase, it is the sunflower that is standing in the garden.)

Punctuation is also crucial to meaning when a participial phrase acts in the same way as a relative clause—that is, when it acts as an adjective immediately following the noun it modifies. Remember that with a relative clause, we used the rule that extra information needs extra commas. We also thought of the commas as hooks that could be used to lift out the extra information. These same principles are true of participial phrases that follow a noun. Also, just as with relative clauses, occasionally it is not clear whether the noun is specific (in which case the participial phrase contains extra information) or general (in which case the participial phrase contains necessary information). Look at the following sentence:

The puppy *chasing its tail* was a comic sight. (In this sentence, since there are no commas to set off "chasing its tail," the participial phrase distinguishes this particular puppy from others. We might visualize a number of puppies—some dozing, some playing, and one in particular chasing its tail.)

The puppy, *chasing its tail,* was a comic sight. (In this sentence, since commas do set off "chasing its tail," the participial phrase contains extra information that could be extracted from the sentence by employing the commas as hooks. Here we should visualize only one puppy.)

Of course, if the participial phrase comes at the beginning or end of this sentence, we automatically need a comma to indicate that the participial phrase modifies the subject:

Chasing its tail, the puppy was a comic sight.

The puppy was a comic sight, *chasing its tail.*

Let's return once more to our original sentence:

Dropping her suitcases, Susan ran toward us.
OR
Susan ran toward us, *dropping her suitcases.*

How should we punctuate this sentence if the participial phrase, like a relative clause, follows the noun it modifies?

Susan, *dropping her suitcases*, ran toward us. (Extra commas indicate extra information here, since "Susan" is a proper noun identifying a specific individual.)

Now let's consider a slight variation on this sentence, one that shows how punctuation affects meaning:

The girl *dropping her suitcases* ran toward us. (The lack of commas indicates that "dropping her suitcases" is a necessary phrase used to identify *which* girl.)

The girl, *dropping her suitcases*, ran toward us. (The extra commas here indicate that "*the* girl" is specific enough, with the definite article "the," to justify viewing the participial phrase as extra information.)

Which version is correct? Because this sentence occurs in isolation, we can argue that both are correct, depending on how we interpret the sentence and visualize the scene described in it. Only in the context of a paragraph would we be able to make a more definitive judgment:

The airport was so crowded that we could barely distinguish any faces. We were beginning to believe that we would never find Cousin Jodie. The girl *dropping her suitcases* ran toward us, but she clearly was chasing a skycap in order to solicit help with her baggage. (The girl remains unidentified, so "dropping her suitcases" is necessary to distinguish her from other girls heading in our direction. The phrase is therefore not set off by commas.)

OR

The airport was so crowded that we could barely distinguish any faces. We were beginning to believe that we would never find Cousin Jodie. Just then we spotted her. The girl, *dropping her suitcases*, ran toward us with tears of relief and joy in her eyes. (Here it becomes clear that "the girl" is actually "Cousin Jodie," and therefore "dropping her suitcases" is extra, not essential, information.)

Once we understand how to identify and punctuate participial phrases, we are ready to move on to diagraming. Since a participle functions as an adjective, participles and participial phrases are diagramed underneath the noun being modified. The participle is placed on a prepositional phrase structure, with the participle itself curved around the angle. As with the infinitive and gerund, a participle can also have an object or complement. Let's look at diagrams for some of the sentences we've already seen.

Dropping her suitcases, Susan ran toward us.

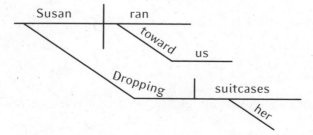

Ralph found his underwear *hanging from his drawer.*

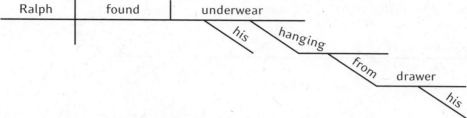

The puppy was a comic sight, *chasing its tail.*

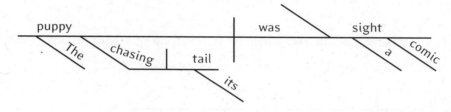

Notice how sometimes punctuation changes the diagram as well:

Kristin watered the sunflower, *standing in the garden.*

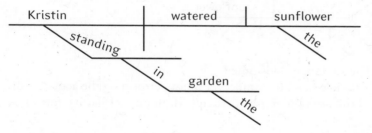

Kristin watered the sunflower *standing in the garden.*

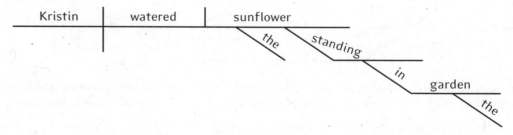

In these sentences, the diagram changes because the comma determines whether the participial phrase modifies the subject or the object. In the following sentences, although the commas do change the way we should visualize the sentence, they don't change the diagram because the participial phrase continues to modify the subject. These two sentences, then, would be diagramed identically:

The puppy *chasing its tail* was a comic sight.

The puppy, *chasing its tail*, was a comic sight.

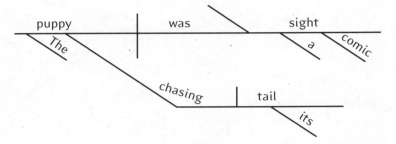

Occasionally a past participle will have a helping verb (a form of *have* or *be*) before it:

Having watered the sunflower, Kristin drank a glass of lemonade.

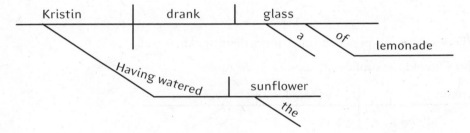

Having been watered, the sunflower blossomed.
(Notice the passive participle here; the sunflower is not performing the action of the participial phrase, and the use of *be* + past participle distinguishes passive form.)

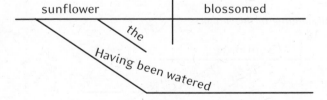

Pre-noun participles are also common. These participles occur before the noun as single words, rather than as participial phrases: a *running* leap, a *watering* can, a *broken* record, *burnt* toast.

The rabbit took a *running* leap toward the fence.

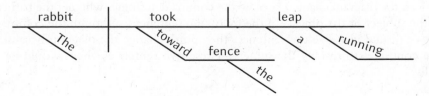

EXERCISE 10.10

In the following sentences, underline the participles and participial phrases and then diagram the sentences.

1. Considering her options carefully, Theresa chose the safest course.

2. Everyone saving money at this bank will receive a bonus interest rate.

3. The children found the goat limping on a cracked hoof.

4. The children found the goat, having searched for hours.

5. In the nursery we saw twenty sleeping babies nestled in their cribs.

see answer key, p. 424

SENTENCE PATTERNS AND VERBALS

Because verbals are formed from verbs and can be followed by objects or complements, we can determine a sentence pattern number for each verbal phrase. First, isolate the verbal phrase and determine if it is an infinitive, a gerund, or a participle. Next, determine the category of the main verb in the verbal phrase. Is it a *be* verb, linking verb, intransitive verb, or transitive verb? Although the verbal phrase does not contain a subject, it often contains a complement or object. Determine what, if anything, follows the verb in the verbal phrase. Is it a complement after a *be* or linking verb or an object after a transitive verb? If you find an object, is there an indirect object or objective complement as well? Once you have identified these elements in the verbal phrase, you can determine the sentence pattern number. Let's see how this works.

Going to a pajama party can be fun.

1. QUESTION:	Are the italicized words an infinitive, a gerund, or a participial phrase?	
ANSWER:	gerund (ends in –ing, acts as subject, can be replaced by "it")	
2. QUESTION:	What category of verb does "going" fall into?	
ANSWER:	intransitive (shows action but only a prepositional phrase follows; no object)	
3. QUESTION:	What sentence pattern does this gerund phrase follow?	
ANSWER:	Pattern 6 (intransitive verb)	

Grinding her teeth, the nervous child finally collapsed in tears.

1. QUESTION:	Are the italicized words an infinitive, a gerund, or a participial phrase?	
ANSWER:	participle because the phrase modifies the subject, "child," and ends in –ing	
2. QUESTION:	What category of verb does "grinding" fall into?	
ANSWER:	transitive (shows action and is followed by an object, "teeth")	
3. QUESTION:	What sentence pattern does this participial phrase follow?	
ANSWER:	Pattern 7 (transitive verb and direct object)	

Elissa set up a trust fund *to become her nephew's benefactress*.

 1. QUESTION: Are the italicized words an infinitive, a gerund, or a participial phrase?

  ANSWER: infinitive (to + verb) used as adverb because the phrase explains *why* Elissa set up the trust fund (and can be preceded by the test phrase "in order to")

 2. QUESTION: What category of verb does "become" fall into?

  ANSWER: linking verb (can be replaced by "be")

 3. QUESTION: What sentence pattern does the infinitive phrase follow?

  ANSWER: Pattern 5 (linking verb + predicate noun, "benefactress")

EXERCISE 10.11

Analyze the verbal phrases in the sentences that follow.

 [A] Underline all verbal phrases.

 [B] Determine if they are infinitive, gerund, or participial phrases.

 [C] Determine the sentence pattern each verbal phrase follows.

 [D] For extra practice, diagram each sentence.

 1. The dream of many people is to write a book.

 2. Handing the waiter her meal, the irate customer asked for the chef.

3. The toddler could not describe the monster hiding in the closet.

4. Being happy is a laudable goal in life.

5. To select Paul as their guide, the tour participants took a vote among themselves.

see answer key, p. 424

SUMMARY OF KEY CONCEPTS IN CHAPTER 10

1. Verbals as nouns: **infinitive (to + verb)**
gerund (ends in –ing)

Replace the infinitive or gerund phrase with "something" or "it," and/or identify its noun function (subject, object, complement, appositive) to determine that it is a noun. Diagram the infinitive on a pedestal using a prepositional phrase structure; diagram the gerund on a pedestal using a step structure.

2. Verbals as adverbs: **infinitive (to + verb)**

The infinitive used as an adverb will modify either the verb (in which case you can precede it by "in order to") or the adjective it follows. The infinitive as adverb is diagramed on a prepositional phrase structure beneath the verb or the adjective it modifies.

3. Verbals as adjectives: **infinitive (to + verb)**
participle (present participle ends in –ing; past participle ends in –ed, –en, –n, –t, or in whatever form an irregular verb changes to when preceded by the auxiliary *have*)

The infinitive phrase and the participial phrase, as adjectives, modify nouns. An infinitive used as an adjective will immediately follow the noun it modifies and is diagramed beneath the noun on a prepositional phrase structure. A participial phrase behaves in one of two ways:

1. If it follows the noun it modifies, punctuate the participial phrase as if it were a relative clause; that is, use extra commas if the participial phrase provides extra information, but no commas if the participial phrase provides necessary information.

2. If it modifies the subject of the sentence, the participial phrase can move to appear at the beginning or at the end of the sentence, as long as it is set off by a comma.

Diagram the participle or the participial phrase beneath the noun it modifies on a prepositional phrase structure, with the participle curving around the angle.

CHAPTER 10 EXERCISE

In the sentences below, underline the infinitive phrases, circle the gerund phrases, and draw a square box around single-word participles and participial phrases. Then diagram each sentence.

1. Ignoring the legal drinking age, Rose began to enjoy two glasses of wine with every meal.

2. Drinking wine with breakfast led to arguments with her protesting parents.

3. After a month, Rose stopped causing everyone concern, dropping wine entirely from her diet.

4. To understand this phenomenon, her parents tried to ask questions.

5. Rose, refusing to explain anything, was already experimenting with her next dietary change.

6. Again no one was eager to eat breakfast with Rose.

7. Pouring mustard on her sweetened cereal, Rose managed to make everyone except herself sick.

see answer key, p. 425

EXERCISES TO REVIEW CLAUSES AND VERBALS

I. The following sentences include all three types of dependent clauses (noun, adverb, and relative) as well as all three types of verbals (infinitives, gerunds, and participles). For a thorough review of all of these structures, diagram the sentences.

1. Aristotle, who established the basic theory of tragedy, used Greek plays to illustrate his points.

2. Aristotle considered tragedy a series of events leading to misery in the life of a noble character.

3. When members of an audience see a tragedy performed on stage, they experience strong emotions.

4. These compelling sensations produce a catharsis that cleanses the emotions of the audience.

5. Although no perfect tragedy exists, Aristotle chose *Oedipus Rex* as his primary example.

6. Governing a land filled with sorrow, Oedipus is ignorant of the deed that has brought his kingdom a terrible pollution.

7. Once he learns the truth, he realizes that he has unknowingly married his own mother.

8. Having offended the gods, he has to purify the land.

9. A turning point of the play occurs at the moment when he realizes his crime of patricide.

10. Compensating for his actions, which have broken cultural norms, is essential.

11. He becomes an isolated figure who must blindly grope his way from the city that he once ruled.

12. The most difficult aspect of his exile is abandoning his two young daughters.

II. Write sentences of your own as directed below. Use the following sentence as a base upon which to build your own:

The hedgehog escaped from the attic.

1. Write a sentence using "escaping" as a gerund.

_____

_____

2. Write a sentence using "escaping" as a participle.

_____

_____

3. Write a sentence using "to escape" as a noun.

_____

_____

4. Write a sentence using "to escape" as an adverb.

_____

_____

5. Write a sentence using "to escape" as an adjective.

_____

_____

6. Write a sentence that begins with an adverb clause. Underline the adverb clause.

_____

_____

7. Write a sentence that contains a relative clause. Underline the relative clause.

_____

_____

8. Write a sentence that contains a noun clause. Underline the noun clause.

_____

_____

9. Write a sentence that contains an appositive. Underline the appositive.

_____

_____

10. Write a sentence that contains a complementary infinitive. Underline the complementary infinitive.

_____

_____

11. Write a sentence that contains both a participial phrase and an adverb clause. Underline the participial phrase, and double underline the adverb clause.

_____

_____

12. Write a compound-complex sentence.

_____

_____

see answer key, p. 427

Usage Problems Associated with Verbs and Verbals

The English verb system, complicated enough in itself, leads to a few common usage errors. In this chapter we will deal first with two usage areas associated with verbs (the subjunctive mood and three pairs of commonly misused verbs) and then go on to examine three usage problems associated with verbals (dangling verbals and elliptical clauses, split infinitives, and use of the possessive with gerunds). Finally, we will look at parallelism, the basic principle that grammatical items in pairs or series within a sentence should be phrased in the same grammatical forms. When a sentence lacks parallelism, the structure of the entire sentence is weakened. We include parallelism here, in the final section of the final chapter devoted to usage, because correcting parallelism problems requires a clear recognition of all the grammatical structures included in this text.

SUBJUNCTIVE MOOD

As we mentioned briefly in Chapter 9, **English verbs have four so-called "moods"**:

INDICATIVE	(by far the most common, since these verbs "indicate" something)
	The shop *is* open.
IMPERATIVE	(verbs that make a demand)
	Open the shop.
CONDITIONAL	(verbs that set up conditions or circumstances under which specific actions or states of existence will come to pass, expressed by the modals "could," "may," "might," "would," and "should")
	If you had opened the shop, I *would have bought* twenty place settings of my favorite china.
SUBJUNCTIVE	(verbs that express a demand or strong recommendation in a noun clause beginning with "that," or verbs that set up a situation contrary to fact)

The employees suggested that the shop *be* closed on holidays. (demand or strong recommendation)

I wish the shop *were* open. (contrary to fact)

In the example sentences for the subjunctive mood, take a close look at the italicized verbs. You will notice immediately that under ordinary circumstances, the rules of standard English would not permit us to say "the shop *be* closed" or "the shop *were* open." What has happened here? How and when do we use the subjunctive mood—which calls for a subjunctive verb form—in English?

If you have ever studied another language, you have probably encountered the subjunctive, a mood that in most languages entails learning separate verb forms and understanding specific circumstances under which the subjunctive is required. As English has evolved over the centuries, it has simplified in this regard and gradually shed most of its subjunctive forms. The subjunctive now remains in only two situations, and even that is in flux. The first situation calling for the subjunctive occurs when a strong suggestion, recommendation, or demand is made in the form of a noun clause beginning with *that*. In this case, the subjunctive is always a one-word verb, not a verb phrase. The second condition under which the subjunctive should be used, when a situation contrary to fact or to reality is hypothesized, seems to be slowly phasing out of everyday speech.

Most of the time, even if you do use the subjunctive form, you are blissfully unaware of it. Only with the *be* verb or with the third person singular form of the verb can we even notice a distinction between the subjunctive verb and the typical present tense, indicative mood of the verb.

Let's compare the present tense and the subjunctive of *be* as called for in the first situation—that is, a strong suggestion, recommendation, or demand.

Present Tense Indicative Mood		Present Tense Subjunctive Mood	
I am	we are	I be	we be
you are	you are	you be	you be
he, she, it is	they are	he, she, it be	they be

INDICATIVE: I am polite.
SUBJUNCTIVE: My job requires that I be polite to customers.

INDICATIVE: They are suspicious of strangers.
SUBJUNCTIVE: Circumstances demand that everyone be suspicious of strangers these days.

INDICATIVE: You are punctual.
SUBJUNCTIVE: I recommend that you be punctual on the day of the final exam.

Now let's take a look at another verb to see how it changes from present tense indicative mood to the subjunctive.

Present Tense *Indicative Mood*		*Present Tense* *Subjunctive Mood*	
I go	we go	I go	we go
you go	you go	you go	you go
he, she, it goes	they go	he, she, it go	they go

Notice that in a verb other than *be*, the only change you can see occurs in third person singular. Although we must remember to add the ending "-s" in the indicative mood, we remove it to indicate subjunctive.

INDICATIVE:	I *go* to Jamaica.
SUBJUNCTIVE:	My job requires that I *go* to Jamaica. (This is the subjunctive mood, but we cannot tell this just from the form of the verb.)
INDICATIVE:	He *goes* to Jamaica.
SUBJUNCTIVE:	His job requires that he *go* to Jamaica. (Here, because we are in third person singular, we can see the subjunctive mood in the form of the verb. The same "-s" ending that we must remember to include in the third person singular, present tense verb is dropped in the subjunctive.)

The second situation that calls for the subjunctive occurs when a situation contrary to reality is hypothesized. This typically requires the past subjunctive form of *be*.

Present Tense *Indicative Mood*		*Present Tense* *Subjunctive Mood*	
I was	we were	I were	we were
you were	you were	you were	you were
he, she, it was	they were	he, she, it were	they were

INDICATIVE:	I *am* rich. / I *was* rich.
SUBJUNCTIVE:	I wish I *were* rich. If I *were* rich, I would quit working immediately. Suppose I *were* rich; I would quit working immediately.

In all three of these sentences we need the subjunctive form because we are expressing a situation contrary to reality. Because this use of the subjunctive appears to be fading slowly from the language, though, you may find that "I wish I *was* rich, "If I *was* rich," or "Suppose I *was* rich" will sound natural to you. You are likely to hear even educated speakers use the indicative rather than the subjunctive in this context.

The subjunctive forms of *be* can be used as helping verbs so that, when expressing hypothetical situations, you can use whatever verb you like.

They wish they *were* fishing rather than working. (Here we cannot see the subjunctive mood in the form of the verb.)

He wishes he *were* fishing rather than working. (Here, because we are in third person singular, the subjunctive form of the verb is evident, since ordinarily we would not say "he were.")

EXERCISE 11.1

Decide whether or not you need the subjunctive in the following sentences. If so, circle the subjunctive form. If you do not need the subjunctive, circle the indicative form.

1. Everyone wishes that it (WAS, WERE) Friday.

2. If Yvette (WAS, WERE) smarter, she would dump her boyfriend.

3. I hoped that everything (WAS, WERE) ready for the party.

4. In the midst of a snowstorm, Cookie often wishes that she (WAS, WERE) living on a tropical island.

5. The manager demanded that each employee (COME, COMES) to work with a spotless uniform.

6. Suppose that a child (WAS, WERE) in charge of the world; how would global politics change?

7. We all wish that chocolate (WAS, WERE) included in one of the basic four food groups.

8. It seems that the cat (WAS, WERE) smarter than the dog when the fire broke out.

9. The doctors have recommended that Victor (DRINK, DRINKS) at least one glass of wine daily.

10. Our professor made us learn that Ben Jonson (WAS, WERE) the first poet laureate of England.

see answer key, p. 430

CONFUSING VERB PAIRS: LIE/LAY, SIT/SET, RAISE/RISE

Three sets of verbs create frequent difficulties for speakers and writers of English: lie/lay, sit/set, and raise/rise. Let's see if we can untangle the confusion, much of which derives from the fact that in each pair one verb is transitive and the other is intransitive.

1 ● *lie/lay*

These two verbs are confused primarily because of their past tense, since the past tense of "lie" is "lay." To be sure you use these verbs correctly, use a two-step process. First, determine which verb to use.

lie =to recline   (intransitive; no object follows)
lay=to place   (transitive; object follows, so one always must "lay something")

Once you have determined which verb is correct, select the appropriate verb form. The three principal parts of each verb are listed below:

base form	past tense	past participle (used with "have")
lie	lay	lain
lay	laid	laid

Using the above chart and the two-step process, let's look at the sentences below.

Most people enjoy *lying* in bed in the morning. (Most people enjoy *reclining* in bed. Notice the spelling of the present participle form, "lying." There is no object since *lie* is an intransitive verb.)

The craftsman was *laying* bricks in a straight line as he built the wall. (The craftsman was *placing* bricks. Here we need the present participle form of *lay*, the transitive verb, since "bricks" serves as object.)

Please *lay* the keys on the table. (Please *place* the keys on the table. Notice that "keys" is the object.)

Yesterday the girls *lay* on the beach for an hour without sunscreen. (Yesterday the girls *reclined* on the beach. "Lay" is the past tense of "lie"; there is no object.)

Those newspapers have *lain* on the porch for a month. (Those newspapers have *reclined* on the porch. Note that objects, not just people, can lie or recline. Here the past participle of *lie*, "lain," is necessary because of the auxiliary "have." There is no object.)

The robin *laid* her eggs in a cozy nest. (The robin *placed* her eggs in a cozy nest. "Laid" is the past tense of "lay," with "eggs" serving as object.)

NOTE: This discussion has omitted *lie* as a verb meaning "to tell a falsehood." This use of the verb rarely causes difficulties. The three principal parts of this meaning of *lie*, though, are "lie" (present), "lied" (past), and "lied" (past participle). The present participle form is "lying."

He *lied* about his age.

He has been *lying* about his age for years.

2 ● *sit/set*

Sit means "to rest" and (like *lie*) is intransitive, with no object; *set* means "to place" and (like *lay*) is a transitive verb and therefore followed by a direct object. Thus one must always "set something." The exception is our idiomatic phrase about the sun: "The sun sets" is intransitive.
    Below are the three principal forms of these two verbs:

base form	past tense	past participle
sit	sat	sat
set	set	set

My mother always *set* the table with pink china.

Meanwhile, my father *sat* in the chair.

He let the dirty dishes *sit* in the sink overnight.

3 ● *rise/raise*

Rise means to ascend and is an intransitive verb, with no object; *raise* means to lift and, as a transitive verb, is always followed by a direct object. Thus we must "raise something."

base form	past tense	past participle
rise	rose	risen
raise	raised	raised

I *raised* the window when I heard the strange sound outside.

I could see that the river was rapidly *rising*.

I *raised* my voice to call for my parents, but they had already *risen* from their beds and were gathering our valuables.

As a quick review, then, here is a chart that might help you remember all three of these verbs.

TRANSITIVE VERBS				
lay	laid	(have) laid	+	object (something)
set	set	(have) set	+	object (something)
raise	raised	(have) raised	+	object (something)

All of these verbs involve placement of a person or object:

Lay the curtains down.

Set the curtains down.

Raise the curtains.

INTRANSITIVE VERBS	lie	lay	(have) lain	=	to recline, to rest
	sit	sat	(have) sat	=	to rest
	rise	rose	(have) risen	=	to ascend

All of these verbs involve autonomous movement; that is, no entity other than the subject is initiating the movement involved, and therefore no direct object appears. Since the base form of all of these verbs includes the letter "i," think of these verbs as being "*i*ntransitive" and showing "I" action—self-initiated action, even when the subject is not "I":

I *lie* down.	The book *lies* open.
I *sit* down.	The book *sits* on the shelf
I *rise* up.	The book *rises* in value each year.

EXERCISE 11.2

Choose the correct verb in each of the sentences below.

1. To make an effective argument, you need to (SIT, SET) down your major points on paper.

2. The teen's parents intended to (LAY, LIE) the groundwork for future discussion about sex.

3. Taxes are (RAISING, RISING) every year.

4. Our poodle likes to (LAY, LIE) on a warm lap.

5. After he has (LAID, LAIN) there for a few minutes, he will fall fast asleep.

6. Then you can (LAY, LIE) a book on top of his head without waking him up.

7. We have even (LAID, LAIN) a phone on top of his sleeping head.

8. When he finally (RAISES, RISES) his head, he looks surprised.

9. We (SIT, SET) him on his hind paws and rub his head.

10. After he has (SAT, SET) there for a while, he returns to (LAYING, LYING) on a warm lap.

see answer key, p. 430

DANGLING VERBALS

In Chapter 10 we discussed the dangers of a dangling participle. Remember that a participle is a word that is formed from a verb but fulfills the function of an adjective. The present participle ends in "-ing," while the past participle either ends in "-ed," "-en," "-n," or "-t" or takes the form of the past participle verb (the *have* form). Most often, a dangling participle occurs when a sentence begins with a participial phrase. This placement indicates that the participial phrase should modify the subject, and so it "dangles" when it does not:

INCORRECT:	*Rushed for time*, the executive's report was left on the kitchen table. (Here the sentence gives us the illogical picture of a report—not an executive—in a hurry.)
CORRECT:	*Rushed for time*, the executive left her report on the kitchen table. (This sentence retains the opening participial phrase, but the phrase now modifies "executive" rather than "report." In the corrected sentence the executive, not the report, is rushed.)

Remember that **when a participial phrase modifies the subject, it can move IF punctuated correctly**:

Rushed for time, the executive left her report on the kitchen table.

The executive, *rushed for time*, left her report on the kitchen table.

The executive left her report on the kitchen table, *rushed for time*.

INCORRECT:	The executive left her report on the kitchen table *rushed for time*. (Here, with no comma to indicate that the participial phrase modifies the subject, we have another dangling participial phrase. In this version, the table is in a rush!)

Less obvious, but just as faulty, are dangling infinitives and dangling gerunds:

INCORRECT:	*To ensure accuracy*, the report was double-checked. (Here the infinitive phrase dangles because the report itself cannot ensure accuracy. Notice that the passive voice of the main clause is a culprit as well.)
CORRECT:	*To ensure accuracy*, a team of experts double-checked the report. (This version gives us a subject—"team"—capable of ensuring accuracy.)
INCORRECT:	By *ensuring accuracy*, the report gained credibility. (Here "ensuring accuracy" is a gerund phrase acting as the object of the preposition "by." However, since the report itself cannot ensure accuracy, we have a dangling gerund phrase.

This sentence needs to include a human agent who can perform the act of ensuring accuracy.)

CORRECT: By *being accurate*, the report gained credibility. (This version gives us a gerund phrase that is within the scope of the subject since the report can *be* accurate even though it cannot *ensure* accuracy.)

CORRECT: By *ensuring accuracy*, the team of experts gave the report credibility. (The gerund phrase now appropriately refers to the team of experts rather than to the report itself.)

Finally, a related problem of dangling arises with the structure known as the elliptical clause. Just as the ellipsis (. . .) is the mark of punctuation indicating that something has been omitted, so in an elliptical clause something has been omitted—frequently the subject and/or part of the verb phrase. What results often looks like a verbal phrase, even though, strictly speaking, it is not.

INCORRECT: *While waiting for the water to boil*, the stove caught on fire. (The italicized words form an elliptical clause because the word group begins with a subordinating conjunction, indicating an adverb clause, and then omits the subject and the *be* auxiliary. The elliptical clause dangles because no noun or pronoun in the sentence is performing the action of the elliptical clause, making it seem as if the stove is doing the waiting.)

CORRECT: *While waiting for the water to boil*, I realized that the stove had caught on fire. (Here the pronoun "I" has been inserted directly following the elliptical clause to make clear that a person, not the stove, was waiting.)

CORRECT: *While I was waiting for the water to boil*, the stove caught on fire. (The simplest way to fix a dangling elliptical clause is to expand it to its full form. There is then no possibility of confusion.)

EXERCISE 11.3

Rewrite the following sentences in order to eliminate dangling verbals and elliptical clauses.

1. Limping on a front paw, the veterinarian examined the stray cat.

_____

_____

2. After administering a routine vaccination, the cat tried wildly to escape.

_____

_____

3. Clawing and hissing, a technician scooped up the animal.

_____

_____

4. To calm its nerves, a sedative was finally administered.

_____

_____

5. We all breathed a sigh of relief knowing that the situation was under control.

_____

_____

6. The veterinarian was caught off guard when, regaining consciousness, we were again attacked by the cat.

_____

_____

7. Although tempted to set it free, the cat was placed in a cage until we could determine what to do next.

_____

_____

see answer key, p. 430

Two final points of usage that arise with verbs involve the question of whether or not to split an infinitive, and how to indicate possession before a gerund or gerund phrase. Both of these issues are relatively minor points ignored by many respected users of English. Observing these rules, though, or at least breaking them deliberately rather than unconsciously, will mark you as a more sophisticated speaker and writer.

SPLIT INFINITIVES

Since an infinitive consists of "to" followed by a verb, a split infinitive occurs when one or more words are inserted between these two elements, as in "to *quickly* speak." Although in general it is advisable to avoid splitting an infinitive, an even better rule to follow is to phrase sentences so that they sound natural. If you must contort a sentence to avoid splitting an infinitive, it is preferable to separate the two parts of the infinitive to achieve a smoothly flowing sentence. In most cases, though, you will find that you can rearrange words or rephrase the sentence entirely in order to avoid this problem.

WORSE:	I asked her *to quietly leave.*
BETTER:	I asked her *to leave quietly.* (Here a simple rearrangement of words resolves the split infinitive.)
WORSE:	*To truly capture* the essence of primitive survival, the adventurers set off into the wilderness with no provisions or equipment.
BETTER:	*To capture* the true essence of primitive survival, the adventurers set off into the wilderness with no provisions or equipment. (Merely re-arranging words is not a viable option in this case. Instead, even though we might contend that a very slight shift in meaning occurs, the best way to avoid splitting the infinitive is to change the adverb "truly" to its adjective form, "true," in order to rephrase the sentence.)

EXERCISE 11.4

Rephrase the following sentences to avoid split infinitives.

1. You must study math for years to clearly understand some of the more complex concepts.

   _____

   _____

2. All ten siblings in Brittni's family insist that they want to always stay close to one another.

   _____

   _____

3. To efficiently manage a restaurant, you need to constantly be on the premises.

_____

_____

see answer key, p. 430

POSSESSIVES WITH GERUNDS

Another usage problem associated with verbals is indicating possession of a gerund. Because a gerund functions as a noun, we must use the same possessive form before a gerund that we would use before any other noun. Consider the following sentences; which one seems grammatically correct to you?

We were excited about *John becoming* a brain surgeon.

We were excited about *John's becoming* a brain surgeon.

Although not everyone can determine the correct choice either by ear or by sight, the second sentence is correct because "becoming" is a gerund—a noun—and before a noun we must use a possessive form. The following two sentences are basically the same in form, although one contains a single-word noun and the other a gerund phrase. The diagram for each one also demonstrates that the possessive before the gerund is the correct form.

We were excited about *John's news.*

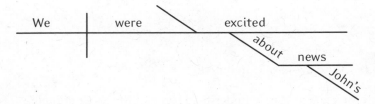

We were excited about *John's becoming a brain surgeon.*

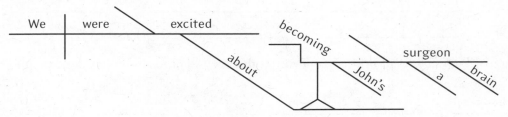

EXERCISE 11.5

Choose the correct form in the sentences below. For extra practice, diagram the sentences.

1. (MARTHA, MARTHA'S) announcing her retirement was a complete surprise.

2. The judges appreciated (US, OUR) entering only one category of competition.

3. Patty's hobby, collecting stamps, led to her (MOTHER, MOTHER'S) increasing her allowance.

see answer key, p. 430

PARALLELISM

A common situation that arises in writing is the parallel phrasing of items in a series. Ideally, each item in any grouping of two or more items should be in the same grammatical structure. Parallelism problems typically occur when a series of three or more items is involved, or when two items are joined by correlative conjunctions. Parallelism is not a usage issue limited to verbs and verbals; in practice, though, many parallelism difficulties do relate to verbs and verbals, as well as to other grammatical elements such as dependent clauses and correlative conjunctions.

Parallelism affects the integrity of the overall sentence and demands an understanding of all the grammatical structures we have studied so far, and so it seems fitting to make it the topic of this final usage section.

1 ● Parallelism in a Series of Three or More

The dancer was *tall*, *blonde*, and *had green eyes*.

The sentence above is not in parallel form because the three descriptors of the subject are not in the same grammatical form. "Tall" and "blonde" are adjectives, but "had green eyes" contains a verb and direct object. One way to visualize this problem is to think of the first part of the sentence as a sentence stem, to be completed in three different ways.

The dancer was   tall.

The dancer was   blonde.

The dancer was   had green eyes.

You can see immediately that the third option for ending this sentence will not work. The first two options result in Pattern 2 sentences; the third option includes a clash between "was" and a transitive verb with direct object ("had green eyes"). Another way to visualize the difficulty is to diagram the sentence.

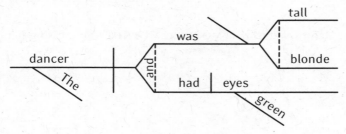

The diagram illustrates that this sentence would be grammatically correct if it contained two conjunctions—in other words, if it were phrased as "The dancer was tall *and* blonde *and* had green eyes." Without two conjunctions, the sentence is awkwardly phrased. To make this sentence parallel, we must **make the grammatical structures match**. We can do this in a variety of ways:

1. The dancer was tall, blonde, and green-eyed. (This is probably the simplest revision. We now have three adjectives following the verb, as indicated by the diagram below.)

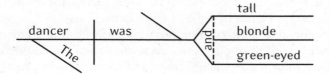

2. The dancer was tall and blonde and had green eyes. (A problem with this revision is that some might object to the repetition of "and.")

3. The tall, blonde dancer had green eyes. (With the adjectives placed before the subject, the entire sentence becomes a Pattern 7; the emphasis changes, though, to the dancer's green eyes.)

4. The green-eyed dancer was tall and blonde. (Changing "had green eyes" into an adjective, "green-eyed," results in a Pattern 2 sentence; this version emphasizes that the dancer is tall and blonde.)

A related problem that often occurs with items in a series is the use of articles. As a rule, either use one article to precede the entire list, or use an article before each item. If some of the items begin with vowels and some with consonants, so that you must vary between "a" and "an," then you have no choice but to include an article with each item in the series.

INCORRECT:	The new manager asked for a cell phone, laptop computer, and a fax machine.
CORRECT:	The new manager asked for a cell phone, laptop computer, and fax machine. (one article)
CORRECT:	The new manager asked for a cell phone, a laptop computer, and a fax machine. (three articles)
INCORRECT:	The new manager asked for a cell phone, laptop computer, and administrative assistant.
CORRECT:	The new manager asked for a cell phone, a laptop computer, and an administrative assistant. (Here three articles are necessary because "administrative assistant," beginning with a vowel sound, requires "an.")

2 ● Parallelism With Correlative Conjunctions

When we are not dealing with a series of three or more, but only two, we still must concern ourselves with parallel form. This is especially true when the two items are joined by **correlative conjunctions**, conjunctions that appear in a double "frame." Correlative conjunctions include the following pairs:

both / and
not only / but also (the "also" may be omitted, but not "but")
either / or
neither / nor
whether / or

When dealing with correlative conjunctions, you must make sure that whatever grammatical structure follows the first conjunction also follows the second. Here is an example:

INCORRECT:	I will *either* cook a turkey *or* a chicken. ("Either" comes before a verb; "or" comes before a noun.)
CORRECT:	I will cook *either* a turkey *or* a chicken. ("Either" and "or" both precede nouns in this sentence.) OR I will *either* roast a turkey *or* fry a chicken. ("Either" and "or" both precede verbs in this sentence.)

"Not only / but also" can be a troublesome pair in terms of syntax. To separate independent clauses, you may use "not only / but" (dropping the "also"); however, using "not only / also" leads to a comma splice. In addition, the use of "not" often calls for the inclusion of a form of *do* as an auxiliary. This in turn may make you doubt whether you have achieved parallelism, since an independent clause beginning with "not only" often places the subject in the middle of the verb phrase. The example below illustrates the changes in syntax necessary to use the "not only / but also" construction as a way of combining two simple sentences into a compound sentence. It also illustrates how easily this construction might lead into a sentence error.

SIMPLE SENTENCES:	Brent made the hockey team. He won a scholarship.
INCORRECT:	*Not only* did Brent make the hockey team, *also* he won a scholarship. (comma splice)
CORRECT:	*Not only* did Brent make the hockey team, *but also* he won a scholarship. (compound sentence)
CORRECT:	*Not only* did Brent make the hockey team, *but* he won a scholarship. (compound sentence)
CORRECT:	Brent *not only* made the hockey team *but also* won a scholarship. (simple sentence with compound verb)

EXERCISE 11.6

Rewrite the following sentences so that they are in parallel form.

1. The apartment could be rented by the week, by the month, or on a yearly basis.

   _____

   _____

2. Barbara likes to read Tolstoy, sketch landscapes, and to run in marathons.

_____

_____

3. Losing his wife to another man, his self-control to liquor, and the loss of his daughter's custody brought Andy to the brink of despair.

_____

_____

4. We wondered whether to watch television or if we should study.

_____

_____

5. The doctor not only located the diseased organ, but he removed it also.

_____

_____

6. The bus driver had to either decide to swerve into the ditch, or he could risk a head–on collision.

_____

_____

7. The project members drank coffee, smoked cigars, and all of the near-tragic events of the day were discussed until dawn.

_____

_____

8. Follow three rules when studying for an exam: start early, study for a short time each day, and you should get a good night's rest before the exam.

_____

_____

9. When Anna was growing up, her parents neither allowed her to have pets nor guests.

_____

_____

10. Both gourmet food and having good friends are obsessions of mine.

_____

_____

11. No respectable zoo can be without a giraffe, elephant, and lion.

_____

_____

12. Not only did the fans cheer as the parading heroes went by, also they threw tons of confetti into the streets.

_____

_____

see answer key, p. 431

SUMMARY OF KEY CONCEPTS IN CHAPTER 11

1. Use the subjunctive mood in two contexts: (a) when a sentence expresses a demand or strong recommendation in a noun clause beginning with "that"; (b) when a sentence sets up a hypothetical situation that is contrary to fact. Except for the *be* verb and the third person singular form of the verb, the subjunctive verb form is identical to the present tense verb form.

2. Distinguish between *lay*, *set*, and *raise* (transitive verbs, followed by a direct object) and *lie*, *sit*, and *rise* (intransitive verbs).

3. Avoid dangling participles, infinitives, gerunds, and elliptical clauses.

4. If at all possible, avoid splitting the infinitive.

5. Use the possessive form before a gerund.

6. Make sure that items in a series are in parallel grammatical form and that correlative conjunctions are correctly placed so that they precede parallel grammatical forms.

CHAPTER 11 EXERCISE

In the sentences below, correct all errors that relate to the concepts covered in this chapter.

If Snow White was a real person, she would not have been able to lay in a deep sleep for many years. Waiting for her prince to arrive, her life would have ended. Because this is a fairy tale, though, anything is possible—him rescuing her, her raising up from an enchanted slumber to gratefully marry him. When thinking about the story, the wicked stepmother comes to mind as well. She lays her plans subtly, sets a trap for Snow White, and all the while she pretends to be a doting parent. She demands that her mirror tells her every day that she is the fairest in the land. To remove competition, Snow White has to be eliminated, but after returning to life, the wicked stepmother is doomed forever. It is rather disturbing to think that many young girls hear this story as they are laying in their beds. Are they wondering if perhaps they, too, will not be able to ever wake up? Could a loving mother turn into a wicked stepmother without the daughter being aware of it? After arguing with her mother, is it possible that this story would come to mind in some way? Perhaps it is time that we set down with our daughters either to more critically analyze fairy tales or we discontinue passing these tales through the generations.

_____

_____

_____

_____

_____

_____

_____

_____

_____

_____

_____

_____

_____

see answer key, p. 432

Punctuation and Capitalization

Punctuation and capitalization, as confusing as their rules may sometimes seem, are often crucial to meaning. Consider the following sentence:

Woman without her man is nothing.

How should it read? Here are two possibilities, showing how punctuation can drastically alter meaning.

Woman, without her man, is nothing.

Woman—without her, man is nothing.

Let's see if we can demystify some of the rules so that you can use punctuation and capitalization thoughtfully, as another way to shape meaning. Even if your sentences are beautifully constructed and you follow the usage rules perfectly, without correct punctuation your ideas will often be unclear or ambiguous.

I ● PUNCTUATION

Comma Rules

The rules for using commas can actually be broken into just a few categories. Some of these rules will already be familiar to you from earlier chapters.

1. **Use a comma before a coordinating conjunction** (remember the FANBOYS acronym—"for," "and," "nor," "but," "or," "yet," "so") when the conjunction separates two independent clauses. (In other words, use a comma before the coordinating conjunction in a compound sentence.)

I would like to go out tonight, *but* I must study these comma rules.

I would like to go out tonight but must study instead. (no comma because "but" separates verbs, not independent clauses, in this sentence)

2. **Use a comma after an adverb clause that begins a sentence**. (Remember that an adverb clause begins with a subordinating conjunction—a word such as "after," "although," "as,"

"because," "if," "since," "unless," "until," "when," "where," "while.") Use a comma before an adverb clause that comes at the end of the sentence only when the adverb clause shows contrast. (In this case, the subordinating conjunction will most likely be one of these: "although," "though," "even though," "whereas," "while.")

> *Although I would like to go out tonight*, I must study these comma rules.

> I must study these comma rules, *although I would like to go out tonight.*

> I would like to go out tonight *because I am tired of studying these comma rules.*

3. **Use a comma after a conjunctive adverb that follows a semicolon**. (Remember that conjunctive adverbs are words that signal transition, such as "however," "therefore," "moreover," "meanwhile," "consequently," "furthermore," "nevertheless," "thus.") Usually, no comma is necessary after the conjunctive adverb "then," and a comma is optional after other one-syllable conjunctive adverbs.

> I must study these comma rules; *therefore*, I cannot go out tonight.

> I will study these comma rules; *then* I will go out.

> I have studied all of the comma rules; *thus* I deserve to go out.
> OR (for more emphasis)
> I have studied all of the comma rules; *thus,* I deserve to go out.

4. **Use a comma after an introductory element** (prepositional phrase, participial phrase, interjection or other introductory word, or a word or phrase that usually serves as a conjunctive adverb).

> Introductory prepositional phrase:

> *After our study session*, I passed the test.

Although you are never wrong to place a comma after an introductory prepositional phrase, the comma is optional if the phrase is short (only two or three words). An exception occurs when the prepositional phrase contains a date. Although the numerals make the prepositional phrase appear short, in actuality you are saying several words when you read the phrase out loud.

> *In the morning* we made our way to New York City. (comma optional)

> *In 1995*, we made our way to New York City. (comma required)

> Introductory participial phrase:
> *Studying the comma rules*, I fell asleep.

> Introductory word (such as "yes," "no," "oh," "well"):
> *Yes*, I have studied the comma rules.

> Introductory conjunctive adverb:
> I have studied the comma rules. *However*, I did not memorize them.
> (Note that at the end of the first sentence, the period could be replaced by a semi-colon.)

5. **Use commas to separate items in a series of three or more**. Do not use commas if all of the items are joined by conjunctions such as "and" or "or."

> We studied commas, semicolons, *and* colons. (Although professionals in fields such as journalism and business often drop the comma before "and," many others— notably lawyers and those in liberal arts disciplines such as English—retain the comma for the sake of clarity. Occasionally newspapers carry stories of lawsuits brought forth because of the presence or absence of the final comma in a series. This comma often influences meaning.)

Occasionally a list will delete the "and" altogether. This rhetorical device, known as asyndeton, gives the impression that the list could continue indefinitely but has been deliberately shortened.

> We studied commas, semicolons, colons.

Conversely, occasionally the "and" is repeated for emphasis, to make the list seem longer, as if it exhausts all the possibilities.

> We studied commas *and* semicolons *and* colons.

6. **Use a comma to separate two adjectives that modify a noun when "and" could substitute for the comma**. Do not insert this comma when the second adjective refers to age, color, or constitutive material.

> Our challenging, fast-paced class deals with all aspects of grammar.

> Our energetic young teacher makes us work hard.

> The large green chalkboard is always covered with sentence diagrams.

> The tall cardboard poster highlights the eight parts of speech.

7. **Use commas to set off all elements (except zip code) in dates and addresses**.

> I finally graduated on May 11, 1985, from Rice University in Houston, Texas. (The international dating system, which uses the month to separate the numerals, avoids the problem of commas in this situation: I finally graduated on 11 May 1985 from Rice University in Houston, Texas.)

> The grammar textbook was mailed to 201 Mullica Hill Road, Glassboro, New Jersey 08028.

Note that when one comma is included within the date or address, another comma is required to signal the end of the date or address:

> I studied French grammar in Paris during May 1995 while on vacation in Europe.

> I studied French grammar in Paris, France, during May, 1995, while on vacation in Europe. (As you can see, the comma between month and year is optional, although nowadays most writers omit it. In MLA style—guidelines set up by the Modern

Language Association, the governing body for scholars and teachers of language and literature—this comma does not appear. If you do insert it, though, you need to place another comma after the year, as in the last example above.)

8. **Use commas to set off extra information within a sentence**. Remember the general rule we mentioned before, in Chapter 7: extra information = extra commas; necessary information = no commas. Extra information can take various forms:

a. Set off nonrestrictive relative clauses.

Mary, who studied her comma rules, made an A on her essay. BUT The person who studied her comma rules made an A on her essay.

b. Set off appositives of more than one word. Set off a one-word appositive when it supplies extra information.

Mary, my friend, studied her comma rules.

My friend, Mary, studied her comma rules. (This sentence implies that Mary is the speaker's only friend, since "Mary" is set off as extra information.)

My friend Mary studied her comma rules. (This sentence implies that the speaker has several friends; the name "Mary" is necessary to distinguish this particular friend.)

One way to remember the difference is to consider the difference in meaning of the sentences below:

Mary's sister Michaela teaches grammar. (Because there is no comma, we assume that Mary has more than one sister; only one teaches grammar.)

Mary's husband, Michael, teaches grammar. (Because legally Mary should have only one husband, commas are necessary here to indicate that her husband's name is extra information.)

A special situation arises when a phrase (often a title) acts as one unit and is therefore treated as a one-word appositive:

William Faulkner's novel *The Sound and the Fury* was an experiment in narrative technique. (This sentence needs no commas because Faulkner wrote many novels; the title is necessary to indicate which novel is under discussion.)

Harper Lee's novel, *To Kill a Mockingbird*, gives us a child's perspective on racial issues in the South. (Because Lee wrote only one novel, the title provides extra information, as indicated by the commas.)

c. Set off interrupting expressions within a sentence; these are often the transitional words included in the conjunctive adverb category.

Mary studied her comma rules. I, however, did not.

Comma rules, to tell the truth, can be rather boring.

You must study the apostrophe rules, too.

d. Set off the name of a person or group being addressed by name.

Mary, please study these comma rules.

Please, Mary, study these comma rules.

Please study these comma rules, Mary.

Ladies and gentlemen, allow me to introduce our grammar expert.

e. Set off a "tag" question (added at the end of a sentence to imply a *yes* or *no* answer).

You are going to study these rules, aren't you?

9. **Use commas with direct quotations**. (Notice the variations below. We will examine direct quotations in more detail later.)

The student said, "I must study these comma rules."

"I must study these comma rules," the student said.

"I must study," the student said, "because we may have a quiz tomorrow." (one sentence quoted)

"I must study," the student said. "We may have a quiz tomorrow." (two sentences quoted)

"Don't interrupt me! I'm studying!" the student shouted.

"Do we have to know all of these rules?" the student asked.

10. **Do *not* use a comma to separate the essential elements of a sentence**. In other words, do not use a comma between a subject and a verb, between a verb and its complement or object, or between an object and its objective complement. Even if you pause in speaking, do not place a comma between the elements of the ten basic sentence patterns. The one exception occurs when the direct object is a direct quotation.

INCORRECT:	Whoever has parked in front of the driveway, must move immediately. (no comma between subject and verb)
CORRECT:	Whoever has parked in front of the driveway must move immediately.
CORRECT:	Whoever has parked in front of the driveway, even for just a few minutes, will be fined. (Although a single comma cannot be placed between subject and verb, two commas can be used to set off an interrupting expression, such as "even for just a few minutes.")

INCORRECT: The manager asked us indignantly and at some length, if we had set off the alarm deliberately. (no comma before the direct object)

CORRECT: The manager asked us indignantly and at some length if we had set off the alarm deliberately.

CORRECT: The manager asked us, indignantly and at some length, if we had set off the alarm deliberately. (commas here to set off a phrase for emphasis)

CORRECT: The manager asked us indignantly, "Did you set off the alarm deliberately?" (Here the comma is correct because the direct object is a direct quotation introduced by an attributive phrase.)

EXERCISE 12.1

To help you review each comma rule, insert commas where needed in the sentences below.

Rule 1 ● comma before coordinating conjunction in compound sentence

1. That wall clock looks expensive but it doesn't work.

2. He likes to buy expensive clothes but hates to pay the bills.

3. The lights went out so the guests had to leave early.

4. The store will have to stay open longer or it will lose money.

5. John has a large garden for he loves to grow vegetables.

Rule 2 ● comma after adverb clause or before an adverb clause that shows contrast

1. When the snow stopped we were able to leave.

2. Because I am tired I am going to bed early tonight.

3. As the stage curtain rose the audience applauded.

4. Dogs crave companionship whereas cats prefer solitude.

5. Although English is offered only in the mornings you can take chemistry at night.

6. Watching television tends to make me passive while listening to the radio energizes me.

7. George is never aware of what is happening around him while he is immersed in a book.

8. We stayed on the beach until the sun went down.

Rule 3 ◉ comma after conjunctive adverb in a compound sentence (optional with one-syllable conjunctive adverbs)

1. I don't know how to play chess; however I would like to learn.

2. My brother loves music; in fact he plays in a local band.

3. Ron is an effective manager; therefore he has been promoted.

4. I heard a strange howling outside the window; then I buried myself beneath the covers.

5. Jay has poor eyesight; consequently he cannot play on the basketball team.

6. I would like to learn many things; for example I have always wanted to take ballet lessons.

7. Historical evidence for the existence of Troy has been found; hence the *Iliad* has taken on new meaning.

Rule 4 ◉ comma after introductory element

1. Wagging its tail the puppy barked in excitement.

2. By four in the afternoon everyone wanted to go home.

3. No I don't want any more ice cream.

4. On every Fourth of July we salute the American flag.

5. Oh I love the mountains in the spring!

6. Reluctantly the students left the classroom.

7. Exhausted by our long day we fell asleep quickly.

8. During the power blackout many people tried to help one another.

9. Opening her umbrella she dashed into the rain.

10. Ignored by the policeman the town drunk always slept in the park.

Rule 5 ● commas to separate items in a series

1. Contemporary women often try to be wives mothers and career professionals.

2. Bill wants to go to the shore his wife wants to go to the mountains and their children don't want to go anywhere.

3. I enjoy biking and skating and swimming.

4. The salesman found a television a blender and a hair dryer in the used car.

5. Sylvia will be happy to read your poem comment on it and return it to you.

Rule 6 ● comma to separate two adjectives before a noun, to take the place of "and"

1. Emerson gave a short interesting speech.

2. The green crunchy lettuce was delicious.

3. The crunchy green lettuce was delicious.

4. The girls were screaming in scared high voices.

5. The intelligent young woman was interesting to talk to.

6. The bright creative man was her husband.

7. The impressive brick structure was actually a facade.

Rule 7 ● comma to separate elements in dates and addresses

1. Susan moved on May 1 1990 from Fort Lauderdale Florida to Cape May New Jersey.

2. A new store opened at 300 North Road San Jose California 95135.

3. People in Charleston South Carolina are very friendly toward visitors.

4. I received my first Christmas gift in December 1977 from the man who would become my husband.

5. My teacher taught in London England from September 1 1992 to June 15 1993.

Rule 8 ● commas to set off extra information

1. The class feels Professor Crow that you should retire.

2. My mother not my father disciplined the children.

3. These peaches believe it or not were grown in my backyard.

4. Everyone admires Larry who always sees the bright side of a bad situation.

5. My twin sister who spends a lot of time at the gym is in excellent shape.

6. A person who spends a lot of time at the gym should be in excellent shape.

7. Watch out for Phil a man whose ambition rules him.

8. The movie starts soon doesn't it?

9. Where did you put my books Tom?

10. And now my friends we will examine the evidence.

11. His wife Belinda speaks French and Spanish.

12. Coin collecting which teaches a great deal about history is also fun.

13. Her favorite food much to our surprise was ketchup sandwiches.

14. Poe died in Baltimore not Philadelphia.

15. We have the right to complain don't we?

Rule 9 ● commas with direct quotations

1. He asked "Who's there?"

2. "No" she insisted "there are no monsters under the bed."

3. Henry said "I'm looking for a mail-order bride."

4. We heard someone shouting "Help!"

5. "You are lying!" the defendant shouted.

6. "Open the door slowly" cautioned the animal trainer.

7. "By the way" the clerk added "you have an overdue fine of $500."

Rule 10 ● no commas between essential sentence parts

1. Learning that we would adopt a baby from Korea led me to make serious changes in my way of thinking about the family unit.

2. The coach shouted to us that we should not give up until the game was over.

3. The coach shouted to us don't give up until the game is over.

4. Whatever happens in the future is beyond our control.

5. Whatever happens in the future according to many philosophers is beyond our control.

see answer key, p. 433

EXERCISE 12.2

Now let's put all of the comma rules together. Insert commas in the following sentences. You should be able to justify each comma by referring to a comma rule.

1. Our speaker today is a man who needs no introduction.

2. Our speaker today Mayor White needs no introduction.

3. The wallet that we found on the sidewalk contained no identification but it did have a substantial amount of cash.

4. Her instructor an expert on Egyptian culture sponsored a trip to Cairo.

5. Believe me you will enjoy your trip to England.

6. Alaska which is the largest state has beautiful mountains and rivers.

7. Before the movie starts you should buy a bag of popcorn.

8. I can't find my shoes my socks or my underwear.

9. I am happy to inform you Mr. Forbes that you are the father of triplets.

10. Near a small quiet pond the hikers could hear the cries of wild geese flying overhead.

11. The math class that I took last semester was challenging.

12. Algebra II which I took last semester was challenging.

13. By Tuesday June 6 Norwood had already sold four vacuum cleaners.

14. A large man who was smoking a cigar sat down next to me although there was a "no smoking" sign in the room.

15. What I like about traveling is seeing new places meeting a variety of people and eating exotic food.

16. A white cat especially a Persian will leave fur throughout your home.

17. I arrived on Tuesday March 18 1999 and found that I was in the wrong city.

18. Betty confided in her best friend whose opinion she valued highly.

19. The meal that was served pleased Uncle Fred who said "May I have more please?"

20. They bought a new painting a rather beautiful landscape.

21. Stephen King's latest book by the way will soon be made into a movie.

22. The crowd that gathered around the accident made the rescue difficult.

23. Having awakened from a nightmare I found it difficult to go back to sleep.

24. We will rehearse the play at school but perform it in the City Theater which has just been built.

25. Some plants surprisingly enough need no sunlight.

26. By the light of the moon we could make out a dim motionless figure near the tree.

27. Pickles not olives were in the tray.

28. My youngest sister who is still in high school wants to be an astronaut.

29. That package must be sent to 30 Overland Street Kansas City Kansas 66102.

30. "I think I'm having an emergency" Catherine said her voice trembling slightly; then a few seconds later she began to scream "Help! Fire!"

31. Because I have a fear of flying I seldom take vacations.

32. I have a fear of flying; therefore I seldom take vacations.

33. Mary Ellen who asked the question did not understand the teacher's answer although she listened carefully.

34. It is important to be polite but it is also important to be assertive.

35. Answering the telephone Clark carried on a conversation while he played a computer game.

see answer key, p. 436

Semicolon Rules

The semicolon takes the place of either a period or a comma. Here are the three situations that call for a semicolon:

1. **Use a semicolon in a compound sentence, to separate two independent clauses that are not joined by a coordinating conjunction.** This use of the semicolon requires two independent clauses with so logical a connection that no conjunction or transition is necessary. In this case the semicolon is taking the place of a period, but the writer has decided that a period would unnecessarily slow down and separate the clauses.

> I heard a loud knock at midnight; I cautiously opened the door.

Often, of course, the semicolon precedes a conjunctive adverb that *does* make the connection between the clauses explicit.

> I opened the door; *however*, I could see nothing when I turned on the light.

We also use the semicolon as a substitute for a comma, a "super-comma" that has been elevated in status to semicolon in order to clarify the connections among the various pieces of the sentence. This usually occurs in the two following situations, both of which involve sentences with at least a few commas so that a semicolon is needed to distinguish major breaking points in the sentences.

2. **Use a semicolon to separate two independent clauses joined by a coordinating conjunction but containing other commas.** In this case, the comma that usually precedes the coordinating conjunction is "crowned" as a semicolon to indicate the most important pause in the sentence, the one between independent clauses. Although there is no hard and fast rule about just how many commas are required to transform the comma in question into a semicolon, most writers require at least three or four commas before they put this rule into practice. A safe guide-

line is that if you have two or more commas in each independent clause, you should use a semi-colon rather than a comma before the coordinating conjunction.

> After ten long, hard years of saving money, Penny invested in Solo Stocks, a new, promising company; *but*, to her dismay, the company quickly went bankrupt.
> BUT
> After ten years of saving money, Penny invested in Solo Stocks, but the company quickly went bankrupt.

3. **Use a semicolon to separate items in a series when the items themselves contain commas.** Once more, what would ordinarily be a comma is "crowned" to become a semi-colon for the sake of clarity.

> I have lived in Houston, Texas; Orlando, Florida; and Little Rock, Arkansas.
> BUT
> I have lived in Houston, Orlando, and Little Rock.
> I depend on my computer, which makes writing faster; my microwave, which makes cooking easier; and my telephone, which keeps me in contact with family and friends.
> BUT
> I depend on my computer, my microwave, and my telephone.

EXERCISE 12.3

Punctuate the following sentences with both commas and semicolons as needed.

1. Negotiations have stopped we will strike at noon.

2. Orphan Annie endured a cruel childhood for a time then she was adopted by Daddy Warbucks.

3. Stacy's childhood was enlivened by Nutty a friendly backyard squirrel Jake her frisky black poodle and Minx her roving tomcat.

4. After buying flour sugar salt and butter I decided to go home and bake shortbread but I found once I checked my telephone messages that my afternoon was no longer free.

5. At 3:00 on Monday afternoon Lisa quit her job at 6:00 the next morning she could not sleep because she was worried about paying the bills and at 10:00 just four hours later she was begging her supervisor to overlook her hasty resignation.

6. The tour group will visit Edinburgh Scotland Dublin Ireland and London England.

7. Thinking creatively the youngster constructed a house out of cardboard although the wind soon blew it down.

see answer key, p. 437

Colon Rule

The common misconception about the colon is that it is used only to introduce a list. Although a colon does usually introduce a list, it can also introduce a word, a phrase, or a clause. The most important requirement, though, is that **a colon must follow a complete sentence.** In addition, that sentence must build up momentum so that the reader expects completion of an idea; the colon implies a strong forward motion into the information contained after the colon, and it also implies that the information contained after the colon is complete rather than partial.

Don't confuse this rule with the first semicolon rule. A semicolon separates two complete sentences; a colon follows a complete sentence, but it does not necessarily precede one. Notice the difference in the sentences below:

TWO INDEPENDENT CLAUSES:	Dale went to the store for several items; he was gone for three hours.
ONE INDEPENDENT CLAUSE:	Dale went to the store for several items: pliers, duct tape, a hammer, and several types of nails.

Although this example shows us the most common colon situation, one in which the colon introduces a list, the examples below illustrate the versatility of this mark of punctuation.

Debra woke up with only one thought in her head: cheesecake. (Here we see a colon introducing one word.)

The trapped animal had only one route of escape: out the window. (Here the colon introduces a phrase.)

Three times she sent her parents the same message: send money immediately. (Here the colon introduces a sentence. Notice that the second sentence does not begin with a capital letter.)

Remember the basic rule of karma: The deeds of one lifetime will have consequences in the next. (Here, as in the example above, the colon introduces a sentence. In accordance with MLA format, though, this time the second sentence begins with a capital letter because it expresses a rule. In MLA style, a rule or principle written as an independent clause begins with a capital letter when it follows a colon.)

Three authors form the backbone of British literature as it has traditionally been taught: Chaucer, Shakespeare, and Milton. (Finally, here the colon introduces a list. Notice that the list itself is not what makes the colon mandatory in this sentence. Rather, we need a colon because the list is preceded by a complete sentence, a sentence that causes us to anticipate that we will learn the names of the three authors.)

INCORRECT: The three authors who form the backbone of British literature as it has traditionally been taught are: Chaucer, Shakespeare, and Milton. (Despite the list, we cannot use a colon here because we do not have a complete sentence before the list. Instead, we have a *be* verb that requires a subjective complement in order to complete the sentence.)

Let's look at one other feature of the colon. When we use a colon before a list, we are indirectly stating that we are offering a complete list. **If we are not offering a complete list, but just a few examples, then the colon is no longer appropriate.**

CORRECT: Last summer I read some challenging authors: Dante, Faulkner, and Joyce.

INCORRECT: Last summer I read some challenging authors: such as Dante, Faulkner, and Joyce.

CORRECT: Last summer I read some challenging authors, such as Dante, Faulkner, and Joyce. (Here a comma sets off the prepositional phrase "such as Dante, Faulkner, and Joyce." The sentence would be grammatically complete without this phrase, and so the extra comma indicates extra information at the end of the sentence.)

INCORRECT: Last summer I read some challenging authors: for example, Dante, Faulkner, and Joyce.

CORRECT: Last summer I read some challenging authors—for example, Dante, Faulkner, and Joyce.
OR
Last summer I read some challenging authors; for example, Dante, Faulkner, and Joyce. (Here a dash or a semicolon sets off the prepositional phrase "for example." The names "Dante, Faulkner, and Joyce" are then introduced by a comma. Notice that this use of the semicolon is relatively infrequent and therefore not included with the earlier semicolon rules.)

Finally, **the phrases "the following" and "as follows" almost always signal the need for a colon.**

Last summer I read the following authors: Dante, Faulkner, and Joyce.

Last summer I read some challenging authors, as follows: Dante, Faulkner, and Joyce. (Notice that in this sentence we need a comma before "as follows" because this part of the sentence contains extra information. We could place a period before "as follows" and still have a complete sentence.)

My list of authors for summer reading was as follows: Dante, Faulkner, and Joyce. (Here no comma is necessary before "as follows" because it completes the idea of the *be* verb.)

EXERCISE 12.4

Punctuate the following sentences with commas, semicolons, and colons as necessary.

1. After all of the arguments that erupted at Joseph's party we never again brought up three topics his failure to graduate from high school his behavior during his wedding and the amount of wine he consumed at the party.

2. Dr. Kee the celebrated botanist was a brilliant engaging person unfortunately his interns were often crushed by his excessive work demands.

3. Certain qualities should be present in every human such as a desire to survive an instinct to preserve one's own species and an ability to empathize with others.

4. Juices that are exceptionally high in Vitamin C include orange grapefruit and tomato juice.

5. Juices that are exceptionally high in Vitamin C include the following orange grapefruit and tomato juice however they also contain a large amount of acid.

6. Beth had one unfulfilled ambition to enjoy high tea in the Pump Room at Bath.

7. The tropical storm damaged everything in its path houses trees and power lines.

see answer key, p. 437

Dash Rules

The dash is an extremely versatile mark of punctuation, often misused. Note that on a keyboard, there is usually no key specifically for the dash. Instead, you must either create a dash if your word processing program includes this option or type the hyphen key twice, with no space between, to form a dash. When writing for general purposes, no space is necessary before and after the dash. However, just as disciplines vary on whether or not to insert a comma before the final "and" in a series, so they vary on this matter. Journalists and business professionals often *do* insert a space both before and after the dash (but never between the two hyphen marks that constitute the dash). There are four situations that call for the dash.

1. **Use a dash to show an interruption in thought.** Many people use the dash when writing informal notes or letters to give the impression of conversational speech, since our spoken sentences often break off from one direction and go in another. You are not likely to use this dash in formal writing.

> Last week—no, wait a minute, I think it was just yesterday—I finally received your letter.

2. **Use a dash to take the place of a colon but to give a less formal impression.** The colon implies formality and dignity; the dash, as even its name indicates, implies informality and energy.

> Last summer I read some challenging authors—Dante, Faulkner, and Joyce.

> Laura repeats a particular word to calm herself down—chocolate.

In this situation, then, a complete sentence must precede the dash.

3. **Use a dash to set off an appositive that contains a series (and therefore already contains commas).** This dash, like the comma "crowned" to become a semicolon, is an "elevated" comma. The dash replaces the comma for the sake of clarity.

CONFUSING:	Three authors, Chaucer, Shakespeare, and Milton, form the backbone of British literature as it has traditionally been taught. (This sentence is unclear. Does it refer to six authors altogether, or do the names "Chaucer, Shakespeare, and Milton" form the appositive for "three authors"?)
CLEAR:	Three authors—Chaucer, Shakespeare, and Milton—form the backbone of British literature as it has traditionally been taught. OR (to make the sentence even more complicated) Three authors—Chaucer, a medieval storyteller; Shakespeare, a Renaissance dramatist; and Milton, a late Renaissance epic poet—form the backbone of British literature as it has traditionally been taught.

Note that in these sentences neither a semicolon nor a colon would be appropriate. The dash is used because the appositive provides extra information, a sort of interruption in thought as described in rule 1 above. Although a single appositive can be set off from the rest of the sentence by commas, an appositive in the form of a series must be set off by dashes. Before going on, let's review the three situations in which commas must be replaced by semicolons or dashes.

Comma "crowned" to become a semicolon before a coordinating conjunction (at least two commas in each independent clause): In 1066, when the Normans invaded England, the political structure, language, and social customs of the Anglo-Saxons were abruptly changed; *but*, over a period of time, certain aspects of Anglo-Saxon culture proved dominant.

Commas "crowned" to become semicolons to separate items in a series already containing commas: Native Britons were invaded by Romans, who brought them many civilizing influences; by Anglo-Saxons, who pushed them into outlying territories; by Vikings, who eventually settled in the northern part of England; and by Normans, who brutally crushed the existing social and political structures in order to impose their own rule.

Commas "elevated" to become dashes to set off an appositive in series form: Many aspects of Anglo-Saxon life—political structure, language, and social customs—were abruptly changed when the Normans invaded England.

4. **Use dashes to replace commas when you want to emphasize extra information in a sentence.** Be sure to make sparing use of dashes for emphasis, or they become irritating to the reader.

Mary—who studied her comma rules—made an A on her essay.

It was Veronica—believe it or not—who lost her passport.

You actually have **three choices about how to set off extra information in a sentence**. **Commas** are the most common choice and do not call attention to the extra information. Use **dashes** to emphasize the extra information. Use **parentheses**, on the other hand, to downplay the extra information. When we read aloud, we tend to lower our tone when we come to words in parentheses; in fact, some people even skip words that are inside parentheses.

See if you can determine the different implications of this sentence when it is punctuated in four different ways:

She's taken up a new hobby, collecting enemies.

She's taken up a new hobby: collecting enemies.

She's taken up a new hobby—collecting enemies.

She's taken up a new hobby (collecting enemies).

EXERCISE 12.5

Punctuate the following sentences, using the comma, semicolon, colon, dash, and parentheses as necessary.

1. On my shopping list were four items that I simply had to buy soap toothpaste tissues and toilet paper.

2. On my shopping list were four items soap toothpaste tissues and toilet paper that I simply had to buy.

3. On my shopping list were the following four items soap toothpaste tissues and toilet paper.

4. I had to buy soap toothpaste tissues and toilet paper however I did not have enough money left over to buy shampoo.

5. The truth of the matter if you really must know is that I hate shopping.

see answer key, p. 437

Hyphen Rules

A mark of punctuation often overlooked is the hyphen. Remember to distinguish on the keyboard between the hyphen (-) and the dash (two hyphens, —). When writing these marks by hand, also make a distinction in length. Here are a few basic rules for hyphen use.

1. **The hyphen is used to join together two or more modifiers that precede a noun**, as in "hard-hitting comments" or "seven-digit number." **The modifiers joined together by a hyphen do not separately modify the noun; instead, they act together as a unit**, becoming in effect one modifier. The hyphen signals this relationship.

> To enter the club, we had to know the seven-digit number used as a code. ("Seven" modifies "digit," not "number," and so the hyphen indicates this fact, turning the two words into a single modifier of "number.")

> She told us a not-to-be-repeated tale. (Here the hyphens join together an entire phrase; be careful, though, not to place a superfluous hyphen before "tale.")

The same modifiers, placed after the noun, would ordinarily not be hyphenated:

> To enter the club, we had to know the code, a number that had seven digits.

> She told us a tale not to be repeated.

2. **When the first modifier before a noun ends in -ly, no hyphen is necessary.**

> The slowly moving train pulled out of the station an hour late. (If this sentence were phrased differently, it would include a hyphen: "The slow-moving train pulled out of the station an hour late.")

When two or more modifiers precede a noun, occasionally a comma rather than a hyphen is appropriate, and sometimes no punctuation at all. Notice the difference between the phrases below that require a hyphen and those that do not.

> five-year plan (The noun being modified is not a "five" plan and not a "year" plan; "five-year" acts as a single unit, and so the hyphen is appropriate.)

> once-in-a-lifetime opportunity (Here the entire phrase is joined by hyphens, but make sure not to place a hyphen before the noun being modified, "opportunity.")

> highly skilled worker (Do not use a hyphen here because the first modifier ends in -ly.)

> friendly, outgoing personality (Here a comma is necessary because we could insert "and" between the two adjectives—"friendly and outgoing personality"—and each one separately modifies the noun: "friendly personality" and "outgoing personality.")

> long red dress (Here, even though each adjective separately modifies the noun, no comma is necessary because the second adjective refers to color; in idiomatic English, we would not say "long and red dress.")

In addition to the basic hyphen rules, there are a few minor ones:

3. **Hyphenate numbers between 21 and 99 when they are spelled out.**

> thirty-five   BUT   one hundred

4. **Hyphenate between syllables of a word when the word breaks at the end of one line and is completed on the next line.** This situation was much more common in the era of typewriters; computers and word processors have made this use of the hyphen practically obsolete.

5. **Hyphenate between a prefix and a root word when the same vowel will appear together twice, unless the word is in common use as a single word.**

> re-enact (the hyphen separates the two *e*'s)
> BUT cooperate (a single word in common use)

Some compound words are also hyphenated, although this is usually a transitory stage before two words become written as one. The single word "teenager," for example, used to be written "teen-ager." When in doubt, consult a recent edition of a dictionary.

EXERCISE 12.6

Place a comma or a hyphen wherever necessary in the following phrases. Note that sometimes you will not need any punctuation.

1. softly falling rain
2. heart stopping thrill
3. faster than lightning speed
4. three part application
5. expensive diamond necklace
6. shy smiling child
7. shyly smiling child
8. one of a kind costume
9. three year old child
10. fast talking salesman
11. dark brown suit
12. three thousand two hundred ninety one dollars

see answer key, p. 438

Slash Mark (Virgule)

The diagonal slash mark, or virgule, imparts three basic meanings, as illustrated in the examples below. Notice that there is no need to space on either side of the virgule. A fourth use of the slash, to separate lines of poetry, usually does entail a space on each side of the virgule.

1. Every investor must be aware that he/she has the potential to lose money as well as to make a profit. (Here the slash mark **indicates "or" and expresses an alternative**: "he or she.")

2. As far as the manager could determine, the employee's proposal sounded like a win/win proposition. It was certainly better than the either/or situation that seemed to be the only alternative. The company wanted its workers/associates to remain happy. (Here the slash mark means something akin to "and." In sentences like these, the virgule **separates two or more words intrinsically related in order to indicate that relationship**. MLA style, however, suggests using the hyphen rather than the slash when the paired terms precede and modify a noun, as in "either–or situation.")

3. The bus was traveling at approximately 90 miles/hour. (Here the slash mark **takes the place of the word "per" to indicate the relationship of two measurements**.)

4. As will be discussed in more detail later, the slash mark is also used to **separate two or three lines of poetry inserted within a prose text**. Here the slash mark

conveys no meaning but is strictly a convention of punctuation. A space is usually inserted on each side of the slash mark in this case.

One of Emily Dickinson's poems begins, "Success is counted sweetest / By those who ne'er succeed."

EXERCISE 12.7

Place the slash mark or virgule wherever needed in the following sentences.

1. As soon as Brecken completes her degree, she will be earning about $90,000 year.

2. We could negotiate the details now, and or we could contact our lawyers.

3. The post of secretary clerk is now open.

4. The menu indicated that the diner's specials included soup, rolls, ice cream, and coffee tea with every meal.

see answer key, p. 438

Apostrophe Rules

Perhaps the punctuation mark that causes the most confusion of all is the apostrophe. One reason confusion reigns is that there are actually two systems of apostrophe use when it comes to showing the possessive for a singular noun ending in -s. Because of the two different systems, writers are often inconsistent and transfer what they know (or think they know) to situations where the apostrophe will not work. Let's see if we can straighten out the confusion to some extent, by looking at the three uses of the apostrophe.

1. Use an apostrophe to indicate the plural of a word used as a word or the plural of a letter. Current MLA practice does not, however, use apostrophes to show the plural of numbers (including dates) or abbreviations.

Pam realized that she had used five *however*'s in her final paragraph.

Everyone wants A's in this class.

Romanticism flourished as a literary movement in England during the early 1800s.

The tourists were relieved to find ATMs throughout Europe.

Do NOT use the apostrophe to show the plural of a regular noun.

INCORRECT: We opened twenty can's of soda.

INCORRECT:	We opened twenty cans' of soda.
CORRECT:	We opened twenty cans of soda.

2. Use an apostrophe to indicate a missing letter or letters in contractions.

The pen didn't write.

Won't you please change your mind? (Notice that "won't" is an unusual contraction because it actually takes the place of "will not.")

It's already five o'clock. (In other words, "It is already five of the clock." Most people do not think about "o'clock" as a contraction, but it is.)

NOTE: Pay special attention to the word "it's." When it contains an apostrophe, it is a contraction for "it is" or "it has."

It's difficult to understand apostrophes.

It's been a long time since I have studied punctuation.

Do NOT use an apostrophe when using "its" as a possessive pronoun.

INCORRECT:	The cat licked it's paw. ("It is" will not make sense here.)
CORRECT:	The cat licked its paw.

3. Use an apostrophe to signal possession for nouns (as in "the *mayor's* office)**.** An apostrophe can also signal possession for indefinite and reciprocal pronouns (as in *"someone's* book" or *"each other's* interest"). Possessive pronouns, however, actually change their form to show possession, so they do not need an apostrophe for this purpose (as in *"his* book" or "that dog of *theirs*").

Possession usually occurs when we see two nouns placed together, with the first one owning the second. Another way of testing for possession is to transform the two nouns into a longer phrase, the phrase that other languages, without the benefit of the apostrophe, would have to use to signal possession. For example, if we see the phrase "my father's job," we notice the juxtaposition of two nouns, "father" and "job" (even if an adjective intervenes, such as "my father's new job"). We can also turn the phrase into "the job of my father," which is the word order used by a language such as French, Spanish, or Italian. This test also helps when you have a phrase that, strictly speaking, does not seem to indicate possession, as in "a month's wages" ("the wages of a month").

Now let's look at the chart below to see how singular and plural nouns show possession.

Singular Noun	Singular Possessive Noun	Plural Noun	Plural Possessive Noun
father	father's	fathers	fathers'

(regular noun with a plural ending in -s; since the English ear is attuned to hearing "-s" at the end of a word to signal possession, add an apostrophe + -s to the singular to show possession but only an apostrophe to show the plural possessive)

| lady | lady's | ladies | ladies' |

(regular noun; spelling changes but plural still ends in -s)

| child | child's | children | children's |

(irregular noun; because the plural does not end in -s, add an apostrophe to show possession and then add -s to satisfy the expectation to hear "-s" for possession)

So far, apostrophe usage may not seem terribly complicated. The confusion settles in when we have a singular noun that ends with "s." Since English speakers associate the ending -s with plural and/or possessive, a singular noun that ends in "s" creates problems. Two systems of handling this situation are in practice. If you are writing for a professional publication, editing guidelines will probably direct you as to which system to use. If you have no guidelines to follow, then you are free to choose for yourself, as long as you are consistent. Both the *Associated Press Manual*, which journalists follow, and the *MLA Handbook* (used by teachers and students of language and literature) use the first system shown below, labeled here as "standard" because it is the preferred practice for professionals in the discipline of English.

	Standard	**Simplified**
Singular Noun	boss	boss
Singular Possessive Noun	boss's	boss'
Plural Noun	bosses	bosses
Plural Possessive Noun	bosses'	bosses'

As you can see, the only form that changes is the singular possessive. The standard style adds an apostrophe + -s to the singular, whether it ends in *s* or in another letter. The simplified style has one rule for all forms: If a noun already ends in -s, whether singular or plural, merely add an apostrophe after the -s.

Few common nouns in English end in "s," but several names do, so this situation is more likely to come up when you are dealing with proper names. Here is a first name that illustrates the difference between the two systems:

	Standard	**Simplified**
Singular Noun	Chris	Chris
Singular Possessive Noun	Chris's	Chris'

Even if we pronounce the last name on this chart with a double "s" sound, only one "s" appears, with an apostrophe following, because the simplified rule specifies that an apostrophe always follows when a possessive noun ends in -s.

Last names create even more of a problem because we frequently refer to an entire family by making a last name plural. Let's look at two common last names, one that does not end in "s" and one that does.

	Standard	**Simplified**
Singular Noun	Ms. Brown	Ms. Brown
Singular Possessive Noun	Ms. Brown's	Ms. Brown's
Plural Noun	the Browns	the Browns
Plural Possessive Noun	the Browns'	the Browns'

Singular Noun	Ms. Jones	Ms. Jones
Singular Possessive Noun	Ms. Jones's	Ms. Jones'
Plural Noun	the Joneses	the Joneses
Plural Possessive Noun	the Joneses'	the Joneses'

Two things may seem confusing to you from this chart:

1. Notice that **a family name (a surname) does not require an apostrophe unless you are indicating possession**.

> We decided to visit the Browns last night.   (plural)

> The Browns' new house is a Victorian mansion.   (plural possessive)

2. **Both styles form the plural by adding –s to a name that does not already end in "s." Likewise, both styles form the plural by adding –es to a name that ends in "s" (or in "x" or "z"**—for example, the Marxes or the Herskowitzes). These names may look strange because we are not used to seeing them spelled out in the plural, but merely adding an apostrophe—as many people do—does not indicate plural form. Save the apostrophe to indicate possession.

Let's look now at two other situations that sometimes cause confusion. First, what happens when you must make a hyphenated noun possessive? The following example illustrates the point:

> I have always enjoyed my mother-in-law's humor. (The hyphenated noun "mother-in-law" is singular, so we merely add an apostrophe + –s to signal possessive singular.)

> I have always enjoyed my sisters-in-law's hospitality. (Here, to make "sister-in-law" plural, we write "sisters-in-law." Since "sisters" indicates the plural, we add an apostrophe + –s at the end of the hyphenated phrase to indicate possession.)

Finally, what happens when we have two or more nouns that possess something? Suppose Holly and Keisha have worked on a project together: The teacher evaluated Holly and Keisha's project. (Here the apostrophe after the second name indicates a joint project.)
BUT
The teacher evaluated Holly's and Keisha's projects. (Here the apostrophe follows both names, indicating two separate, individual projects. Even the noun "projects" becomes plural rather than singular in this sentence.)

EXERCISE 12.8

Add apostrophes (and, where necessary, an additional "s" if you are following standard style) as needed in the following sentences. You may use either standard or simplified style as long as you are consistent.

1. While it was parked at the curb overnight, Ernies car was hit.

2. He was fined for contempt of court on the judges order.

3. The fine china cup had lost its original handle.

4. Mr. Clarks geography class is intimidating for junior high students.

5. On my brothers twenty-first birthday, he gambled and drank for the first and last time.

6. My mother-in-laws recipe for homemade pasta is the best Ive ever had.

7. These boys grades are disgraceful!

8. In my doctors opinion Im overworked and must take a vacation.

9. My mothers job was in the childrens department.

10. If youre interested in going on the school trip, you must have both parents consent.

11. The Simpsons could not decide what to do with their free Saturday evening.

12. The girls locker room is directly across from the boys gym.

13. Yeats poetry explains his unique mythological system.

14. Its three oclock, so I must leave for my best friends party.

15. The Blakes car is a classic Mustang.

see answer key, p. 438

Underlining or Using Quotation Marks for Titles

Every time that you write the title of a published work, you need to indicate that it is a title either by underlining (or italicizing) the title or by placing quotation marks around the title. **When you underline or italicize a title, you are indicating that it is of substantial length and constitutes one unit; when you use quotation marks, you are indicating that it is (1) of short length or (2) contained within a larger volume of work**. Note that you do not underline or italicize the titles of your own papers—unless they are officially published.

Long Works	newspaper
	magazine or journal
	book
	movie
	TV series (implying a collection of individual shows in the series)
	music collection or musical work of significant length

Short Works   newspaper, magazine, or journal article
chapter within a book
TV show (individual program or an episode in a series)
song or titled portion of a long musical work

In addition, we usually underline or italicize the names (titles, in a sense) of ships, airplanes, space vehicles, and works of art.

EXERCISE 12.9

Underline/italicize or use quotation marks as necessary to punctuate the titles in the following sentences.

1. My favorite Hemingway novel is The Sun Also Rises.

2. During the holiday season many churches advertise productions of Handel's masterpiece, the Messiah.

3. Chapter 12, Punctuation and Capitalization, is a very long one.

4. Perhaps the most famous plane at the Smithsonian is the Spirit of St. Louis.

5. Leonardo da Vinci's Mona Lisa is always surrounded by admirers at the Louvre.

6. Sesame Street is an enormously popular television series for children.

7. Poe's story The Fall of the House of Usher gave me nightmares as a child.

8. The first song to project the Beatles to stardom was I Wanna Hold Your Hand.

9. Many business executives read the Wall Street Journal on a daily basis.

10. Newsweek recently published an informative article entitled What You Need to Know About Political History.

see answer key, p. 439

Other Uses of Underlining and Quotation Marks

1. **Use underlining (or italics) to indicate emphasis.** As with the dash, which can also be used to emphasize, be sparing in your use of this technique.

> I will not be held accountable for this misjudgment. (no added emphasis)

> I will *not* be held accountable for this misjudgment. (emphatic)

2. **Use underlining (or italics) to indicate a foreign word or phrase.**

> Caroline possessed a *savoir faire* that all of her peers envied.

If the foreign word or phrase is in common use in English, underlining or italicizing is not necessary.

> At the birthday party, none of the children could split open the pinata.

3. **Use underlining (or italics) to indicate that you are using a word as a word, not for its actual meaning.** Although this rule reflects MLA style, you should be aware that many texts (including this one) also use quotation marks to set off a word used as a word. You may need to exercise judgment as to whether quotation marks or underlining (italics) will make your meaning clearer.

> An overused word in English is *and*.

> *Bonfire* has an interesting word origin.

> "How many times have you used the word *no* today?" asked the toddler's mother.

4. **Use quotation marks to indicate a direct quotation**, as opposed to an indirect quotation. An indirect quotation is introduced either by *that* to indicate an indirect statement or by a question word (who, whom, whose, if, whether, when, where, how, why) to indicate an indirect question. Notice that the word order of the indirect question does not change as it normally would when phrasing a question. When you write an indirect question, you are stating a question, not asking it.

> INDIRECT: The reporter asked if anyone had survived the crash.

> DIRECT: The reporter asked, "Did anyone survive the crash?"

When you insert a quotation within a quotation, you need single quotation marks to indicate the embedded quotation.

> The cynical professor began the semester by repeating over and over, "Alexander Pope said, 'A little learning is a dangerous thing,' so this class may be hazardous."

If we rearrange this sentence a bit, we come up with an interesting situation when the single quotation marks and the double quotation marks appear together:

> The cynical professor began the semester by repeating over and over, "Alexander Pope said, 'A little learning is a dangerous thing.'"

Although the sentence above is punctuated correctly, many writers and publishers prefer to break the rule. In order to make the sentence more pleasing to the eye, they insert the period between the single and the double quotation marks:

> The cynical professor began the semester by repeating over and over, "Alexander Pope said, 'A little learning is a dangerous thing'."

Look again at comma rule 9 to review how commas are used in direct quotations. **Remember especially that a comma or period at the end of a direct quotation is tucked *inside* the ending quotation marks, as in the examples above. Semicolons and colons are placed *outside* ending quotation marks. If the quotation itself ends with a question mark, the question mark appears inside the quotation marks; if the entire sentence is a question, then the question mark appears outside. The same is true for an exclamation point.**

> The students asked, "Will we have a test on these rules?" (Only the quoted words form the question.)

> Did the students say, "We enjoy studying punctuation"? (The sentence as a whole is a question, but the quoted words are a statement.)

> Did the students ask, "Will we have a test on these rules?" (Here, since both elements of the final sentence are set up as questions, only one question mark is necessary.)

> The students exclaimed, "We love studying punctuation!" (Only the quoted words are exclaimed.)

> How wonderful that the students said, "We love studying punctuation"! (The sentence as a whole is an exclamation, but the quoted words are a statement.)

> How wonderful that the students exclaimed, "We love studying punctuation!" (Again, since both elements of the final sentence are set up as exclamations, only one exclamation mark is necessary.)

Now let's refine a bit on the information in comma rule 9:

a. There are **three ways to introduce a direct quotation**, as indicated below.

> The students complained, "There are too many rules of punctuation." (This is the normal pattern, with attribution—who is speaking—indicated first and then the direct quotation.)

> The students made the following complaint: "There are too many rules of punctuation." (Here a colon is needed because a complete sentence precedes the direct quotation.)

> The students complained that there were "too many rules of punctuation." (Here no punctuation is needed because the two elements of this sentence, the unquoted and the quoted words, flow together smoothly to form one sentence.)

b. What happens when, using MLA style, you are quoting and **need to include a parenthetical reference at the end of the quotation**? The answer differs depending on whether you are dealing with prose, poetry, or drama, and also whether the passage being quoted can be classified as short or long.

SHORT QUOTATIONS

Short Prose Quotation, with quoted author in parenthetical reference

One mythological expert explains Helen of Troy's ultimate fate: "On the fall of Troy Menelaus recovered possession of his wife, who had not ceased to love him, though she had … deserted him for another" (Bullfinch 185).

Short Prose Quotation, with author indicated outside of parenthetical reference

Thomas Bullfinch explains Helen of Troy's ultimate fate: "On the fall of Troy Menelaus recovered possession of his wife, who had not ceased to love him, though she had … deserted him for another" (185).

Notice that in both of these examples, the ending period *follows* the parentheses. Also, the page number of the quotation appears within the parentheses, along with the author's name if it has not already been mentioned in the text.

NOTE: A short prose quotation consists of four or fewer lines as you type it onto the page.

Short Poetry Quotation

Frost evokes a quiet, rather somber mood when he writes, "Whose woods these are I think I know, / His house is in the village, though; / He will not see me stopping here" (1-3).

Note that when you are quoting three or fewer lines of poetry and including them within the text, you should separate the lines with slash marks. The line numbers from the poem you are quoting, not the number of the page on which the lines are found, are included in the parentheses.

NOTE: A short poetry quotation consists of three or fewer lines of poetry as those lines are set up by the poet.

Short Quotation from Drama

During her sleepwalking scene, Lady Macbeth hints at the foul deeds she and her husband have committed: "Out, damned spot! Out, I say! … Yet who would have thought the old man to have had so much blood in him?" (*Macbeth* 5.1.34, 38-39).

If a play is broken up into acts, scenes, and line numbers, indicate that information in the parenthetical reference. Otherwise, indicate page number in parentheses.

NOTE: A short quotation from drama consists of four or fewer lines of prose, as you type the passage onto the page, or three or fewer lines of poetry, as set up by the dramatist.

LONG QUOTATIONS

For prose, a long quotation consists of more than four lines as you type the passage onto your page. For poetry, including poetic drama, a long quotation consists of more than three lines of poetry as set up by the poet or dramatist. In both cases, the basic conventions are the same:

Indent ten spaces from the left margin to create a block quotation.

Omit quotation marks around the quoted passage.

Place the period *before* the parenthetical reference at the end.

In MLA style, double-space block quotations. (Nothing is single-spaced, including the entries in the Works Cited section.)

Let's expand on one of our passages and see how a long quotation appears.

Thomas Bullfinch explains Helen of Troy's ultimate fate:

On the fall of Troy Menelaus recovered possession of his wife, who had not ceased to love him, though she had yielded to the might of Venus and deserted him for another. After the death of Paris she aided the Greeks secretly on several occasions, and in particular when Ulysses and Diomed entered the city in disguise to carry off the Palladium. She saw and recognized Ulysses, but kept the secret and even assisted them in obtaining the image. Thus she became reconciled to her husband, and they were among the first to leave the shores of Troy for their native land. (185-86)

Using the Ellipsis and Square Brackets

While looking at the previous examples of direct quotations, you have probably recognized the ellipsis (…) as a way of indicating that words have been omitted from a quotation. Knowing how to use the ellipsis to indicate omitted material, and square brackets to indicate added material, is useful for writers who must handle direct quotations but want to manipulate them so that they will fit more smoothly into the flow of the overall text.

1. **An ellipsis of three dots indicates that words have been omitted from the direct quotation**. No ellipsis is needed at the beginning or end of a direct quotation if it is clear that words have been omitted. The only time you invariably must use an ellipsis is when words are omitted from the middle of a passage. Let's look again at the example used above, concentrating this time on the ellipsis.

Thomas Bullfinch explains Helen of Troy's ultimate fate: "On the fall of Troy Menelaus recovered possession of his wife, who had not ceased to love him, though she had … deserted him for another" (185).

2. What happens when the ellipsis does not occur in the middle of a sentence?

a. Ellipsis at end, followed by parenthetical reference

Thomas Bullfinch explains Helen of Troy's ultimate fate: "On the fall of Troy Menelaus recovered possession of his wife …" (185). (Here the ellipsis makes clear that, although the quoted words constitute a complete sentence, the original sentence did not end at this point.)

b. Ellipsis at end, not followed by parenthetical reference

On page 185, Thomas Bullfinch explains Helen of Troy's ultimate fate: "On the fall of Troy Menelaus recovered possession of his wife...." (Notice that four dots end this sentence, indicating that a period follows the ellipsis.)

c. Ellipsis to indicate omission of one or more sentences

Thomas Bullfinch explains Helen of Troy's ultimate fate:

On the fall of Troy Menelaus recovered possession of his wife, though she had yielded to the might of Venus and deserted him for another. After the death of Paris she aided the Greeks secretly on several occasions, and in particular when Ulysses and Diomed entered the city in disguise to carry off the Palladium.... Thus she became reconciled to her husband, and they were among the first to leave the shores of Troy for their native land. (185–86)

Four dots—a period (with no space after "Palladium") followed by an ellipsis—indicate that "Palladium" ends a sentence and that one or more sentences have been omitted.

d. Ellipsis to indicate omission from middle of one sentence to end of another

Thomas Bullfinch explains Helen of Troy's ultimate fate: "On the fall of Troy Menelaus recovered possession of his wife .... Thus she became reconciled to her husband, and they were among the first to leave the shores of Troy for their native land" (185–86).

Here four dots—an ellipsis (with a space after "wife") followed by a period—indicate that the sentence ending with "wife" has not been quoted in its entirety, and that one or more sentences that follow are also missing.

e. Ellipsis to indicate omission from middle of one sentence to middle of another

Thomas Bullfinch explains Helen of Troy's ultimate fate: "On the fall of Troy Menelaus recovered possession of his wife ... and they were among the first to leave the shores of Troy for their native land" (185–86).

In this quotation, an ellipsis but no period appears because there is no way to indicate where the original sentence ended. It is also impossible to determine whether the quotation omits partial sentences or omits one or more complete sentences before picking up again mid-sentence.

3. When omitting one or more lines of poetry in a block quotation, use a line of spaced periods to indicate ellipsis.

In "Holy Sonnet 10," John Donne powerfully expresses the concept of triumph over death:

Death, be not proud, though some have called thee
Mighty and dreadful, for thou art not so;

. . . .
One short sleep past, we wake eternally
And death shall be no more; Death, thou shalt die. (1-2, 13-14)

4. **Square brackets indicate that the writer has altered or added to quoted material.** Square brackets indicate exactly what changes have been made. On the other hand, occasionally a writer will retain the exact original wording of a quotation even if it is in error, from the standpoint of either grammar or content. To indicate that the error is in the direct quotation, not the fault of the current writer, the Latin abbreviation *sic* (meaning "thus" or "in this way") is placed in square brackets directly behind the faulty information.

    a. Square brackets to indicate material inserted into a direct quotation

       In one of his poems, Yeats asks if Leda "put on his [the swan's] knowledge" (13).

    b. Square brackets to indicate a change in capitalization or in verb tense in order to facilitate the merging together of the writer's own words and quoted material

       Thomas Bullfinch mentions that "[o]n the fall of Troy Menelaus recovered possession of his wife" (185). (In the original version, the sentence begins with "On"; the "o" is changed to lower case here and therefore placed in square brackets.)

       According to Thomas Bullfinch, Helen secretly helps the Greeks several times, even helping two Greek warriors to steal the Palladium, the talisman protecting Troy. These actions recompense for her earlier desertion, so that she and her husband "[are] among the first to leave the shores of Troy for their native land" (185–86). (The verbs of the original version are in past tense; in this paraphrase the verbs have been changed to present tense, necessitating square brackets to specify the verb tense change in the phrase that is directly quoted.)

    c. Square brackets with *sic* to indicate an exact reproduction of the original

       The catalog specifies, "An English major must take fore [*sic*] composition classes."

EXERCISE 12.10

Punctuate the following sentences as necessary.

    1. I absolutely must have one of those dolls the elderly woman exclaimed

    2. The elderly woman exclaimed I absolutely must have one of those dolls

    3. The client asked his attorney What does the Latin word uxor mean in this document

    4. Have you ever heard someone say I told you so

5. The eager reporter quoted the local official as saying I refuse to be intimidated by the corrupt political situation that has prevailed here for years. I predict the imminent arrest or departure of several key figures in the community

6. The eager reporter misquoted the local official as saying the following I refuse to be intimidated by several key figures in the community

7. I am a sensitive human the teenager told her friends I simply can't believe that my parents would treat me this way

8. In perhaps the most famous love poem ever written, Elizabeth Barrett Browning proceeds to count the ways in which she loves. (Hint: The original line, just in case you don't know it offhand, is "How do I love thee? Let me count the ways.")

9. To modernize the first line of Browning's poem, Sherry changed the archaic pronoun so that the line now reads as follows How do I love you? Let me count the ways

10. As she walks through London, Mrs. Dalloway muses about her friend Peter Walsh For they might be parted hundreds of years, she and Peter; she never wrote a letter and his were dry sticks; but suddenly it would come over her, If he were with me now what would he say?—some days, some sights bringing him back to her calmly, without the old bitterness; which perhaps was the reward of having cared for people; they came back in the middle of St. James's Park on a fine morning—indeed they did (Woolf 5)

11. As she walks through London, Mrs. Dalloway muses For they might be parted hundreds of years, she and Peter; she never wrote a letter and his were dry sticks; but suddenly it would come over her … (Woolf 5)

12. Why do Virginia Woolf's novels remind me of poetry inquired Allison

see answer key, p. 439

EXERCISE 12.11

Rewrite the following direct quotations in indirect quotation form.

1. "You should schedule an annual physical," said the doctor to the elderly patient.

_____

_____

2. Harry's wife shouted, "You never pay attention to me!"

_____

_____

3. All of the officers agreed, "Membership in our club should be closed until further notice."

_____

_____

4. "Did anyone get a good look at the suspect?" asked the police officer.

_____

_____

see answer key, p. 440

EXERCISE 12.12

Read the passage below from Shakespeare's *King Lear* (Act 1, Scene 2, lines 103–114). Then, using ellipses and square brackets as necessary, punctuate correctly the quotation from it that follows. You do not need to include parenthetical references for this exercise.

ORIGINAL:

These late eclipses in the sun and moon portend no good to us. Though the wisdom of nature can reason it thus and thus, yet nature finds itself scourg'd by the sequent effects. Love cools, friendship falls off, brothers divide: in cities, mutinies; in countries, discord; in palaces, treason; and the bond crack'd 'twixt son and father. This villain of mine comes under the prediction; there's son against father: the King falls from bias of nature; there's father against child. We have seen the best of our time. Machinations, hollowness, treachery, and all ruinous disorders follow us disquietly to our graves.

FOR YOU TO PUNCUATE: These late eclipses in the sun and moon portend no good to us. Love cools, friendship falls off, brothers divide: the bond is crack'd 'twixt son and father. We have seen the best of our time. Machinations and all ruinous disorders follow us.

see answer key, p. 440

2 ● CAPITALIZATION

Along with punctuation, capitalization provides visual cues to help readers make sense of the words before them on the page. You have no doubt encountered the capitalization rules before, so what follows is a brief summary of them.

1. **In general, capitalize the pronoun "I" and all nouns that refer to specifically named persons, places, or things.**

He enjoys reading historical documents.
He enjoys reading the Declaration of Independence.

We are math majors.
We are English majors. (Capitalize "English" because it is derived from a proper noun, "England.")

We are taking algebra.
We are taking Algebra I.

The tour group traveled north in the fall.
The tour group traveled to the North in the fall. (Capitalize "North" because it refers to a specific region. In the first sentence, "north" is an adverb indicating a direction rather than a noun specifying a place. Note that seasons of the year are not capitalized.)

Few people in my family graduate from high school.
Few people in my family have graduated from Parsons High School.

Jenny introduced her mother and her uncle to the senator from New York.
Jenny introduced Mother and Uncle Bill to Senator Clinton from New York.

The capital of Maine is Augusta.
The capitol is in Washington, DC. (Notice the difference in spelling as well as in capitalization. The capitol is a specific building in the city known as the capital of the US.)

2. **When dealing with titles, capitalize the first and last words. In accordance with MLA style, capitalize all nouns, pronouns, verbs, adjectives (except articles), adverbs, subordinating conjunctions, and interjections.** Do not capitalize articles, prepositions, or coordinating conjunctions unless they occur as the first or last words of the title.

The Day That All Clocks Stopped

Prayers and Possibilities

This Pledge Is a Travesty

Girls Also Can Win at the Game of Life

Remember that, unless it is your own title, you also must either place the title of each published work in quotation marks or underline/italicize it.

EXERCISE 12.13

A. Capitalize as necessary in the following sentences.

1. my mother has always loved italian dressing, but i have always preferred russian.

2. dad and mom would like to sail to jamaica for valentine's day.

3. the local animal hospital has been placing ads in the paper for veterinary assistants.

4. the pitman animal hospital has been placing ads in the pitman news for veterinary assistants.

5. although our family is from the south, aunt jean and her husband have always wanted to live in the northwest, preferably near seattle.

6. the navy does an excellent job recruiting students from st. george's academy.

7. the boston tea party is an event that almost all american school children can explain.

8. the names in the old testament of the bible can be very difficult to spell correctly.

9. my uncle worked in the summer as a district manager for pennsylvania bell.

10. after passing a battery of tests, kevin rose to the rank of secretary I in the university system.

B. Capitalize and use either quotation marks or underlining/italicizing for the following titles.

1. the origin of all board games (book)

2. the best way to lose all enemies and feel no fear (magazine article)

3. how to succeed in college (published essay)

4. cats are human, too (children's song)

5. learn to run your own business (newspaper article)

see answer key, p. 440

SUMMARY OF KEY CONCEPTS IN CHAPTER 12

A useful way to review the rules that follow is to write a sentence to demonstrate each one.

Comma Rules:

1. Use a comma before a coordinating conjunction (FANBOYS).

2. Use a comma after an introductory adverb clause, and before a subordinating conjunction that shows contrast (although, though, even though, whereas, while).

3. Use a comma after a conjunctive adverb that follows a semicolon.

4. Use a comma after an introductory element in a sentence.

5. Use commas to separate items in a series of three or more.

6. Use a comma to separate two adjectives that modify a noun when *and* could substitute for the comma.

7. Use commas to set off all elements (except zip code) in dates and addresses.

8. Use commas to set off extra information in a sentence.

9. Use commas with direct quotations.

10. Do not place a comma between essential sentence parts.

Semicolon Rules:

1. Use a semicolon in a compound sentence to separate two independent clauses not joined by a coordinating conjunction.

2. Use a semicolon to separate two independent clauses joined by a coordinating conjunction but containing other commas.

3. Use a semicolon to separate items in a series when the items themselves contain commas.

Colon Rule:

A colon must follow a complete sentence and is used to introduce the word, phrase, clause, or list that the sentence builds up to.

Dash Rules:

1. In informal writing, use a dash to indicate a disruption in thought.

2. Use a dash to take the place of a colon but to give a less formal impression.

3. Use a dash to set off an appositive that contains a series.

4. Use dashes to replace commas when you want to emphasize extra information in a sentence.

Hyphen Rules:

1. The hyphen joins together two or more modifiers that precede a noun and act as a single modifier rather than separately modifying the noun.

2. When the first modifier before a noun ends in –ly, no hyphen is necessary.

Slash Mark (Virgule) Rules:

1. The slash mark indicates "or," as in "he/she."

2. The slash mark indicates "and," as in "He was a teacher/friend to all of us."

3. The slash mark indicates "per," as in "ten feet/second."

4. Use the slash mark to separate lines of poetry inserted within a prose text.

Apostrophe Rules:

1. Use an apostrophe for special plurals (plurals of a letter or of a word used as a word).

2. Use an apostrophe to indicate a missing letter or letters in contractions.

3. Use an apostrophe to signal possession for nouns (or for indefinite and reciprocal pronouns).

4. Do NOT use an apostrophe to signal possession for other pronouns or to signal regular plurals.

Miscellaneous Rules:

1. Use underlining or italicizing to indicate titles of lengthy or complete works; use quotation marks to indicate titles of short works or works that make up part of a larger whole.

2. Use ellipses to indicate omitted material when quoting from a source.

3. Use square brackets to indicate a change or addition to the original material when quoting from a source.

4. When a comma or period is needed at the end of a quotation, place the comma or period inside the quotation marks, even if the comma or period does not appear in the original quotation. Colons and semicolons are placed outside quotation marks.

CHAPTER 12 EXERCISE

Add capitalization and punctuation to the following sentences as necessary.

1. While we were at the little league game we bought some candy and soda however the game was so exciting that we forgot the candy and spilled the soda.

2. Janet who is the new president of the historical research club is a well organized efficient person.

3. Some students prefer british literature while others prefer american literature each literary tradition has its own unique strengths.

4. The icing on the cake at Boris birthday party looked delicious but it tasted to our dismay like glue.

5. After we had stayed up all night we decided to have breakfast together at the regent café then we slept until noon.

6. The smiths used to live in el paso a border town with excitement opportunity and flair.

7. Sharons twin sister who recently took a vacation decided to move to honolulu hawaii rather than return to trenton new jersey.

8. My favorite holidays are christmas when I receive presents my birthday when I receive phone calls from all of my friends and valentines day when I receive boxes of chocolate.

9. If I am reading the lease correctly the rent at crossbones apartments includes the following items gas electricity and water.

10. Throughout the years of childhood most of us develop a strong sure sense of identity yet sadly enough we may later give up our individuality due to social pressure.

11. The repairman insisted that he could not locate the on off switch.

12. The three countries that we visited sweden norway and denmark form what is known as scandinavia.

13. Jean Smith the cardiologist Angelo Martinez the dentist and Alan Wilson the psychiatrist meet for lunch on the twenty third of every month.

14. The payroll department collects the workers time cards each week and then prepares everyones paycheck.

15. Lillian Hellman americas first great female playwright entitled her first play the childrens hour.

16. The kind gentle creatures seemed to have descended from the spaceship that was hovering in the background although I couldnt be sure.

17. Bridge my parents hobby chess my oldest sisters passion and three dimensional puzzles my favorite pastime are all time consuming activities luckily though we all manage our time wisely.

18. During our class on friday october 31 three subjects repeatedly came up ghosts witches and vampires.

19. Sergio finally proposed to Maria my mother said but she turned him down.

20. Four foods spaghetti cheeseburgers hot dogs and burritos constitute Elizabeths normal diet.

21. That delicately framed portrait is unusual isnt it

22. The five pointed star figures prominently in the books first chapter entitled the symbolism of stars.

23. Who said a rose is a rose is a rose

24. The victorian period is associated with the industrial revolution middle class morality and the foundations of twentieth century science.

25. When I attended stetson university all of the freshmen were required to read the great gatsby.

26. Poetry wrote William Wordsworth is emotion recollected in tranquillity.

27. Dan Burns the coach made it clear that each member of the team would be held responsible for his her actions.

28. The police officer asked if the driver had been wearing a seat belt at the time of the accident.

29. In 1895 my grandfather and grandmother settled into a quiet simple life in the southwest corner of mississippi.

30. As the fairy waved her wand the witch disintegrated into dust and ashes shrieking with horror and rage.

see answer key, p. 441

Sentence Transformations

The best writers, at least from a stylistic point of view, are those who can be versatile, who know how to mold language to suit their purposes. The ten basic sentence patterns that we have already learned can be combined and expanded through the use of dependent clauses and verbal phrases. In addition, sentences can be transformed in a variety of ways to shift the emphasis or heighten the effect of a sentence. This chapter will examine ways of transforming sentences. Some will already be familiar to you, but some may not. The next time you are editing a piece of your writing, see if you can enhance your writing style by calling some of these transformations into play.

FOUR TYPES OF SENTENCES

Besides classifying sentences by structure as simple, compound, and complex, we can classify sentences according to their function. Most of us learn in elementary school that there are four types of sentences: declarative, interrogative, imperative, and exclamatory. Probably, though, you learned simplified facts about these sentences, so let's take a closer look now.

Declarative sentence—A declarative sentence makes a statement.

> George's mother bought him a car for graduation.

Interrogative sentence—An interrogative sentence asks a question. Notice that whenever we ask a question, the verb is automatically split in two by the subject. This means that the verb in a question, unless it is the *be* verb, must be a verb phrase of at least two words. If no auxiliary is apparent, then "do," "does," or "did" is used in place of a standard helping verb.

> *Did* George's mother *buy* him a car for graduation?
>
> When *will* George's mother *buy* him a car?
>
> *Is* the car for George?
>
> (NOTE: This final question does not consist of a verb phrase because the *be* verb is the one exception to the rule that a question needs a two-part verb.)

Imperative sentence—An imperative sentence gives a command. Typically, the subject is an understood "you," although for emphasis the "you" can actually be stated in an imperative sentence. Notice that in an imperative sentence, only a one-word verb is used; if we add an auxiliary, even a modal indicating the imperative, we end up with a declarative sentence.

> *Close* the door. ("You must close the door" is declarative.)

> You *leave* right now. ("You must leave right now" is declarative.)

When we diagram an imperative sentence, we can indicate the understood "you" by placing an "x" in the subject spot or by placing "you" in square brackets.

> Close the door.

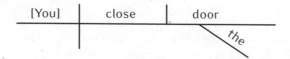

Exclamatory sentence—Probably your conception of the exclamatory sentence is that it ends with an exclamation mark. This *may* be true, but this is not what makes a sentence exclamatory. In fact, declarative and imperative sentences can also end in an exclamation mark. The exclamation mark's only function is to express strong emotion.

> George's mother bought him a car for graduation! (declarative sentence)

> Close the door! (imperative sentence)

So then, what *does* constitute an exclamatory sentence, if not the exclamation mark? An exclamatory sentence has had its syntax rearranged for the purpose of highlighting a modifier by bringing it close to the beginning of the sentence. The two words capable of doing that in English are *how* and *what*. Although both words can begin an interrogative sentence as well, in this case they are not used to ask a question but to emphasize a quality.

DECLARATIVE:	The new professor seems obnoxious.
EXCLAMATORY:	How obnoxious the new professor seems!
	How obnoxious the new professor seems.
	OR
	What an obnoxious professor she seems to be!
	What an obnoxious professor she seems to be.

Notice that the exclamatory versions can end in either a period or an exclamation mark, depending on the tone of voice the writer wishes to indicate. What transforms the sentence from declarative to exclamatory is the rearrangement of syntax. By beginning with "how" or "what" and then moving the modifier "obnoxious" near the beginning of the sentence—and thereby emphasizing the modifier—we have formed an exclamatory sentence.

EXERCISE 13.1

Transform the following declarative sentence into an interrogative, imperative, and exclamatory form.

The butler diligently polishes the gleaming silver tea set every day.

_____

_____

_____

see answer key, p. 442

CLEFT SENTENCES

Another structure used to emphasize certain elements within a sentence is the cleft sentence. The cleft sentence is broken into two parts, the first part building to the climax of the second. A cleft sentence begins with one of two words, "it" or "what." Here is a shorthand formula of the two cleft structures:

It + *be* + highlighted item

Noun clause beginning with What + *be* + highlighted item

Let's look at an example.

Declarative: The ghost of a sad woman visited my room last night.

Cleft with "it":   It + *be* + highlighted item

It was *the ghost of a sad woman* that visited my room last night.

It was *my room* that the ghost visited last night.

It was *last night* that the ghost visited my room.

Notice how, by varying what follows the stem "It was," a writer can vary the emphasis of each sentence.

Cleft with "what":   Noun clause beginning with *what* + *be* + highlighted item
          What visited my room last night was *the ghost of a sad woman*.

The suspense is built up even more in the cleft sentence beginning with "what." Versatility is limited here, but the climax of the sentence has a stronger effect.

EXERCISE 13.2

Using the same sentence as in Exercise 13.1, form a cleft sentence beginning with "What" and as many cleft sentences as possible beginning with "It."

The butler diligently polishes the gleaming silver tea set every day.

_____

_____

_____

_____

_____

_____

see answer key, p. 443

PASSIVE SENTENCES

In Chapter 9 we discussed the difference between a verb in active voice, in which the subject performs the action, and a verb in passive voice, in which the subject is acted upon. Remember that the passive verb always consists of two parts, a form of *be* and the past participle of the main verb. Other auxiliaries, of course, may also be included.

ACTIVE: Carol typed the report without complaint.

PASSIVE: The report was typed by Carol without complaint.

Most writers have received years of well-intended advice to "avoid the passive," and the example above demonstrates that in general this is good advice. In most cases transforming a sentence into passive voice makes it unnecessarily wordy and colorless. Rather than avoiding the passive altogether, though, you should know how and when to use it. The passive voice is helpful primarily in two situations:

1. If you do not know who or what performed an action, or if that information is not necessary or useful, use the passive.

The computer *was repaired* yesterday.

Here the essential information is that the computer was repaired; the identity of the person who actually did the repair is either unknown or insignificant.

2. If you want to emphasize the helplessness, victimization, or passivity of the subject, or if you want to avoid assigning responsibility or blame, use the passive.

Just a few decades ago, psychiatric patients *were* often *subjected* to electric shock therapy as a matter of routine. (This sentence emphasizes victimization and hence evokes pity for the subject.)

Katrina's engagement ring *was thrown* into the trash by accident. (Passive voice here indicates that either we do not know, or do not wish to name, the identity of the person who committed the mistake.)

EXERCISE 13.3

A. First determine whether the verb in each sentence below is written in active or passive voice; then decide, based upon the content of the sentence, if the sentence is most effective in that voice. If you disagree with the chosen voice of the sentence, rewrite it.

1. The videotape was erased by the mischievous children.

   _____

   _____

   _____

2. Arthur was crowned king after he removed the sword from the stone.

   _____

   _____

   _____

3. The lone survivor of the plane crash was besieged by questions from media representatives.

   _____

   _____

   _____

4. Someone stole the tooth hidden beneath Amelia's pillow.

   _____

   _____

   _____

5. The delicate design was woven into the cloth with threads of gold.

_____

_____

_____

B. Write two sentences of your own to illustrate the effective use of passive voice. Be able to justify your use of passive.

_____

_____

_____

_____

_____

_____

see answer key, p. 443

"THERE" AS EXPLETIVE

Somewhat related to the passive—because it, too, is a weak construction—is the sentence that uses "there" as an expletive. We examined this construction in Chapter 8, because this type of sentence, in which the subject follows the verb, often results in subject-verb agreement errors. The basic formula for a sentence using "there" as expletive is the following:

There + *be* **+ subject**

You should be aware that this sentence is a viable construction, that can be used for variety, but it should be placed sparingly in any piece of writing. Notice in the diagram below how "there" is clearly an expletive, not a subject.

There is a distinct pattern in Dante's epic.

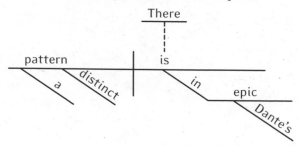

The sentence is stronger if rephrased to eliminate the expletive: Dante's epic has a distinct pattern. The diagram demonstrates that every word now counts.

EXERCISE 13.4

A. In the sentences below, determine whether "there" is used as an expletive or as an adverb. If the sentence uses "there" as an expletive, rephrase it to eliminate "there." Which version sounds stronger?

1. There was a red fox helping itself to the cat food in the Smiths' yard last night.

   _____

   _____

2. There were good reasons for the decision.

   _____

   _____

3. No one was there when we knocked on the door.

   _____

   _____

B. Write two sentences of your own using "there" as an expletive. Decide whether this is the most effective construction or if the sentence would be stronger if rephrased.

   _____

   _____

   _____

   _____

   _____

   _____

see answer key, p. 443

ANTICIPATORY APPOSITIVE

Somewhat related to the cleft sentence is the sentence that contains an anticipatory appositive. By beginning with the pronoun "it," the sentence forces us to anticipate what "it" will turn out to be. This sentence has the following structure:

It + *be* + adjective + appositive for "it" in the form of noun clause, gerund, or infinitive

The anticipatory appositive structure, like the cleft sentence, has the effect of building up suspense in a sentence. At the same time, the adjective that follows the *be* verb gives the reader an emotional context for how to absorb the information in the appositive.

Let's take a look at how this sentence structure works and also at how to diagram it. Notice that the appositive structure is placed next to "it" and is enclosed by parentheses.

It is exciting that we have met again. (The noun clause "that we have met again" is the appositive for "It.")

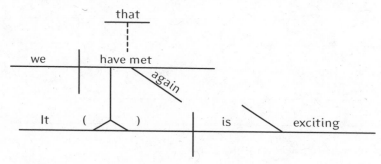

It is exciting meeting you again. (The gerund phrase "meeting you again" is the appositive for "It.")

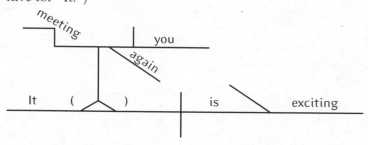

It is exciting to meet you again. (The infinitive phrase "to meet you again" is the appositive for "It.")

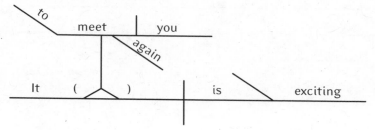

All of these sentences could easily be rephrased:

That we have met again is exciting.

Meeting you again is exciting.

To meet you again is exciting.

Can you detect the difference in the effect of these sentences? The anticipatory appositive, as its name implies, forces us to "anticipate" the semantic subject of the sentence, thereby enhancing the importance of that subject.

EXERCISE 13.5

In the following sentences, underline the appositive for "It." Then diagram each sentence.

1. It is important to eat a nutritious breakfast.

2. It has been wonderful babysitting the grandchildren.

3. It is incredible that you survived the accident.

see answer key, p. 444

SENTENCE APPOSITIVE

Another type of appositive is one that sums up the idea of the entire sentence. Placed at the end of the sentence, it is preceded by either a comma or a dash (for added emphasis). In Chapter 8, when we addressed the problem of broad-reference "which," many of our corrections involved the use of sentence appositives, although we did not label them at that point. Let's take a look at such a sentence:

INCORRECT: Every day he ate a pound of candy, which contributed to his weight problem. (Although you will often hear people use broad-reference "which," and will also see it in print occasionally, remember that technically the relative pronoun "which" is capable of relating back only to the noun it follows. Although the logic of this sentence is apparent, from a grammatical viewpoint "candy"—not the act of eating a pound of candy every day—is responsible for the weight problem here.)

CORRECTION: Every day he ate a pound of candy, a *habit* that
(with sentence appositive):   contributed to his weight problem. (Now that the sentence structure eliminates the comma before the relative pronoun, "that" is a better word choice than "which.")

The distinguishing features of the sentence appositive are that the structure begins with a noun, and that the noun and the modifiers that follow the noun constitute a summary or comment on the entire sentence.

Now let's take a look at how to diagram a sentence appositive, using the sentence above. Notice that the sentence appositive occupies its own separate but equal structure, not joined in any way to the main diagram.

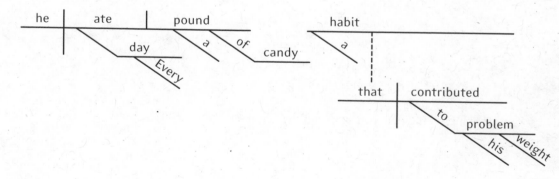

EXERCISE 13.6

In the following sentences, underline the sentence appositives and then diagram the sentences.

1. No one in class remembered the teacher's birthday—an oversight that led to trouble.

2. All of the players memorized the coach's instructions, an action resulting in victory.

3. The Smiths celebrated their fiftieth anniversary, an extraordinary event in our community.

4. Michael asked when his mother would feel better, a question that no one could answer.

see answer key, p. 444

NOMINATIVE ABSOLUTE, OR ABSOLUTE PHRASE

Just as the sentence appositive is a noun structure that occurs at the end of the sentence, the nominative absolute (also known as an absolute phrase) is a noun structure that typically occurs at the beginning of the sentence. It can also, though, appear at the end. When it does appear at the end of a sentence, how can we distinguish the nominative absolute from the sentence appositive? The sentence appositive sums up or comments on the idea of the entire sentence. The **nominative absolute**, on the other hand, **performs one of two functions. It either explains a cause or condition that permitted or resulted in the action of the sentence, or it provides focus on a particular detail related to the sentence.** In form, the nominative absolute consists of a headword noun followed by a prepositional phrase, an adjective or adjective phrase, a noun phrase, a participle, or a participial phrase.

Because it is a noun structure identical in grammatical form (although not in function) to the sentence appositive, we diagram the nominative absolute in the same way as the sentence appositive. When the nominative absolute begins the sentence, we diagram it to the left of the main diagram; when it ends the sentence, we diagram it to the right.

> *The car repaired*, we decided to complete our drive to Florida. (Here the nominative absolute explains the condition under which we decided to complete the drive.)

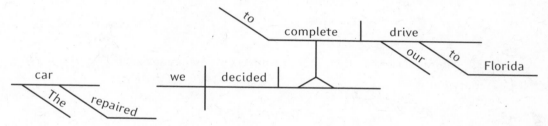

> The police officer paused at the door, *her hand on her revolver*. (Here the nominative absolute acts like the zoom lens on a camera, focusing on a particular detail in order to give us a better overall impression of the action of this sentence.)

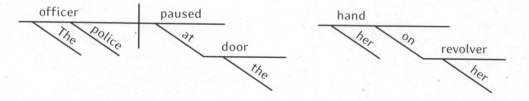

EXERCISE 13.7

In the following sentences, underline the nominative absolute. Then diagram each sentence.

1. The ink spilling onto the table, the words on the document gradually disappeared.

2. Its fur wet, the puppy looked at me hopefully through the open door.

3. The alarm clock rang loudly, its bell near my ear.

4. Marcia walked forward, her hands shaking as she threw the bridal bouquet.

see answer key, p. 445

EXERCISE 13.8

See if you can distinguish between the sentence appositive and the nominative absolute. Underline and label these structures in the sentences below. Then diagram each sentence.

1. My father never completed high school, a fact that he usually concealed from strangers.

2. His family in need of income, my father never completed high school.

3. My father confessed that he never completed high school, his voice stuttering.

4. The package fell to the floor, its contents spilling everywhere.

5. Its wings flapping wildly, the bird tried to escape from the cat—a reminder of nature's rule, "survival of the fittest."

see answer key, p. 446

SUMMARY OF KEY CONCEPTS IN CHAPTER 13

1. By function, sentences can be categorized as declarative, interrogative, imperative, and exclamatory. An exclamatory sentence is defined not by its ending punctuation but by the fact that it begins with "how" or "what," with the syntax of the sentence rearranged to highlight a modifier.

2. A cleft sentence can be used to build suspense. Cleft sentences follow one of two structures:

> It + *be* + highlighted item

> Noun clause beginning with "what" + *be* + highlighted item

3. The passive voice is appropriate in two situations:

   a. Either we do not know the agent of the action of the sentence, or that information is insignificant.

   b. We want to emphasize the helplessness, victimization, or suffering of the grammatical subject.

4. "There" as expletive is a weak sentence construction and can lead to subject-verb agreement problems. Use this structure sparingly.

5. The anticipatory appositive, like the cleft sentence, builds anticipation:

> It + *be* + adjective + appositive for "it" in form of noun clause, gerund, or infinitive

6. The sentence appositive (noun structure that occurs at the end of a sentence) sums up the idea of the entire sentence and can be used to correct the broad-reference "which" problem.

7. The nominative absolute (noun structure that appears at the beginning or end of a sentence) performs one of two functions:

   a. It explains a cause or condition that permitted or resulted in the action of the sentence.

   b. It provides focus on a particular detail related to the sentence.

CHAPTER 13 EXERCISE

Using the base sentence given below, write sentences as directed. You will need to add information, so be prepared to use some imagination. This exercise will review all of the sentence structures that we have learned in this text: sentences 1-6 will help you review what you learned in Chapters 5, 6, and 7 about expanding a simple sentence, sentences 7-11 will help you review what you learned in Chapter 10 about verbals, and sentences 12-20 will help you review the transformations you learned in Chapter 13.

The mischievous children locked their eccentric governess in the closet.

1. a compound sentence containing a coordinating conjunction

_____

_____

_____

2. a compound sentence containing a conjunctive adverb

_____

_____

_____

3. a complex sentence containing a noun clause

_____

_____

_____

4. a complex sentence containing an adverb clause

_____

_____

_____

5. a complex sentence containing a relative clause

_____

_____

_____

6. a compound-complex sentence

_____

_____

_____

7. a sentence containing a gerund

_____

_____

_____

8. a sentence beginning with a participial phrase

_____

_____

_____

9. a sentence containing an infinitive used as a noun

_____

_____

_____

10. a sentence containing an infinitive used as an adverb

_____

_____

_____

11. a sentence containing an infinitive used as an adjective

_____

_____

_____

12. an interrogative sentence

_____

_____

_____

13. an exclamatory sentence

_____

_____

_____

14. a passive sentence

_____

_____

_____

15. a cleft sentence beginning with "it"

_____

_____

_____

16. a cleft sentence beginning with "what"

_____

_____

_____

17. a sentence containing an anticipatory appositive

_____

_____

_____

18. a sentence containing a sentence appositive

_____

_____

_____

19. a sentence beginning with a nominative absolute

_____

_____

_____

20. a sentence ending with a nominative absolute

_____

_____

_____

see answer key, p. 447

Additional Exercises

EXERCISE I ● PARTS OF SPEECH (CHAPTER I)

Label each of the underlined words in the passage below as one of the eight parts of speech.

According to classical mythology, Earth belonged to gigantic gods known as <u>Titans</u>. After deposing their father, Saturn, <u>three</u> gods divided the world <u>among</u> themselves. Jupiter <u>ruled</u> the earth and all living creatures, Neptune ruled the ocean, <u>and</u> Pluto ruled the underworld, the land of the <u>dead</u>.

One <u>day</u> a <u>lesser</u> god, Prometheus, amused <u>himself</u> by shaping a figure <u>from</u> earth and water. In the earth <u>was</u> a seed <u>he</u> had never seen before. As the sun <u>beat</u> upon the figure, the seed grew <u>quickly</u>, and the figure sprang to life. Prometheus named <u>this</u> new creature Man.

Prometheus wanted to give Man <u>a</u> gift. He rode <u>into</u> the sky, dipped his torch into the sun, and then handed the gift of fire to Man. Although Man profited <u>immensely</u> from the gift, Prometheus <u>suffered</u> terribly. <u>Alas</u>, he endures <u>eternal</u> punishment, chained to a rock and condemned to have his liver eaten by a vulture.

EXERCISE II ● SENTENCE PATTERNS 1-5 (CHAPTER 2)

Write the number of the sentence pattern whenever a blank follows a sentence in the passage below. For extra practice, diagram the sentences for which you have identified a sentence pattern number.

The first age of the world was the Golden Age. ___ Flowers bloomed constantly. The weather was perfect. ___ Innocence was everywhere. ___ Humans lived in peace with each other and with the gods. After a while, Jupiter became restless. ___ He divided the year into seasons. Eventually humans fought among themselves for land. They also fashioned weapons. The world passed from the Silver Age to the Bronze Age to the Iron Age. The condition of humans remained a downward spiral. ___

EXERCISE III ● SENTENCE PATTERNS 1-10 (CHAPTERS 2 & 3)

Write the number of the sentence pattern in the blank following each sentence. For extra practice, diagram each sentence as well.

Because of the evil in the world, Jupiter announced to the other gods his new plans. ___ A flood would destroy everything. ___ They consented to Jupiter's scheme. ___ After days of rain, only Mount Parnassus rose above the flood waters. ___ Deucalion and Pyrrha clung to the rocks. ___ Unlike other humans, they had always been pure in heart. ___ Their plight made Jupiter suddenly sympathetic. ___ The gods gave the couple a reprieve from death. ___ The waters receded. ___ Then the humans walked to a nearby temple. ___ At the direction of the oracle, they threw stones behind themselves. ___ The stones turned into people. ___ Their obedience gave the world a new population. ___ The gods judged these humans an improvement on the former race. ___

EXERCISE IV ● NOUN CLAUSES (CHAPTER 6)

Underline the noun clauses in the following paragraph and identify the function of each one. For extra practice, diagram each sentence.

Phaeton traveled to the Palace of the Sun. He knew that this palace was where his father lived. He approached Apollo, his father, and asked him for a gift. Apollo promised he could have whatever he wanted. Phaeton asked if he could drive his father's chariot across the sky. Apollo knew that this was extremely dangerous, but he could not break his promise. He also could not dissuade his son. Finally, with many warnings about what could happen, he handed the reins of his chariot to Phaeton. The chariot flew wildly, and much of the earth burned. At last Apollo threw a thunderbolt at Phaeton. He died instantly. This action is what saved the earth from destruction by fire.

EXERCISE V ● ADVERB AND RELATIVE CLAUSES (CHAPTER 7)

Underline the adverb clauses and circle the relative clauses in the passage below. For extra practice, diagram each sentence.

As Pluto was driving his chariot through the vale of Enna, he spotted a beautiful maiden who was gathering flowers. He took Proserpina to the underworld, where he treated her with utmost kindness. Although she missed her mother, she loved Pluto. When Ceres learned of her daughter's plight, she begged Jupiter for help. He could not order the maiden's release because she had eaten pomegranate seeds during her stay in the underworld. Jupiter finally made a deal with Ceres. Her daughter would live with her for half of each year; however, she would live with Pluto for the other half. Whenever Proserpina is with Ceres, it is summer. Winter begins when she returns to Pluto.

EXERCISE VI ● VERBALS (CHAPTER 10)

Underline verbal phrases in the passage below and identify the verbals as infinitives, gerunds, or participles. Then diagram each sentence. (In addition to verbals, you will also find a noun clause, an adverb clause, and a relative clause in this passage.)

A young hero named Jason decided to undertake a dangerous adventure. Sailing with a group of young men on the *Argo*, he landed at Colchis to claim the famous golden fleece. The king agreed to give him the golden fleece under one condition. Jason had to accomplish two tasks before receiving his prize. The king ordered him to yoke two fire-breathing bulls and to sow dragon's teeth. What the king had commanded was extremely dangerous.

The king's daughter, Medea, had fallen in love with Jason. Exercising her magic powers, she gave him a charm to protect himself. When Jason undertook his first task, he was able to yoke the bulls without difficulty. Then he was able to defeat the warriors who sprang up from the dragon's teeth. Jason, returning to Greece with Medea, became king. Winning the golden fleece was the happiest accomplishment of his life.

APPENDIX • TWO

Verb Conjugations (*See* and *Be*)

CONJUGATION OF THE VERB *See*

For purposes of illustration, you will find below all possible forms of the verb *see*. In ordinary practice, however, you are unlikely to encounter any of the perfect progressive aspects of the verb in passive voice. Notice how awkward these verb phrases sound when you say them aloud and how difficult it would be to find situations in which to use them.

ACTIVE VOICE   PASSIVE VOICE

Present

I see	we see	I am seen	we are seen
you see	you see	you are seen	you are seen
he, she, it sees	they see	he, she, it is seen	they are seen

Past

I saw	we saw	I was seen	we were seen
you saw	you saw	you were seen	you were seen
he, she, it saw	they saw	he, she, it was seen	they were seen

Future (for emphasis, *shall* can be substituted for *will* in any future form)

I will see	we will see	I will be seen	we will be seen
you will see	you will see	you will be seen	you will be seen
he, she, it will see	they will see	he, she, it will be seen	they will be seen

Present Perfect

I have seen	we have seen	I have been seen	we have been seen
you have seen	you have seen	you have been seen	you have been seen
he, she, it has seen	they have seen	he, she, it has been seen	they have been seen

Past Perfect

I had seen	we had seen	I had been seen	we had been seen
you had seen	you had seen	you had been seen	you had been seen
he, she, it had seen	they had seen	he, she, it had been seen	they had been seen

Future Perfect

I will have seen	we will have seen	I will have been seen	we will have been seen
you will have seen	you will have seen	you will have been seen	you will have been seen
he, she, it will have seen	they will have seen	he, she, it will have been seen	they will have been seen

Present Progressive

I am seeing	we are seeing	I am being seen	we are being seen
you are seeing	you are seeing	you are being seen	you are being seen
he, she, it is seeing	they are seeing	he, she, it is being seen	they are being seen

Past Progressive

I was seeing	we were seeing	I was being seen	we were being seen
you were seeing	you were seeing	you were being seen	you were being seen
he, she, it was seeing	they were seeing	he, she, it was being seen	they were being seen

Future Progressive

I will be seeing	we will be seeing	I will be being seen	we will be being seen
you will be seeing	you will be seeing	you will be being seen	you will be being seen
he, she, it will be seeing	they will be seeing	he, she, it will be being seen	they will be being seen

Present Perfect Progressive

I have been seeing	we have been seeing	I have been being seen	we have been being seen
you have been seeing	you have been seeing	you have been being seen	you have been being seen
he, she, it has been seeing	they have been seeing	he, she, it has been being seen	they have been being seen

Past Perfect Progressive

I had been seeing	we had been seeing	I had been being seen	we had been being seen
you had been seeing	you had been seeing	you had been being seen	you had been being seen
he, she, it had been seeing	they had been seeing	he, she, it had been being seen	they had been being seen

Future Perfect Progressive

I will have been seeing	we will have been seeing	I will have been being seen	we will have been being seen
you will have been seeing	you will have been seeing	you will have been being seen	you will have been being seen
he, she, it will have been seeing	they will have been seeing	he, she, it will have been being seen	they will have been being seen

CONJUGATION OF THE VERB *Be* ● ACTIVE VOICE

As the most irregular verb in English, *be* has more irregular forms than other verbs. In addition, we frequently use *be* when we need to express the subjunctive mood (expressing something that is contrary to fact, as in "She wishes she *were* single again," or occurring in a noun clause following a demand or recommendation, as in "Her husband demanded that she *be* home by midnight.") Because of the nature of *be*, it is not practical to conjugate all its possible forms. The future progressive of *be* ("will be being") is almost always expressed through the future ("will be"); likewise, the perfect progressive tenses sound redundant and are usually expressed in a different way. You are almost certainly going to say, for example, "I have been happy" rather than "I have been being happy." Listed below, then, are the forms of *be* in actual use among speakers of English.

INDICATIVE MOOD

Present

I am	we are
you are	you are
he, she, it is	they are

SUBJUNCTIVE MOOD

Present

I be	we be
you be	you be
he, she, it be	they be

Past

I was	we were
you were	you were
he, she, it was	they were

Past

I were	we were
you were	you were
he, she, it were	they were

Future (for emphasis, *shall* can be substituted for *will* in any future form)

I will be	we will be
you will be	you will be
he, she, it will be	they will be

Present Perfect

I have been	we have been
you have been	you have been
he, she, it has been	they have been

Past Perfect

I had been	we had been
you had been	you had been
he, she, it had been	they had been

Future Perfect

I will have been	we will have been
you will have been	you will have been
he, she, it will have been	they will have been

Present Progressive

I am being	we are being
you are being	you are being
he, she, it is being	they are being

Past Progressive

I was being	we were being
you were being	you were being
he, she, it was being	they were being

Irregular and Troublesome Verb Forms

Base Form	Past Tense	Past Participle (follows *have* or *be*)
arise	arose	arisen
awake	awoke, awakened	awakened
beat	beat	beaten
become	became	become
begin	began	begun
bend	bent	bent
bet	bet	bet
bind	bound	bound
bite	bit	bitten
bleed	bled	bled
blow	blew	blown
break	broke	broken
breed	bred	bred
bring	brought	brought
build	built	built
burst	burst	burst
buy	bought	bought
cast	cast	cast
catch	caught	caught
choose	chose	chosen
cling	clung	clung
come	came	come
cost	cost	cost
creep	crept	crept
cut	cut	cut
deal	dealt	dealt
dig	dug	dug
dive	dived, dove	dived
do	did	done
drag	dragged	dragged
draw	drew	drawn

Base Form	Past Tense	Past Participle (follows *have* or *be*)
dream	dreamed, dreamt	dreamed, dreamt
drink	drank	drunk
drive	drove	driven
eat	ate	eaten
fall	fell	fallen
feel	felt	felt
find	found	found
fit	fit, fitted	fit, fitted
flee	fled	fled
fly	flew	flown
forget	forgot	forgot, forgotten
forgive	forgave	forgiven
freeze	froze	frozen
get	got	got, gotten
give	gave	given
go	went	gone
grind	ground	ground
grow	grew	grown
hang (suspend)	hung	hung
hang (execute)	hanged	hanged
hide	hid	hidden
hit	hit	hit
hurt	hurt	hurt
keep	kept	kept
know	knew	known
lay	laid	laid
lead	led	led
leave	left	left
lend	lent	lent
let	let	let
lie	lay	lain
lose	lost	lost
make	made	made
mean	meant	meant
prove	proved	proved, proven
put	put	put
raise	raised	raised
read	read	read
rid	rid	rid
ride	rode	ridden
ring	rang	rung
rise	rose	risen

Base Form	Past Tense	Past Participle (follows *have* or *be*)
run	ran	run
see	saw	seen
set	set	set
shake	shook	shaken
shed	shed	shed
shine	shone	shone
shoot	shot	shot
shrink	shrank, shrunk	shrunk, shrunken
shut	shut	shut
sink	sank, sunk	sunk
sit	sat	sat
slay	slew	slain
slide	slid	slid
slit	slit	slit
sneak	sneaked	sneaked
speak	spoke	spoken
speed	sped	sped
spend	spent	spent
spin	spun	spun
spread	spread	spread
spring	sprang, sprung	sprung
stand	stood	stood
steal	stole	stolen
stick	stuck	stuck
sting	stung	stung
stink	stank	stunk
strike	struck	struck, stricken
strive	strove	striven
swear	swore	sworn
sweep	swept	swept
swim	swam	swum
swing	swung	swung
take	took	taken
teach	taught	taught
tear	tore	torn
tell	told	told
think	thought	thought
throw	threw	thrown
thrust	thrust	thrust
wake	woke, waked	woken, waked
wear	wore	worn
weave	wove, weaved	woven, weaved

Base Form	Past Tense	Past Participle (follows *have* or *be*)
weep	wept	wept
win	won	won
wind	wound	wound
wring	wrung	wrung
write	wrote	written

Summary of Clauses and Verbals

Each grammar text must decide whether to group clauses and verbals by structure (clause or phrase?) or by function (noun? adjective? adverb?). Because we have followed the principle of structure, this appendix groups clauses and verbals (plus the adverbial objective) according to their function as nouns, adverbs, or adjectives.

NOUN STRUCTURES

NOTE: All noun forms are diagramed on a pedestal. Also, all noun clauses and phrases can be replaced with "something" or "someone" and serve a noun function (subject, object, complement, or appositive).

I. NOUN CLAUSE	Begins with interrogative (diagramed within the noun clause)	who, whom, what = pronouns whose, which = adjectives when, where, why, how = adverbs
	OR Begins with expletive (diagramed above the noun clause)	if, that, whether, whether or not
2. GERUND	Verb form that ends in –ing	
	Can be followed by a complement or an object	
	Diagram on a pedestal with a "step"	
3. INFINITIVE	To + base form of verb	
	Can be followed by a complement or an object	
	Diagram on a pedestal with a prepositional phrase structure	

ADVERB STRUCTURES

NOTE: Adverb clauses can move within a sentence; so can most adverb phrases.

I. ADVERB CLAUSE	Begins with a subordinating conjunction (after, although, as, before, because, even though, if, once, since, unless, until, when, whenever, where, wherever, whereas, whether or not, while)
	Place a comma after an introductory adverb clause.
	No comma necessary when an adverb clause ends the sentence unless the subordinating conjunction indicates contrast (while, whereas, although, though, even though)
	Diagram on a second "tier" beneath the independent clause, joining the clauses together by a connecting line between the verbs of the two clauses. Write the subordinating conjunction on the dotted line.
2. INFINITIVE	To + base form of verb
	Can be followed by a complement or an object
	Diagram on prepositional phrase structure beneath the verb (if it is a movable adverb) or beneath the adjective (if it modifies the adjective it follows and therefore cannot move).
2. ADVERBIAL OBJECTIVE	Noun used as adverb
	Diagram on prepositional phrase structure, so that adverbial objective can be written on horizontal line, beneath the verb.

ADJECTIVE STRUCTURES

I. RELATIVE CLAUSE	Begins with a relative pronoun (who, whom, whose, which, that) or a relative adverb (when, where, why)
	Diagram on a second "tier" beneath the independent clause, with a dotted line joining the relative pronoun or adverb to the noun or pronoun being modified. (In an effectively written sentence, this means that you will join the relative pronoun or adverb to the word it follows.) Do not write anything on the dotted line. Insert the relative pronoun wherever it belongs in the relative clause; place the relative adverb beneath the verb.

Use a comma to set off nonrestrictive relative clauses, when extra information is provided in the relative clause; do not use a comma to set off restrictive information, when the relative clause provides necessary information.

2. INFINITIVE

To + base form of verb

Can be followed by a complement or an object

Diagram on a prepositional phrase structure beneath the noun being modified.

3. PARTICIPLE

Verb form that ends in "-ing" or past participle form of verb

Can be followed by a complement or an object

Diagram on a prepositional phrase structure beneath the noun being modified, with participle written around the inside of the angle.

Use a comma to set off an introductory participial phrase or an ending participial phrase that modifies the subject.

Use a comma with an internal participial phrase that provides extra information about the noun it follows.

Be watchful for dangling participles.

Diagraming Summary

BASIC PRINCIPLES

1. Place subject and verb on a baseline, split in two by a vertical line. The subject and all of its modifiers will be placed to the left of the vertical line; the verb and all of its modifiers (the predicate) will be placed to the right of the vertical line.

The unusual flower bloomed during the night.

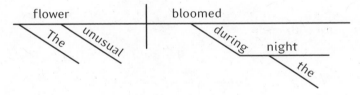

2. Subjective complements and objective complements are indicated by a diagonal or slash line pointing back in the direction of the word they modify.

The flower is *beautiful*.   We considered it *beautiful*.

3. Direct objects are indicated by a straight line that does not cut through the baseline.

Joan planted the *flower*.

4. An indirect object is always placed underneath the verb, on a prepositional phrase structure.

Joan's mother gave *her* the bulb.

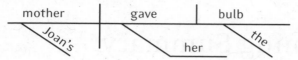

5. In sentence patterns 2, 4, and 9, the subjective or objective complement may be in the form of a prepositional phrase. If so, place the prepositional phrase on a pedestal.

Joan's mother was *in a good mood*.

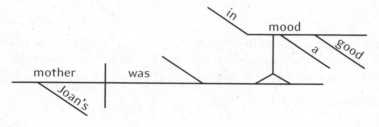

Joan considered her *out of step* with reality.

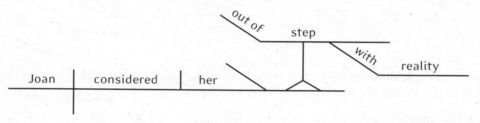

6. Noun structures—noun clauses, gerunds, and infinitives used as nouns—are placed on pedestals. The gerund structure has a "step"; the infinitive is placed on a prepositional phrase structure.

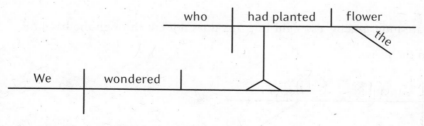

We wondered *who had planted the flower*.

Planting the flower was Joan's job.

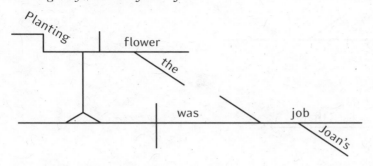

To plant a flower can be fun.

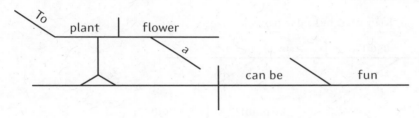

7. An adverb clause is placed on a second tier below the independent clause. Join the verbs of the main clause and the adverb clause with a dotted line and write the subordinating conjunction on the dotted line.

After Joan planted the bulb, she forgot about it.

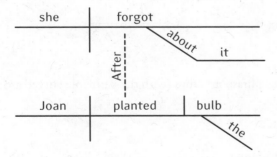

8. A relative clause is also placed on a second tier below the independent clause. Join the relative pronoun or relative adverb to the noun or pronoun it modifies in the main clause. Do not write anything on the dotted line.

The bulb *that Joan planted* was huge.

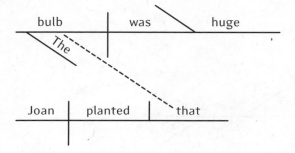

9. An infinitive used as an adverb or adjective is diagramed on a prepositional phrase structure beneath the word it modifies.

To plant the bulb, Joan used her new trowel.

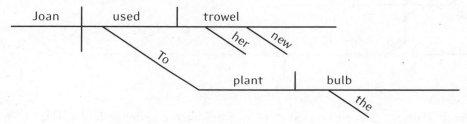

The best time *to plant* is in the fall.

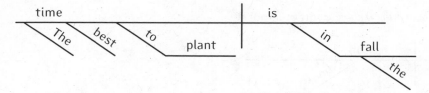

10. A participle is diagramed on a prepositional phrase structure (with the participle curved around the inside angle) beneath the noun it modifies.

Planting the bulb, Joan hummed happily.

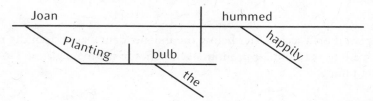

11. An adverbial objective (noun used as adverb) is diagramed on a prepositional phrase structure beneath the verb.

Joan saw the bloom *this morning*.

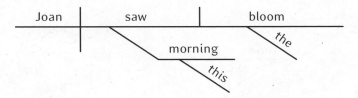

12. Diagram expletives above the diagram. There are three categories of expletives: "as" to introduce an objective complement; "if," "that," "whether," and "whether or not" to introduce a noun clause; and "there" when it is not used as an adverb or interjection.

A local committee named Joan *as* the most creative gardener on her block.

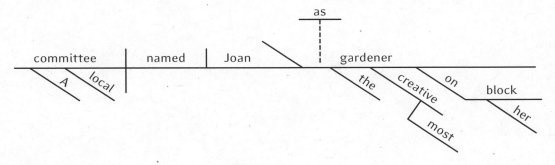

Joan wondered *if* she could win again.

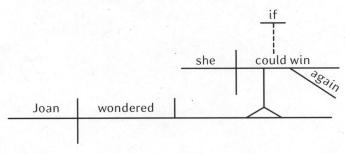

There was a butterfly on the flower.

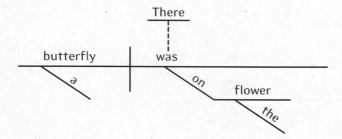

Commonly Confused Words

Although the list that follows is by no means exhaustive, you'll recognize many of the most troublesome word pairs below. Remember that, when you use a spell checker on a computer, it will not show an error if you have chosen the wrong word. That holds true for the commonly confused words below as well as for homonyms, word pairs that sound exactly alike but are spelled differently (such as "flower" and "flour" or "pail" and "pale"). A spell checker can recognize whether letters have been put together correctly, but you must do the thinking to make sure that you have chosen the right word in the first place.

1. accept / except

Confusion arises because these two are often pronounced identically. If you remember that the prefix "ex-" means "out," you can distinguish between the two.

> I wanted to *accept* his offer of marriage.

> I was afraid that, *except* for him [*out*side of him], no one would ever love me.

2. advice / advise

"Advice" is the noun; "advise" is the verb. Although the meanings have no correlation, if you recognize that "advertise" is a verb, then remember that so is "advise."

> I would *advise* you to postpone marriage until after you graduate from college.

> I realize, though, that my *advice* will probably go unheeded.

3. affect / effect

This pair is complicated because each word has two different meanings. Most of the time, "*affect*" shows *a*ction and is a verb, while "effect" is a noun. In some situations, though, "affect" can be used as a noun while "effect" can be used as a verb, although the meaning of each word changes drastically.

> Usual Definitions: affect = verb; to change or influence; can also mean to feign or make a display of liking or using something
>
>   effect = noun; a result

> The patient was adversely *affected* by the medication.

Its *effect* was a rapid increase in blood pressure and heartbeat.

The nurse *affected* a calmness that she did not truly feel as she reassured the patient.

Secondary Definitions: affect = noun; emotional disposition, with the implication that it may be a cultivated one

effect = verb; to cause or bring about

The prisoner's *affect* was strangely disquieting to those in power.

Her passive resistance had *effected* massive revolts as citizens rose up in protest against their oppressive government.

4. allusion / illusion / delusion
When you make an "*allusion*," you are making a reference to something else, dropping a name; when you have an "*illusion*," you are under the influence of your imagination; when you have a "*delusion*," you are mistaken about something, so that your perception *detracts* from reality. There is often a thin line between "illusion" and "delusion," but "delusion" carries with it a negative connotation.

The professor made several *allusions* to the works of metaphysical poets.

She had an *illusion* of herself as a fashion model.

She suffered from the *delusion* that everyone was bent on making her life miserable.

5. already / all ready
"Already" is an adverb that means "previously" or "so soon." When written as two words, "all ready" is an indefinite pronoun followed by an adjective.

Hester had *already* repented for her sins.

Was it *already* time to face her accusers?

The congregation was *all ready* to condemn Hester for immoral behavior.

6. altar / alter
An "*altar*" is a place to pray; "*alter*," the verb, means "to change" or "to make different." If you know how to spell "alternative," an option for changing or making something different, then you will be able to remember how to spell "alter."

Mary Colleen knelt at the *altar*.

She knew that it was time to become serious about *altering* her life.

7. as, as if / like
When you are not sure which of these two words to choose, remember that "as" is a subordinating conjunction and must be followed by a subject and a verb. "Like" is a preposition and must be followed by an object, without a verb. One way to remember the difference is to associate the ending "s" on "as" with the term "subordinating."

Joey hops around *as* a restless monkey does.

Joey hops around *as if* he were a restless monkey.

Joey hops around *like* a restless monkey.

8. between / among
"Between" is a preposition signaling two; "among" signals more than two.

Between you and me, what is going on here?

Can we keep the secret *among* the five of us?

9. bring / take
These two words imply two different directions. To "bring" is to come closer to the subject of the action, the "*I*" of the sentence; to "take" is to go "*away*" from the subject of the action.

Bring the report to me in the morning.

Please *take* away these dirty dishes.

10. capital / capitol
"Capitol" has only one meaning, the building in which a legislative body meets. Visualize the "o" as the site of an impressive building. (Many capitols are topped by domes, and so visualizing such a capitol may also help.) All other meanings will be spelled "capital."

Fred invested his *capital* wisely.

Begin each sentence with a *capital* letter.

Your performance on this project has been *capital*.

The *capital* of Texas is Austin.

The mayors met in the state's *capitol* building.

11. compliment / complement
"Compliment," a noun or a verb, refers to praise; one mnemonic device is to associate "compl*i*ment" with pretty eyes (*i*'s). "Complement" can also be either a verb or a noun and carries with it the meaning of completion.

The interior decorator felt that burgundy accents would *complement* the gray carpet.

After following his advice, we have received many *compliments* on how the room looks.

12. conscience / conscious
"Conscience," a noun (remember its component word "science") is the moral dimension of our being, the entity that makes us feel responsible for our actions. "Conscious," an adjective, means "aware." If you remember the phrase "consci*ous* of us," you should avoid confusion.

Richard III's *conscience* haunted him at the end of his life.

He was *conscious* of the many murders he had committed.

13. **continual / continuous**

Something that is "continual" happens at regular intervals; something that is "continuous" is ongoing, without interruption. Think of the "uou" in "continuous" as a never-ending circle to help you remember that this is the word that implies a never-ending occurrence. The difference in meaning is sometimes so slight that either word will work in a given sentence, as in the examples below, but the impression made by each word is somewhat different. Choose between these two carefully.

> Her *continual* [ongoing and frequent] complaints made everyone unhappy.
> OR
> She *continually* complained.

> Her *continuous* [without pause] complaints made everyone unhappy.
> OR
> She *continuously* complained.

In some sentences, the word choice makes a real difference:

> The water ran *continuously*. (Watch out for a huge water bill!)

> The water bill *continually* grew. (The water bill arrives at intervals.)

14. **desert / dessert**

Since all of us would like more than one dessert after dinner, remember that this sweet treat contains a double "s." While "dessert" is a noun, "desert" can be either a verb ("to abandon") or a noun ("an arid location").

> I must *desert* your pleasant company and return to work immediately after dinner.

> That means, unfortunately, that I will miss *dessert*.

> It is extremely difficult for humans to survive in a *desert*.

15. **different from / different than**

Although many people use the construction "different than," "different from" is actually the preferred form.

> This pumpkin pie is certainly *different from* any other that I've tasted.

16. **everyday / every day**

"Everyday" is an adjective and will almost always precede a noun; "every day" is an adverb.

> Carol thought of herself as just an *everyday* housewife.

> She kept the house running efficiently *every day*.

17. **farther / further**

"Farther" measures distance, so that we use it to determine how "far" away something is. "Further" is used for entities that cannot be empirically measured.

> I would like to drive a little *farther* today. (We can measure the miles.)

> I would like to explore this issue *further*. (We cannot measure this.)

18. fewer / less

The problem of differentiating between these two words relates to the fact that English contains both mass and count nouns. Use "fewer" with nouns that can be counted, and use "less" with mass nouns, those that cannot be counted singly.

To lose weight, eat *fewer* calories.

It also helps to eat *less* sugar and fat.

19. fiancé / fiancée

Words borrowed from the French, this pair denotes masculine and feminine, respectively. The prospective husband is the "fiancé"; the prospective bride is the "fiancée." A few other words in English retain the added "e" ending to mark the feminine, as in "protégé" (masculine) and "protégée" (feminine) or "confidant" (masculine) and "confidante" (feminine).

The excited young *fiancé* picked out a tuxedo while his *fiancée* shopped for a wedding dress.

20. hanged / hung

A man or a woman can be hanged (notice the "a" in all of these words); objects are hung.

The outlaw was *hanged* at sundown.

His hat, gun, and belt had been carefully *hung* on the wall of the jail before his execution.

21. healthful / healthy

Something that is good for you is "healthful," causing you to become "healthy."

Scientific studies have repeatedly shown that fresh fruits and vegetables are *healthful*.

To stay *healthy*, you should eat several servings of fresh fruits and vegetables daily.

22. hopefully / hopeful

In ordinary speech, most of us are likely to confuse the adverb form ("hopefully") and the adjective form ("hopeful").

INCORRECT:	Hopefully, we can solve this problem quickly. (This is wrong because we cannot solve the problem *hopefully*.)
CORRECT:	We hope that we can solve this problem quickly. OR We are hopeful that we can solve this problem quickly. OR We looked at the professor hopefully as she pondered how to solve the problem.

23. imply / infer

You might find it easier to make the distinction between these two verbs if you think of the corresponding nouns, "implication" and "inference." An implica*tion* is a sugges*tion*; an infer-ence is a surmise, a guess. The difference here is that one person *implies* (suggests, hints at) some-thing; another person *infers* (surmises, concludes) what has been implied.

> Kay's friend *implied* that she was bored.

> Kay *inferred* that she was expected to alleviate her friend's boredom.

24. irregardless, regardless

Put simply, there is no such word as "irregardless." The "ir–" prefix is negative, as is the "-less" suffix. Follow the general rule of avoiding a double negative and you end up with "regardless" as the only possible option. (Most likely the confusion results from the fact that we say "regu-lar" and "irregular," but in this pair the "ir–" prefix is the only negative and therefore correct.)

> *Regardless* of the consequences, we must see this *irregular* situation through to the end.

25. its / it's

Although we have already mentioned the confusion here, it's worth looking at this troublesome pair one more time. Remember that "its" is a possessive pronoun and that pronouns do NOT require an apostrophe to indicate possession. "It's" is always a contraction for either "it is" or "it has."

> *It's* hard saying good-bye for the final time.

> American culture does not like to admit *its* powerlessness over death.

26. moral / morale

"Moral" can be a noun ("ethical principle") or an adjective ("virtuous," "ethical"). "Morale," pronounced with the stress on the second syllable, is a noun that refers to one's emotional state. One way to remember this is to associate the word "ego" with "moral*e*," since ego suffers if one's morale is low. It may also help if you remember that the opposite of "moral" is "immoral"; there is no opposite of "morale," since it is a noun rather than an adjective.

> Aunt Velma was a *moral* person who would have condemned her children's *immoral* behavior after the funeral. She had tried to teach them better *morals*. The *moral* of this story is that parents cannot always be successful in imparting their own *morals* to their children.

> Uncle Lou's *morale* declined rapidly after his wife's unexpected death.

27. a number / the number

"A number," when followed by a prepositional phrase, is a plural indefinite noun; "the number" is always singular.

> A child suffers from stress. (Here the verb "suffers" agrees with the singular "child.")

> *A number* of children suffer from stress. (Notice the plural verb "suffer.")

The number of children suffering from stress is impossible to determine. (Notice that the singular verb "is" agrees with "the number," meaning one particular number if we actually counted the children suffering from stress.)

28. number / amount

"Number" is the correct term when referring to count nouns; "amount" is correct when referring to mass nouns, entities that cannot be counted.

Because of her restless nature, Gina had lived in *a number* of cities.

Because of her frequent moves, the *amount* of clutter she had accumulated was small.

29. personal / personnel

Like "moral" and "morale," these words are pronounced differently. "Personal" (emphasis on the first syllable) is an adjective that means "relating to a person," while "personnel" (emphasis on the final syllable) refers to a number of people, usually employed in the same activity or business. The double "n" in "personnel" will help you think of this word as applying to more than one person.

Peggy and Jack asked us a few *personal* questions during our initial conversation.

All of the accounting *personnel* will be required to work overtime during tax season.

30. principle / principal

No doubt you've heard the mnemonic "The principal is your pal," but this saying is misleading. It implies that the only meaning of "principal" is a school administrator, but that is not true. "Principal" can also refer to a sum of money on which one earns interest or, as an adjective, can mean "chief" or "major." On the other hand, "principle" *does* have just one meaning. Therefore, remember that "princip*le*" = ru*le*," and that all other meanings must be spelled "principal."

The retiree was living off the interest of $1 million in *principal*.

I disagree with you in *principle*, but it seems that in practice we are in accord.

I never did learn the *principles* of geometry.

I spent many hours in the *principal's* office.

The *principal* export of England is wool.

31. prophecy / prophesy

"Prophecy" is the noun in this pair, with the last syllable pronounced "see." On the other hand, "prophesy" is a verb, with the last syllable pronounced "sigh." One way to distinguish between the two is to remember that the verb form ends in "sy," which we can think of as a shorthand form of "say," also a verb.

Jeremiah *prophesied* mass destruction, but no one believed his *prophecies*.

32. real / really

As the "-ly" ending indicates, "really" is the adverb form, while "real" is an adjective. As an adjective, "real" can appear either before a noun or following a *be* or linking verb, as a predicate adjective.

Last night a *real* emergency occurred in our town.

The emergency was *real*, not simulated.

All of the townspeople were *really* frightened.

33. stationary / stationery

"Stationary" means to remain in one place; "stationery" is used for writing letters.

The girl sat *stationary* for hours as she wrote her thank you notes.

She had chosen to write on gold leaf *stationery*.

34. sure / surely

Just as with "real" and "really," remember that "sure" is the adjective (meaning "certain") and that "surely" is the adverb (meaning "certainly").

I am *sure* that this recipe will work.

I am *surely* hungry.

35. then / than

"Then" means "when" or indicates a subsequent action; "than" always has to do with a comparison.

First we cut down the Christmas tree; *then* we dragged it home.

Since I will get paid tomorrow, I'll think about my bills *then*.

On pancakes, I like honey better *than* syrup.

36. versus / verses

"Versus" means "against," as in "*us* against them." "Verses," on the other hand, refers to poetry or song, or to the divisions within Bible chapters.

The lawsuit involved company owners *versus* tenants in subsidized housing.

One of the tenants composed a song that devoted many *verses* to the horrendous living conditions that had prompted the lawsuit.

37. whose / who's

Just as with "its" and "it's," we have here a pronoun in possessive form (the relative or interrogative pronoun "whose") and a contraction ("who's," meaning "who is" or "who has").

Whose responsibility is it to take out the trash?

Who's been lax about doing this chore?

PRACTICE

Circle the correct word in the following sentences.

1. The (PRINCIPAL, PRINCIPLE) known as the Golden Rule is an ecumenical one.

2. (IT'S, ITS) motor racing, the sports car finally slowed to a stop.

3. I would like to (COMPLIMENT, COMPLEMENT) you on your excellent study habits.

4. A bigot believes that one group of people is innately better (THEN, THAN) another.

5. Will Donna's newly inherited fortune (AFFECT, EFFECT) her circle of friends?

6. Nostradamus is famous for his many (PROPHECIES, PROPHESIES).

7. The archer preferred to practice on a (STATIONARY, STATIONERY) target.

8. The (DESERT, DESSERT) becomes cool at night.

9. Frieda's aunt is completely (DIFFERENT FROM, DIFFERENT THAN) anyone else in the family.

10. Nolan decided to (ALTAR, ALTER) his will after his daughter married a millionaire.

11. The divorce documents read "Romeo (VERSUS, VERSES) Casanova."

12. The counselor (ADVICED, ADVISED) the distraught student to calm down.

13. My little sister always (AFFECTS, EFFECTS) an air of helplessness so that she can get her way.

14. *War and Peace* is a (REAL, REALLY) long novel.

15. (FEWER, LESS) people showed up for the concert than the organizers had expected.

16. (CONSCIENCE, CONSCIOUS) of her striking beauty, the model managed to alienate most of her friends.

17. The voters had to decide (BETWEEN, AMONG) a Republican, a Democrat, a Socialist, and a Green Party candidate.

18. Making restitution is one way of relieving a guilty (CONSCIENCE, CONSCIOUS).

19. What will be the (AFFECT, EFFECT) of enlarging the ozone hole?

20. Some people contend that the (PRINCIPAL, PRINCIPLE) cause of divorce is boredom.

21. The magician tricked us with an optical (ALLUSION, ILLUSION).

22. Grayson was unwilling to (ACCEPT, EXCEPT) the blame.

23. "Is everyone (ALL READY, ALREADY) for the first day of kindergarten?" asked Mrs. Clark.

24. She behaves (AS, LIKE) her mother commands.

25. The periodic but (CONTINUAL, CONTINUOUS) ringing of the telephone punctuated their conversation.

26. "How much (FARTHER, FURTHER) do we have to go?" asked the child for the tenth time.

27. The severely depressed prisoner (HANGED, HUNG) himself in his cell.

28. Blueberries are an extraordinarily (HEALTHFUL, HEALTHY) food for several reasons.

29. (IRREGARDLESS, REGARDLESS) of the law, Antigone knew that she was morally right.

30. After reading the contract carefully, the customer (IMPLIED, INFERRED) that the warranty she had just purchased was basically worthless.

31. The psychiatrist was struggling to understand the (ILLUSIONS, DELUSIONS) of the enraged patient.

32. It takes special training to work in a (PERSONAL, PERSONNEL) office, even for a small company.

33. Susan Anthony was (SURE, SURELY) brave to rebel against the conventional standards for women of her time.

34. The neighborhood was curious about (WHOSE, WHO'S) house was for sale.

35. Each of Aesop's fables ends with a (MORAL, MORALE).

36. Joe introduced us to his (FIANCÉ, FIANCÉE), Michele.

37. Heated arguments are an (EVERYDAY, EVERY DAY) occurrence in some households.

38. What is the (CAPITAL, CAPITOL) of Arkansas?

39. To participate in the field trip, the campers had to (BRING, TAKE) permission slips to their counselors.

40. (A NUMBER, THE NUMBER, THE AMOUNT) of women who elect to become engineers is still small.

41. In a strong relationship, the qualities of one partner (COMPLIMENT, COMPLEMENT) those of the other.

42. Marguerite at last is free of arthritic pain and (HOPEFULLY WILL STAY, IS HOPEFUL THAT SHE WILL STAY) that way.

43. The commencement speaker made several (ALLUSIONS, ILLUSIONS) to mythological figures.

ANSWERS TO PRACTICE FOR APPENDIX 6

1. principle
2. Its
3. compliment
4. than
5. affect
6. prophecies
7. stationary
8. desert
9. different from
10. alter
11. versus
12. advised
13. affects
14. really
15. Fewer
16. Conscious
17. among
18. conscience
19. effect
20. principal
21. illusion
22. accept
23. all ready
24. as
25. continual
26. farther
27. hanged
28. healthful
29. Regardless
30. inferred
31. delusions
32. personnel
33. surely
34. whose
35. moral
36. fiancée
37. everyday
38. capital
39. bring
40. The number
41. complement
42. is hopeful that she will stay
43. allusions

ANSWER KEY

EXERCISE 1.1 (p. 19)

The <u>governess</u> insisted that the <u>children</u> should not be allowed to indulge their <u>whims</u>. She instructed the <u>butler</u>, <u>Percy Shaw</u>, to ignore their <u>complaints</u>; as she put it, "These spoiled <u>darlings</u> need to learn the <u>meaning</u> of <u>discipline</u>!"

EXERCISE 1.2 (p. 24)

   1

"<u>That</u> is not acceptable," proclaimed the schoolmaster, rocking <u>himself</u> emphatically back

     3   4   5   .6

and forth on <u>his</u> heels. "<u>I</u> want to know the person <u>who</u> is responsible for <u>this</u> suggestion.

               7   8   9

Should students have the right to determine <u>their</u> own grades? <u>It</u> is a preposterous idea! <u>I</u> will

     10 11   12   13

assign grades to <u>you</u> as <u>I</u> see fit, and <u>anyone</u> wishing to argue with <u>me</u> may do so. Grades are

14   15   16   17   18   19

<u>my</u> prerogative. <u>You</u> will not grade <u>yourself</u>, nor will <u>you</u> grade <u>one another</u>. <u>Who</u> would ever

think of such a thing?"

    1. That = demonstrative pronoun
    2. himself = reflexive pronoun
    3. his = possessive pronoun, functioning here as adjective (determiner)
    4. I = nominative or subjective pronoun
    5. who = relative pronoun
    6. this = demonstrative pronoun, functioning here as adjective (determiner)
    7. their = possessive pronoun, functioning here as adjective (determiner)
    8. It = nominative or subjective pronoun
    9. I = nominative or subjective pronoun
    10. you = objective pronoun
    11. I = nominative or subjective pronoun
    12. anyone = indefinite pronoun

13. me = objective pronoun
14. my = possessive pronoun, functioning here as adjective (determiner)
15. You = nominative or subjective pronoun
16. yourself = reflexive pronoun
17. you = nominative or subjective pronoun
18. one another = reciprocal pronoun
19. Who = interrogative pronoun

EXERCISE 1.3 (p. 30)

1. D	6. C	11. A
2. B	7. B	12. C
3. B	8. D	13. D
4. D	9. C	14. B
5. A	10. B	15. D

EXERCISE 1.4 (p. 31)

                                            INT   INT   T

The hands of the clock <u>were moving</u> slowly while Gretchen <u>walked</u> to town. She <u>had</u>
                      T   INT

a serious look on her face as she <u>approached</u> the shop where her mother <u>had worked</u> for the
                              T   BE

past ten years. Today she <u>would enter</u> the shop for her final good-bye before she <u>was</u> on her
                      T   INT   INT

way to America. As she <u>pushed</u> open the heavy door, she <u>did</u> not <u>weep</u>. Instead, she <u>smiled</u> so
           L

that she <u>might appear</u> happy and confident.

EXERCISE 1.5 (p. 33)

<u>The</u> <u>choppy</u> <u>blue</u> waters of <u>the</u> normally <u>quiet</u> lake battered <u>Michael's</u> <u>worn</u> <u>old</u> boat. As <u>a</u> veteran of <u>many</u> <u>fierce</u> storms, it looked both <u>defiant</u> and <u>triumphant</u> as <u>high</u> waves slapped against <u>its</u> <u>chipped</u> bow.

(In the first sentence, note that although "Michael" is a noun, the possessive form, "Michael's," is an adjective. Likewise, in the last sentence the word "its" is a possessive pronoun in form but functions as an adjective.)

EXERCISE 1.6 (p. 34)

Sarah and Manuel sat <u>forlornly</u> on the porch steps. They talked <u>very</u> <u>quietly</u> as they considered what life would <u>now</u> be like. With their grandmother's death, life had changed <u>irrevocably</u> <u>for-ever</u>, and they could <u>not</u> bear going <u>inside</u>.

EXERCISE 1.7 (p. 37)

The barking dog chased the frantic squirrel <u>around the house</u> [ADV] and <u>under a bush</u> [ADV]. It was a scene <u>of pathetic comedy</u> [ADJ]. <u>For several moments</u> [ADV] the squirrel's escape seemed hopeless, but fortune suddenly reversed itself. The dog collapsed <u>in exhaustion</u> [ADV], and we breathed a sigh <u>of relief</u> [ADJ].

EXERCISE 1.8 (p. 37)

1. Dylan is the one from whom Luigi always seeks advice.
2. Animal rights is an issue about which I care deeply.
3. For which flavor of ice cream are you going to ask?
4. Rochester is the man with whom Jane Eyre fell in love.

EXERCISE 1.9 (p. 40)

<u>Although</u> Lady Grimshaw offered us <u>both</u> tea <u>and</u> coffee, we refused to take advantage of her hospitality, <u>for</u> the hour was late; <u>however</u>, we agreed to return within a few days.

1. Although = subordinating conjunction
2. both/and = correlative conjunction
3. for = coordinating conjunction
4. however = conjunctive adverb

CHAPTER 1 EXERCISE (p. 42)

Part I

ADJ ADV ADJ N V-T P PREP ADJ N PREP ADJ ADJ N
A strangely familiar portrait faced me during my dinner at the ancestral estate.
CONJ P V-BE ADV ADV ADJ P V-L ADJ PREP ADJ N PREP
Because I am not usually superstitious, I felt upset by the effect of
ADJ N INTER ADJ N V-T P N PREP N CONJ P
that experience. Oh, that portrait gave me nightmares for days, but they

ADV	V-INT	CONJ	P	V-T	ADJ	N	PREP	ADJ	N	CONJ	ADJ
finally	stopped	when	I	investigated	the	history	of	the	house	and	its

N	ADJ	N	PREP	ADJ	N	V-BE	ADJ	N	PREP	P
owner.	The	subject	of	the	portrait	was	an	ancestor	of	mine

CONJ	V-INT	PREP	ADJ	ADJ	N	PREP	ADJ	ADJ	N
and	had fallen	to	a	grisly	death	in	the	previous	century.

Part II

1. book = noun
2. book = (transitive) verb
3. book = adjective
4. up = adverb

5. up = (transitive) verb
6. up = preposition
7. since = preposition
8. since = subordinating conjunction

Part III

Sample sentence containing eight parts of speech:

Oh, all children want love, but they often lack appreciation for parental discipline.

Oh = interjection
all = adjective
children = noun
want = verb
love = noun
but = conjunction

they = pronoun
often = adverb
lack = verb
appreciation = noun
for = preposition
parental = adjective
discipline = noun

EXERCISE 2.1 (p. 48)

1. <u>Photographs</u> of children in various settings | <u>adorn</u> the walls of the gallery.

2. I | <u>have improved</u> my writing skills.

3. <u>Gratitude</u> and <u>self-discipline</u> | <u>are</u> signs of maturity.

4. The <u>people</u> of the village | <u>were</u> angry about the increased taxes.

5. The <u>clerk</u> in our office | <u>should have been</u> aware of the growing technical difficulties of the job.

EXERCISE 2.2 (p. 50)

1. Pattern 1
2. Pattern 3
3. Pattern 2
4. Pattern 1
5. Pattern 2
6. Pattern 3
7. Pattern 1

EXERCISE 2.3 (p. 54)

1. Pattern 2
2. Pattern 2
3. Pattern 3
4. Pattern 3
5. Pattern 1
6. Pattern 2

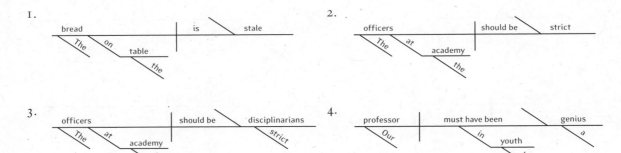

5.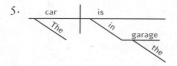

6.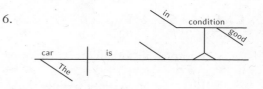

CHAPTER 2 EXERCISE (p. 59)

Part I. A-C

1. The <u>party</u> <u>is</u> here. (*be* verb)

2. The <u>computer</u> (on the desk) <u>was</u> new. (*be* verb)

3. The <u>computer</u> <u>was</u> (on the desk.) (*be* verb)

4. The farewell <u>present</u> <u>should have been</u> John's idea. (*be* verb)

5. The new <u>perfume</u> <u>smelled</u> delightful. (linking verb)

6. <u>Flies</u> <u>are</u> a nuisance (during a picnic.) (*be* verb)

7. <u>Candy</u> <u>can be</u> harmful (in large quantities.) (*be* verb)

8. Our business <u>venture</u> gradually <u>became</u> an embarrassment. (linking verb)

9. The pink <u>slipper</u> <u>was</u> (under the bed.) (*be* verb)

10. (After ten minutes,) Theresa's <u>face</u> <u>grew</u> red (with impatience.) (linking verb)

Part I. D-E

1. Pattern 1

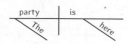

2. Pattern 2

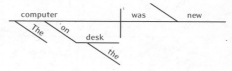

3. Pattern 1

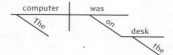

4. Pattern 3

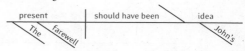

5. Pattern 4

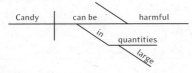

6. Pattern 3

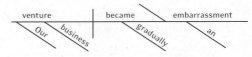

7. Pattern 2

8. Pattern 5

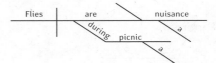

9. Pattern 1

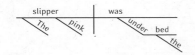

10. Pattern 4

Part II

A. A Pattern 2 sentence ends with a predicate adjective; a Pattern 3 sentence ends with a predicate noun (or predicate nominative).

B. A Pattern 2 sentence contains a *be* verb; a Pattern 4 sentence contains a linking verb. Both end with a predicate adjective. A Pattern 3 sentence contains a *be* verb; a Pattern 5 sentence contains a linking verb. Both end with a predicate noun (or predicate nominative).

C. The back slash mark in Patterns 2 through 5 indicates that the subjective complement refers back to the subject. The back slash mark points toward the subject.

D. A prepositional phrase should be diagramed on a pedestal when it is a predicate adjective; that is, it follows a *be* or linking verb and is essential to complete the meaning of the sentence. Patterns 2 and 4 could contain a pedestal.

E. A linking verb can be replaced by a form of the verb *be*.

EXERCISE 3.1 (p. 66)

1. Pattern 6

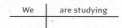

2. Pattern 7

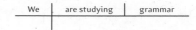

3. Pattern 6

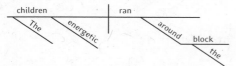

4. Pattern 8

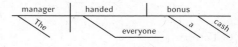

5. Pattern 7

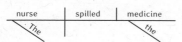

6. Pattern 8

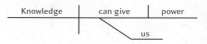

7. Pattern 6

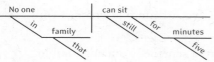

8. Pattern 8

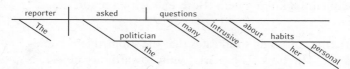

EXERCISE 3.2 A (p. 68)

1.

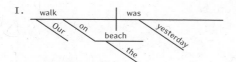

2.

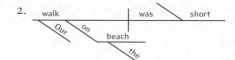

3.

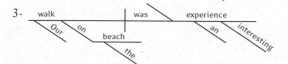

4.

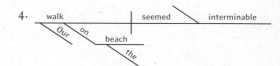

5.
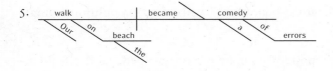

6.
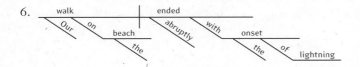

7.
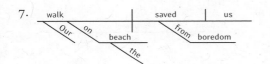

8.
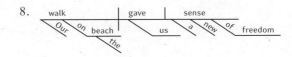

EXERCISE 3.2 B (p. 70)

1. Pattern 1 ends with an adverb of time or place; Pattern 2 ends with a predicate adjective; Pattern 3 ends with a predicate noun or predicate nominative.
2. The slanted line indicates that the subjective complement (the predicate adjective or predicate noun) refers back to the subject. The predicate adjective modifies the subject; the predicate noun renames the subject.
3. The difference is that Pattern 2 contains a form of the *be* verb; Pattern 4 contains a linking verb. Likewise, Pattern 3 contains a form of the *be* verb, while Pattern 5 contains a linking verb. Patterns 2 and 4 end with a predicate adjective; Patterns 3 and 5 end with a predicate noun (or predicate nominative).
4. Pattern 2 ends with a predicate adjective; Pattern 3 ends with a predicate noun.
5. Pattern 4 ends with a predicate adjective; Pattern 5 ends with a predicate noun.
6. A linking verb can be replaced by a form of the *be* verb.
7. Action verbs can be intransitive (no direct object following the verb) or transitive (direct object follows the verb).
8. An intransitive verb has no direct object; a transitive verb is followed by a direct object.
9. Pattern 6 contains an intransitive verb; Pattern 7 contains a transitive verb.
10. A direct object answers the question "whom" or "what" after the verb. The indirect object answers the question "to whom, "for whom," "of whom," "to what," "for what," or "of what."
11. The vertical line indicates that there is no relationship between the subject and the direct object; they are two different entities. The diagonal line is like an arrow pointing back to the subject, or like the curve of a circle encompassing the subjective complement and the subject. The vertical line is like a wall separating the subject from the direct object.

12. The indirect object is always diagramed beneath the verb, on a prepositional phrase structure.
13. The indirect object occurs first.
14. Patterns 2 and 4 could include a prepositional phrase placed on a pedestal IF the predicate adjective is a prepositional phrase rather than a single-word adjective. Because these sentences contain no prepositional phrases used as predicate adjectives (and thus necessary to complete the meaning of the sentence), we find no pedestals in this exercise.

EXERCISE 3.3 (p. 73)

1. Pattern 4

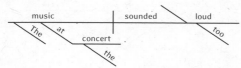

2. Pattern 6

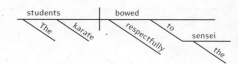

3. Pattern 7

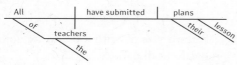

4. Pattern 8

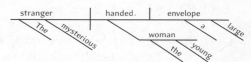

5. Pattern 1

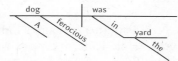

6. Pattern 3

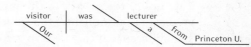

7. Pattern 2

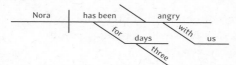

8. Pattern 5

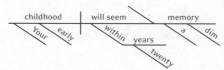

9. Pattern 2

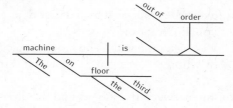

10. Pattern 7

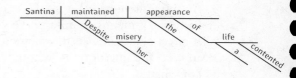

EXERCISE 3.4 (p. 79)

1. Pattern 6
2. Pattern 8
3. Pattern 10
4. Pattern 7
5. Pattern 9
6. Pattern 7
7. Pattern 9
8. Pattern 9

1.

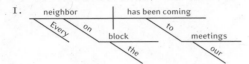

2.

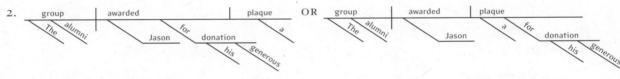 OR

3.

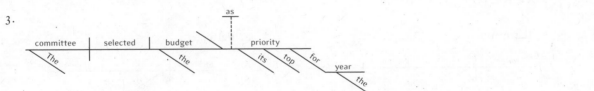

4.

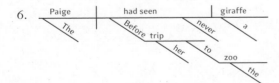

5.

6.

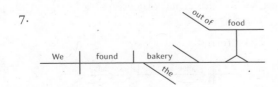

7.

8.

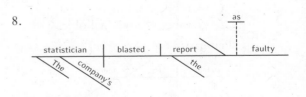

EXERCISE 3.5 (p. 82)

1. Pattern 6

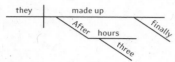

2. Pattern 7

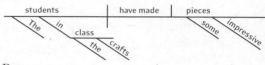

3. Pattern 6

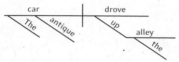

4. Pattern 7

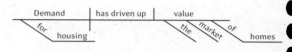

5. Pattern 7

EXERCISE 3.6 (p. 84)

1. Pattern 7

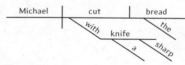

2. Pattern 7

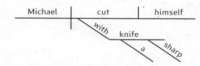

3. Pattern 3

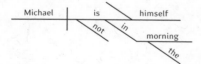

EXERCISE 3.7 (p. 87)

1. October = noun
2. October = adverbial objective
3. times, year = adverbial objectives
4. time = noun

1. Pattern 3

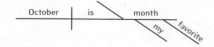

2. Pattern 7

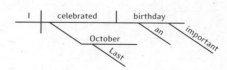

3. Pattern 7

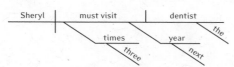

4. Pattern 7

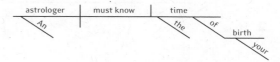

EXERCISE 3.8 (p. 89)

1. Pattern 6

2. Pattern 7

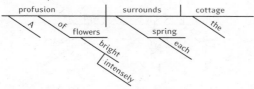

3. Pattern 4

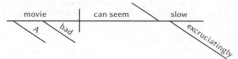

4. Pattern 7

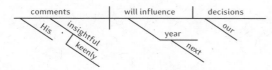

CHAPTER 3 EXERCISE (p. 93)

Part II

1. Pattern 2
2. Pattern 6
3. Pattern 9
4. Pattern 7
5. Pattern 6
6. Pattern 7
7. Pattern 7
8. Pattern 7
9. Pattern 10
10. Pattern 10
11. Pattern 8
12. Pattern 9
13. Pattern 4
14. Pattern 8
15. Pattern 5
16. Pattern 7
17. Pattern 2
(or possibly Pattern 1, if "beyond our reach" is
interpreted as meaning physically impossible to locate)

1.
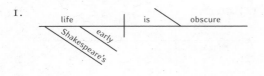

2.
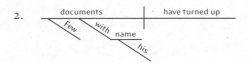

3.
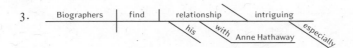

4.
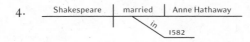

5.

6.

7.
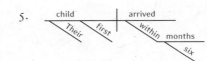

8.
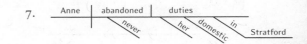

9.
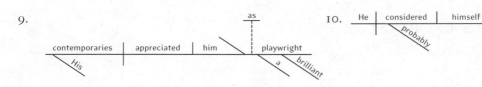

10.

11.
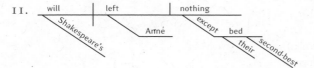

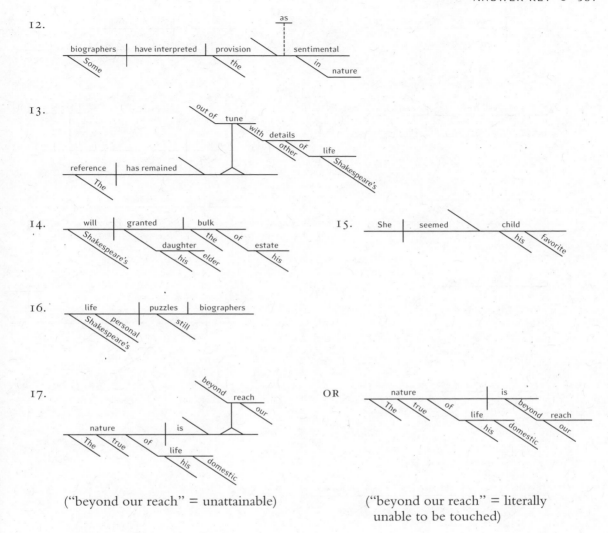

12.

13.

14.

15.

16.

17.

("beyond our reach" = unattainable)

OR

("beyond our reach" = literally
unable to be touched)

Part III

1. Pattern 8
2. Pattern 6
3. Pattern 7
4. Pattern 2
5. Pattern 1

6. Pattern 7
7. Pattern 6
8. Pattern 2
9. Pattern 6
10. Pattern 7

1.

2.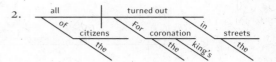

3.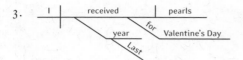

4.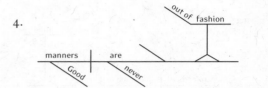

5.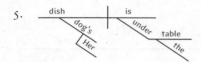

6.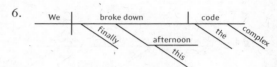

7.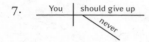

8.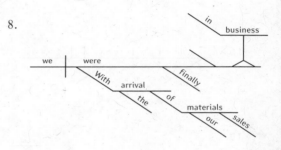

9.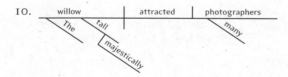

10.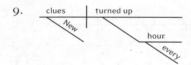

EXERCISE 4.1 (p. 104)

1. well
2. really, well
3. bad
4. bad
5. badly
6. well
7. surely
8. really
9. badly, well
10. sure, Surely

EXERCISE 4.2 (p. 108)

1. All of the students felt *bad* after learning of the professor's illness.
2. Which of these two books did you enjoy *more*?
3. Patricia is the *youngest* student in kindergarten.
4. Brenda always studied hard so that she could do *well* on the tests in her grammar class.
5. After my bout with the flu, I finally felt *well* again.
6. Who is *most* irresponsible—Ned, Tad, or Jason?
7. Mark's goal is to be *more handsome* than his father.
8. Jesse drives *dangerously*.

EXERCISE 4.3 (p. 110)

1. The union negotiators are asking for *only* a small increase in salary.
2. Feed the fish *with small bones in it* to the cat.
3. The noise *from the planes overhead* was tremendous.
4. The child was *almost* in tears by the end of the first day of camp.
5. Good parents want *only* what is best for their children.
6. Tell us *just* the facts of this situation, not your opinion.
7. The picture *above the fireplace* caught everyone's attention.
8. The magician has *even* one more trick up his sleeve.
9. *Not* all items are on sale.
10. We have *only* seven days left before graduation.

CHAPTER 4 EXERCISE (p. 114)

Part I

1. Which one of the twins is the *smarter*?
2. Sarah broke *only* one of the rules, but it was *just* too much to forgive.
3. No one could hear the student who spoke the *most quietly*.
4. The circumstances were *worse* than we had imagined.
5. The veterinarian felt *bad* about the animals that had to be euthanized.
6. The news about the flooding in Texas left us *really* worried about our friends there.

7. CORRECT
8. Margarine tastes better than butter if you eat it *quickly*.
9. CORRECT
10. Kittens *surely* can be curious.
11. Once she felt well, the elderly widow resumed living *with her sister* in the mansion on the corner.
12. The artist's talent was *unique*, as recognized by *almost* all the spectators.

EXERCISE 5.1 (p. 121)

1. Chaucer was not a nobleman, nor was he a commoner.
2. Solitary travel was not safe in the fourteenth century, so the pilgrims traveled together.
3. Chaucer and his contemporaries could write in Latin or English.
4. Chaucer could also write in French, yet he chose English.

EXERCISE 5.2 (p. 124)

1. Mary is my best friend, so I must remember her birthday.
2. The friends were quietly conversing; meanwhile, a burglary was going on in the next room.
3. I am not athletic; I can, however, play tennis and golf.
4. The door opened; then a mysterious figure stepped inside.
5. We waited for hours, but the bus did not appear; finally, we walked into town.
6. Husbands and wives should not reveal their personal lives or their fantasies to strangers.
7. Vegetarianism is admirable; nevertheless, it is not an easy choice.

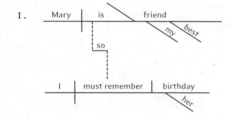

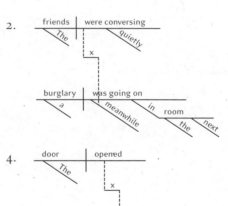

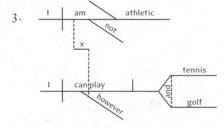

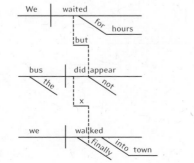

6.

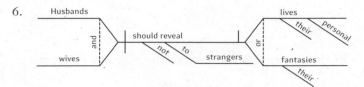

7.

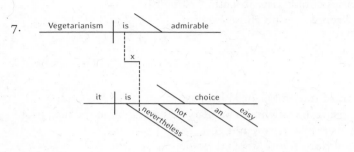

CHAPTER 5 EXERCISE (p. 127)

Part I

1. S
2. CD
3. S
4. CD
5. CD

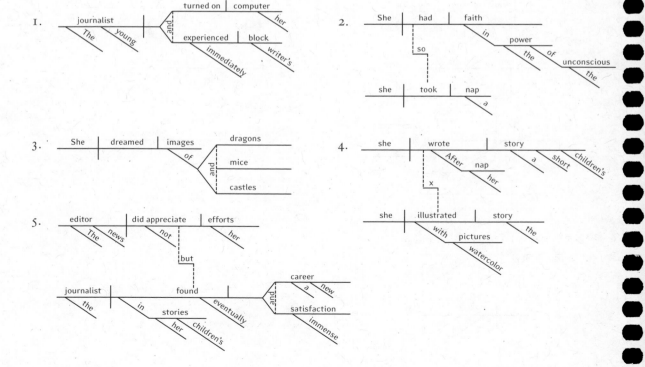

Part II

1. Natasha was frightened of flying, for she had once seen a plane crash.
2. Her entire family was planning a trip overseas; Natasha, however, was reluctant to go.
3. Her mother arranged for her to see a special counselor, so Natasha began working on a series of exercises designed to reduce her fear.
4. After a few months of therapy, Natasha thought that she had overcome her fear; she believed she was cured.
5. She even sat on an empty plane and imagined herself feeling relaxed in the sky. (*no change*)
6. Natasha had done all she could, yet she was not completely prepared for the actual experience of flying.
7. As the jet's engines revved up on the runway, Natasha closed her eyes and breathed deeply; then she fainted.
8. When she regained consciousness, she found herself looking out at wispy clouds of white and at last enjoying the wonder of air travel. (*no change*)
9. Natasha had finally conquered her fear, so she began flying frequently.
10. Family members now refer to Natasha as a professional traveler; moreover, she is happy to share her story with others who are still wrestling with their fear of flying.

Part III (Answers will vary.)

1. The dog was whining at the door, for it was wet and cold outside.
2. Daisy had saved her allowance for months, so she bought the bicycle she wanted.
3. The restaurant has an excellent reputation; however, our meals were not quite as good as we had expected.
4. Nicole was certain that she had seen a ghost, and her roommate agreed with her.
5. Most people believe that wealth will bring them happiness, but the story of Midas proves that this is not necessarily true.

EXERCISE 6.1 (p. 133)

1. <u>What is unusual about the Navajo culture</u> is its respect for all living things. [S]
2. Navajos see <u>how all inhabitants of the natural world are related</u>. [DO]
3. They offer <u>whoever can grasp this concept</u> a sense of unity and connection. [IO]
4. Their explanation of this unity is <u>that the same Supreme Being created all living things</u>. [SC]
5. One of their beliefs, <u>that the Navajo were once victims of a great flood</u>, appears in other cultures as well. [APP]
6. They also believe <u>that the number four is sacred</u>. [DO]
7. With four seasons, four directions, four winds, four sacred mountains, and four sacred colors, the Navajo relate this number to <u>why the universe operates smoothly</u>. [OP]
8. They find progress through four worlds as <u>what is necessary for spiritual growth</u>. [OC]
9. I often wonder <u>when other cultures will discover the wisdom of the Navajo</u>. [DO]
10. Our reaction to their concept of oneness may determine <u>whether humans will survive in the centuries to come</u>. [DO]

EXERCISE 6.2 (p. 138)

1. The messenger asked <u>who was at home</u>. (direct object)
   SENTENCE = Pattern 7; NOUN CLAUSE = Pattern 1
2. <u>What will happen at the party</u> is a secret. (subject)
   SENTENCE = Pattern 3; NOUN CLAUSE = Pattern 6
3. Jay wondered <u>whose advice he should accept</u>. (direct object)
   SENTENCE = Pattern 7; NOUN CLAUSE = Pattern 7
4. Last week the students in the advanced class debated <u>which novel they should read</u>. (direct object) SENTENCE = Pattern 7; NOUN CLAUSE = Pattern 7
5. No one knew <u>whether the performance would continue</u>. (direct object)
   SENTENCE = Pattern 7; NOUN CLAUSE = Pattern 6
6. <u>How Erica would handle her new fortune</u> was <u>what all of us wondered</u>. (subject, subjective complement/predicate noun) SENTENCE = Pattern 3; FIRST NOUN CLAUSE = Pattern 7; SECOND NOUN CLAUSE = Pattern 7
7. Your announcement about <u>where we could find half-price theater tickets</u> helped us immensely. (object of preposition) SENTENCE = Pattern 7; NOUN CLAUSE = Pattern 7
8. Nancy's claim, <u>that she did not love him</u>, baffled Sam. (appositive)
   SENTENCE = Pattern 7; NOUN CLAUSE = Pattern 7
9. Nancy claimed <u>she did not love Sam</u>. (direct object)
   SENTENCE = Pattern 7; NOUN CLAUSE = Pattern 7
10. We asked <u>when the membership drive would begin</u>. (direct object)
    SENTENCE = Pattern 7; NOUN CLAUSE = Pattern 6

1.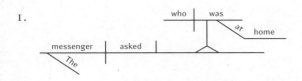

2.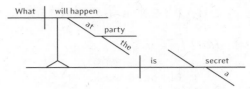

3.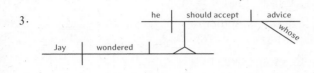

4.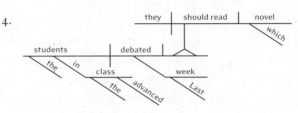

5.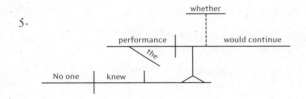

6.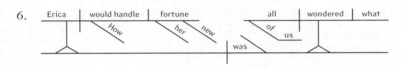

7.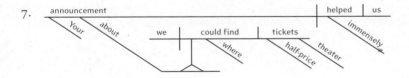

8.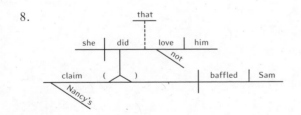

9.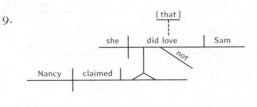

10.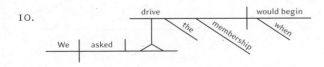

CHAPTER 6 EXERCISE

Part I

1. No one has asked (if) the university can afford twenty new professors.
   (SENTENCE PATTERN = 7; NOUN CLAUSE PATTERN = 7)

2. The question in the minds of many citizens is (whether or not) terrorism can stop.
   (SENTENCE PATTERN = 3; NOUN CLAUSE PATTERN = 6)

3. The burglar thought (that) he could easily escape detection.
   (SENTENCE PATTERN = 7; NOUN CLAUSE PATTERN = 7)

4. (Which) job was most desirable was the foremost question in Ellen's mind.
   (SENTENCE PATTERN = 3; NOUN CLAUSE PATTERN = 2)

5. The children discovered (where) their parents had been hiding the presents.
   (SENTENCE PATTERN = 7; NOUN CLAUSE PATTERN = 7)

6. Your concern, (why) this office has never returned your call, is important.
   (SENTENCE PATTERN = 2; NOUN CLAUSE PATTERN = 7)

7. The reporter interviewed all of the neighbors about (what) had happened.
   (SENTENCE PATTERN = 7; NOUN CLAUSE PATTERN = 6)

8. We debated (whose) situation seemed worse.
   (SENTENCE PATTERN = 7; NOUN CLAUSE PATTERN = 4)

9. The expert salesperson gave (whoever) would listen to her spiel a bonus gift.
   (SENTENCE PATTERN = 8; NOUN CLAUSE PATTERN = 6)

10. The ancient Greeks considered poetry (what) made life worthwhile.
    (SENTENCE PATTERN = 10; NOUN CLAUSE PATTERN = 9)

1.

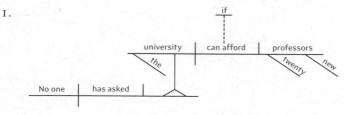

2.   3.

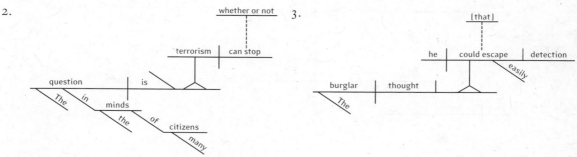

4.

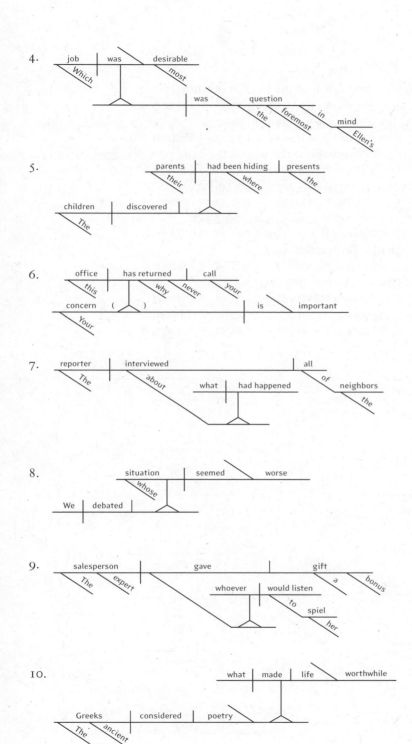

5.

6.

7.

8.

9.

10.

EXERCISE 7.1 (p. 148)

1. <u>After the party ended</u>, we could not find the keys to our hotel room.
   INDEPENDENT CLAUSE = Pattern 7; ADVERB CLAUSE = Pattern 6
2. Bonnie's father bought her a new car for graduation, <u>even though she could not drive</u>.
   INDEPENDENT CLAUSE = Pattern 8; ADVERB CLAUSE = Pattern 6
3. The children held their complaints about the school <u>until the new principal arrived</u>.
   INDEPENDENT CLAUSE = Pattern 7; ADVERB CLAUSE = Pattern 6
4. Dogs are sociable creatures, <u>whereas cats are usually solitary</u>.
   INDEPENDENT CLAUSE = Pattern 3; ADVERB CLAUSE = Pattern 2
5. Wanda will ask me twenty questions <u>unless I can avoid her</u>.
   INDEPENDENT CLAUSE = Pattern 8; ADVERB CLAUSE = Pattern 7
6. <u>Wherever Lucy goes</u>, Charlie Brown follows her.
   INDEPENDENT CLAUSE = Pattern 7; ADVERB CLAUSE = Pattern 6
7. Everyone will suffer <u>if civility vanishes from our social interactions</u>.
   INDEPENDENT CLAUSE = Pattern 6; ADVERB CLAUSE = Pattern 6
8. <u>If civility vanishes from our social interactions</u>, everyone will suffer.
   INDEPENDENT CLAUSE = Pattern 6; ADVERB CLAUSE = Pattern 6

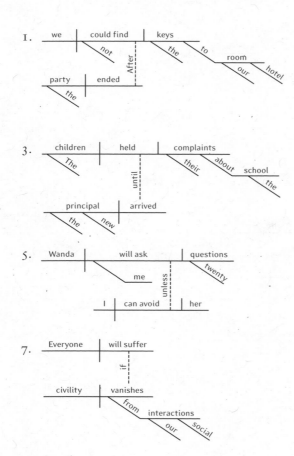

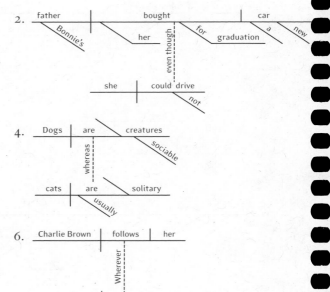

8. same as 7 except for changes in capitalization: "everyone" (now in lower case) and "if" (now capitalized to signal that the adverb clause begins the sentence)

EXERCISE 7.2 (p. 151)

1. <u>If we are grateful for small things</u>, we understand their importance in our lives.
   INDEPENDENT CLAUSE = Pattern 7; ADVERB CLAUSE = Pattern 2

2. I wondered (if the bus would ever arrive.)
   SENTENCE = Pattern 7; NOUN CLAUSE = Pattern 6

3. <u>Since their relationship began</u>, both of them have been extremely jealous.
   INDEPENDENT CLAUSE = Pattern 2; ADVERB CLAUSE = Pattern 6

4. Bob's dilemma, (where he should invest his inheritance,) is an enviable one.
   SENTENCE = Pattern 3; NOUN CLAUSE = Pattern 7

5. Bob asked (where he should invest his inheritance.)
   SENTENCE = Pattern 7; NOUN CLAUSE = Pattern 7

6. <u>Wherever Bob invests his inheritance</u>, he wants a good return on his capital.
   INDEPENDENT CLAUSE = Pattern 7; ADVERB CLAUSE = Pattern 7

7. <u>While the thunder roared</u>, the dog cowered beneath the bed.
   INDEPENDENT CLAUSE = Pattern 6; ADVERB CLAUSE = Pattern 6

8. People learn lessons about life from (whomever they admire during their childhood.)
   SENTENCE = Pattern 7; NOUN CLAUSE = Pattern 7

9. (What our schools need now) is leadership, <u>although I am not advocating more government intervention</u>. INDEPENDENT CLAUSE = Pattern 3; NOUN CLAUSE = Pattern 7; ADVERB CLAUSE = Pattern 7

10. <u>Once we reconcile ourselves to Dean's resignation</u>, we will give assistance to (whoever assumes his duties.) INDEPENDENT CLAUSE = Pattern 7; ADVERB CLAUSE = Pattern 7; NOUN CLAUSE = Pattern 7

1.

2.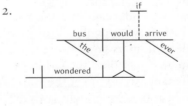

3.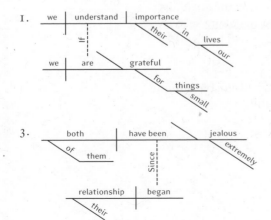

4.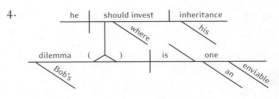

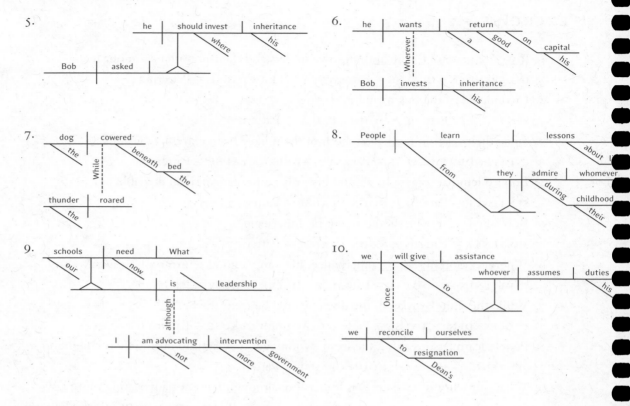

EXERCISE 7.3 (p. 155)

1. The town <u>where I grew up</u> is extremely small.
2. People <u>who have extensive classroom experience</u> are valuable resources for beginning teachers.
3. The printer <u>which we hooked up to the computer</u> is not working properly.
4. The year <u>when they eloped</u> was a difficult one for her parents.
5. I do not understand the reason <u>why we must negotiate secretly</u>.
6. A person <u>whose will is strong</u> can live through bad times.
7. The swimmers saw a turtle <u>that was injured</u>.
8. The manager fired the worker <u>whom she did not like</u>.
9. The table <u>we found at the yard sale</u> is actually a valuable antique.
10. The car <u>that we bought last year</u> is very reliable.

EXERCISE 7.4 (p. 158)

1. Simon, <u>who had just started his diet</u>, woke up at midnight because he was hungry.
2. This old doll, <u>which has been in the closet for years</u>, might be extremely valuable.
3. Wanda framed the first check <u>that she received from her publisher</u>.
4. Many elderly people nostalgically recall their youth as a time <u>when life was simpler</u>.
5. The children <u>who were playing at the end of the block</u> could not hear the shouts of their parents. (Without commas, the relative clause identifies *which* children.)
   OR
   The children, <u>who were playing at the end of the block</u>, could not hear the shouts of their parents. (With commas, the relative clause provides extra information. This sentence can be punctuated with or without commas because, without more context, we do not know how precisely the definite article, "the," defines which children are being referred to here. Note from the diagram below that, with or without commas in the sentence, the sentence diagram remains the same.)
6. Stamp collecting, <u>which can consume much time and money</u>, is an educational hobby.
7. The fugitive concealed the reason <u>why he had no identification</u>.

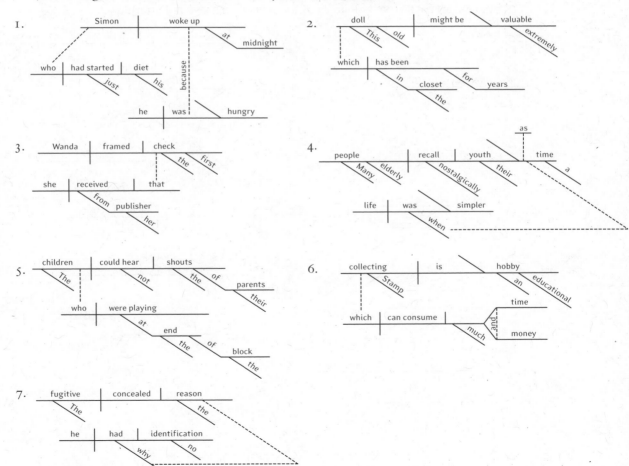

EXERCISE 7.5 (p. 162)

1. Juliet, <u>who has been my friend for ten years</u>, now lives in France.
   INDEPENDENT CLAUSE = Pattern 6; RELATIVE CLAUSE = Pattern 3
2. This young woman, <u>whom many of us admired for her multiple talents</u>, has become a well-known photographer.
   INDEPENDENT CLAUSE = Pattern 5; RELATIVE CLAUSE = Pattern 7
3. She published the first photograph <u>that she submitted to a magazine</u>.
   INDEPENDENT CLAUSE = Pattern 7; RELATIVE CLAUSE = Pattern 7
4. The explanatory letter <u>she wrote</u> caught the attention of the editor.
   INDEPENDENT CLAUSE = Pattern 7; RELATIVE CLAUSE = Pattern 7
5. Juliet still remembers the desolate place <u>where she took the photo</u>.
   INDEPENDENT CLAUSE = Pattern 7; RELATIVE CLAUSE = Pattern 7
6. Photography, <u>which requires intelligence and creativity</u>, is a perfect match for Juliet's natural gifts.
   INDEPENDENT CLAUSE = Pattern 3; RELATIVE CLAUSE = Pattern 7
7. I understand the reasons <u>why Juliet has been so tremendously successful in this field</u>.
   INDEPENDENT CLAUSE = Pattern 7; RELATIVE CLAUSE = Pattern 2

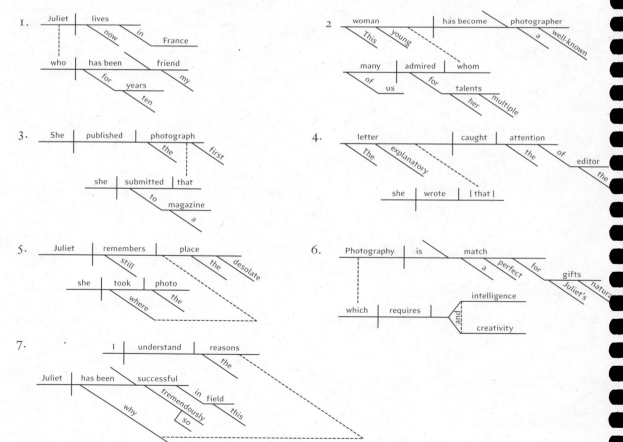

EXERCISE 7.6 (p. 164)

1. Relative clause
2. Appositive
3. Relative clause
4. Relative clause
5. Appositive that contains a relative cause

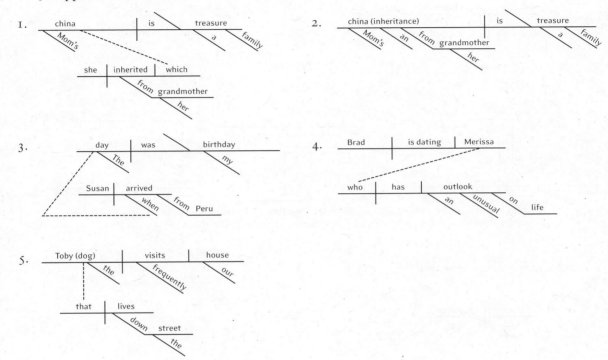

CHAPTER 7 EXERCISE (p. 170)

Part I

1. <u>After we found the puppy</u>, we took it to the animal shelter. [A]
2. The puppy <u>that we found</u> was friendly and playful. [R]
3. Helen's computer, <u>which was quite old</u>, remained reliable. [R]
4. Helen's computer remained reliable, <u>although it was quite old</u>. [A]
5. Everyone <u>who was on the team</u> appreciated Coach Tina. [R]
6. Bethany, <u>who was on the team</u>, appreciated Coach Tina. [R]
7. Coach Tina complimented the team <u>because each player had worked hard during the season</u>. [A]

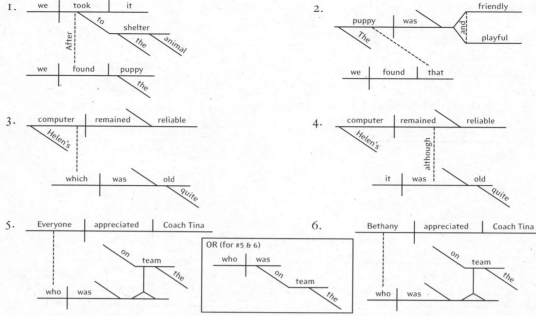

In 5 and 6, diagraming "on the team" on a pedestal, as a Pattern 4 sentence, emphasizes team membership; diagraming "on the team" beneath the verb, as a Pattern 1 sentence, emphasizes physical location.]

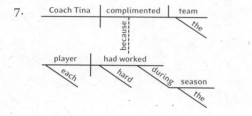

Part II

1. Princess Lila, <u>who had slept for a century</u>, suddenly awakened. [R]
2. The evil fairy <u>whom the queen had employed as a guardian</u> had finally died. [R]
   OR
   The evil fairy, <u>whom the queen had employed as a guardian</u>, had finally died. [R]
3. The princess thought <u>that she had slept for a short time</u>. [N]
4. The first conversation <u>that she held</u> confused her. [R]
5. <u>When she heard an unfamiliar language</u>, she grew frightened. [A]
6. She grew even more frightened <u>until she looked in a mirror</u>. [A]
7. The sight of her own face reassured her at the moment <u>when she needed a friend</u>. [R]
8. <u>Although most princesses depend on handsome princes</u>, Lila took matters into her own hands. [A]

9. She took responsibility for <u>what happened from that moment</u>. [N]
10. Soon Lila wondered <u>if her memories of an earlier lifetime were real</u>. [N]

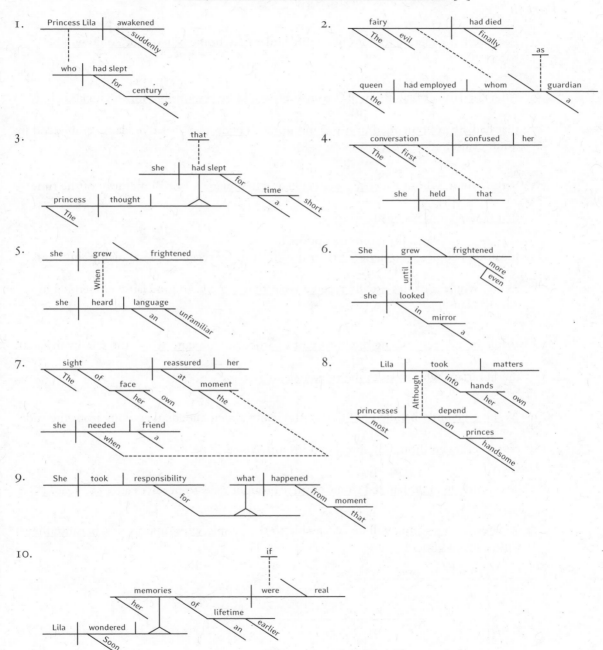

CHAPTER 7 EXERCISE

Part III

1. <u>Because I am allergic to dogs</u>, [A] we must find a new home <u>where our collie will be happy</u>. [R]

2. <u>After the lawyer read the will</u>, [A] I realized <u>I would be responsible for the locked chest</u> [N] <u>that had always remained in my grandmother's bedroom</u>. [R] (relative clause embedded in noun clause)

3. Seth Brown, <u>whom everyone respected as a fine pianist</u>, [R] lost all memory of the tune <u>that had been in his head</u>. [R]

4. Idealistic people, <u>who fight for their dreams</u>, [R] [commas optional] usually receive several disappointments in life, <u>whereas cynics usually receive</u> [A] <u>what they expect</u>. [N] (noun clause embedded in adverb clause)

5. <u>While he was researching the history of a particularly obscure word</u>, [A] the scholar irritated the librarians <u>who were in the reference area</u>. [R]

6. <u>As she efficiently handled her duties</u>, [A] the waitress demanded an apology from the rude customer, <u>even though he protested his innocence</u>. [A]

7. The note <u>the child handed to his mother</u> [R] brought tears to her eyes <u>after she read it</u>. [A]

8. <u>Whatever you decide</u> [N] will be acceptable to the people <u>who support you</u> [R] <u>because they trust your judgment</u>. [A]

1.

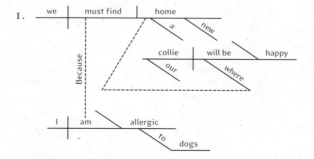

2.

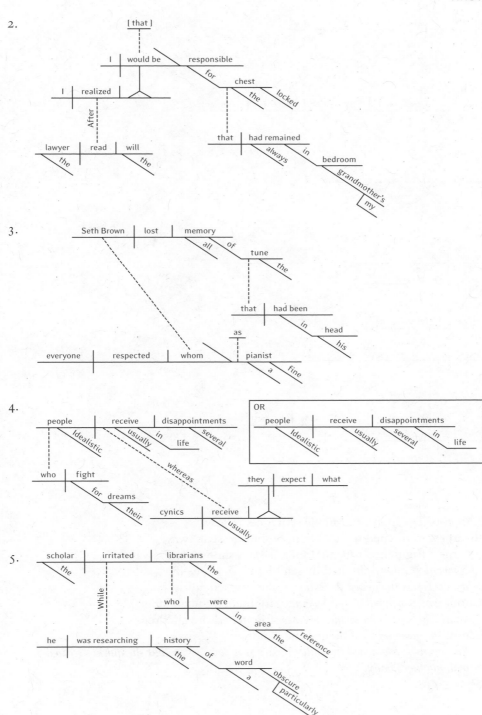

3.

4.

5.

6.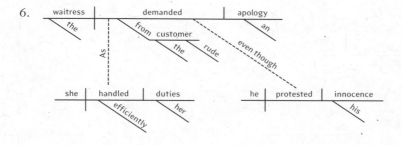

7.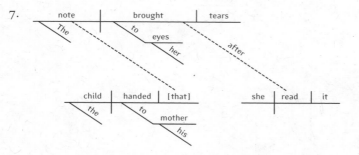

8.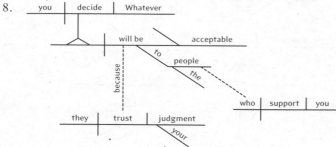

Part IV

Answers will, of course, vary, but example sentences follow.

- a. The governess frightened the children, *so* she was sent away.
- b. The governess frightened the children; *therefore*, she was sent away.
- c. *What the governess said* frightened the children.
- d. *Because the governess frightened the children*, she was sent away.
- e. Miss Eaton, *who was hired as the governess*, frightened the children.
- f. The woman *who was hired as the governess* frightened the children.
- g. Miss Eaton, *the governess*, frightened the children.
- h. *Because the governess frightened the children*, she was sent away, *but she quickly secured a position with another family.*

Part V

Answers will vary, but here is an example of how to combine the sentences in this passage:

Great Expectations, a novel by Charles Dickens, tells the story of Pip, a young orphan who lives with his rather cruel, cold sister and her good-hearted husband. Eventually Pip attracts the attention of a wealthy woman named Miss Havisham. Years ago, she was jilted on her wedding day. She still wears her wedding dress and has the wedding cake; in fact, nothing has changed since the day of the jilting. Even the clock has been stopped. She has taken in a young girl named Estella, with whom Pip falls in love. Miss Havisham has trained Estella to break the hearts of young men, a skill that allows Miss Havisham some measure of satisfaction since it is a way of imposing vengeance upon men in return for her own jilting. Pip, Estella, and Miss Havisham are three of the most memorable characters created by Charles Dickens, an author famous for distinctive characters.

EXERCISE 8.1 (p. 185)

1. were	9. Does
2. was	10. was
3. is	11. wants
4. were	12. were
5. was	13. were
6. are	14. were
7. has	15. has
8. have	

EXERCISE 8.2 (p. 188)

Sentences 2 and 5 have been rephrased.
1. Someone left keys on the table.
2. All of the people who saw the film said that they disliked the ending.
3. The Spanish Club decided to revamp its constitution.
4. It took several days before the jury returned with a verdict. [OR its verdict]
5. Anyone who lived through the 1960s can relate memories of the era.

EXERCISE 8.3 (p. 192)

1. who	7. he [has been]
2. Who	8. him
3. whoever	9. Whoever
4. whom	10. whom
5. them	11. they [could]
6. We	12. Jill and I

EXERCISE 8.4 (p. 194)

1. one another's
2. themselves
3. me
4. each other
5. them

EXERCISE 8.5 (p. 196)

Revised by using second person:

For many people, being the perfect host is not as easy as it seems. While you are cooking, you are simultaneously supposed to be engaging in witty conversation. And how do you check the toilet paper supply or change the bed sheets without feeling as if you are invading the guest's privacy? The perfect host is just a myth; he never really existed. [OR The perfect host is just a myth; he or she never really existed. OR The perfect host is just a myth that never really existed.]

Revised by using third person plural:

For many people, being the perfect host is not as easy as it seems. While they are cooking, they are simultaneously supposed to be engaging in witty conversation. And how do they check the toilet paper supply or change the bed sheets without feeling as if they are invading the guest's privacy? Perfect hosts are just myths; they never really existed.

EXERCISE 8.6 (p. 197)

Notice that in the examples below, the first sentence rephrases the original, while the second retains the original sentence but places a noun before the relative clause. The relative clause now modifies the noun, not the entire sentence preceding it. You may also find other ways to correct the broad-reference "which" errors of the original sentences.

1. Hemingway's trademark, using short sentences, makes his style the antithesis of Faulkner's. OR Hemingway's trademark is to use short sentences, a style that is the antithesis of Faulkner's.
2. Spending all of my money on graduate school depressed me. OR All of my money was spent on graduate school, a huge expense that depressed me.
3. Because he hated classical music, he was incompatible with Rhonda. OR He hated classical music, a trait that made him incompatible with Rhonda.

CHAPTER 8 EXERCISE (p. 199)

Revised by using third person plural:

Students must know how to study effectively and efficiently. They can study with other students, for example, and help one another. The "buddy method," as it is called, usually works better than having students working by themselves. Studying in pairs or groups is especially helpful for those who are in need of motivation and discipline; it also helps if students compare notes to see if they agree on the key concepts to be learned. Students can usually improve their grades substantially just by being able to distinguish major points from minor ones. An entire class can improve its average if everyone studies together. The "buddy method" is such an effective tool that it should not be kept a secret. Between you and me [OR Between us], we can spread the word to many other students and thereby achieve widespread scholastic success.

Revised by using second person:

You must know how to study effectively and efficiently. You can study with another student, for example, and help each other. The "buddy method," as it is called, usually is more effective than having a student working alone. Studying in pairs or groups is especially helpful if you are in need of motivation and discipline; it also helps if you compare notes to see if you agree with others on the key concepts to be learned. You can usually improve your grade substantially just by being able to distinguish major points from minor ones. An entire class can improve its average if everyone studies together. The "buddy method" is such an effective tool that it should not be kept a secret. Between you and me, we can spread the word to many other students and lead the way to widespread scholastic success.

EXERCISE 9.1 (p. 205)

1. Past perfect progressive
2. Future perfect
3. Present progressive
4. Past
5. Present perfect
6. Past perfect progressive
7. Future progressive
8. Future perfect progressive

EXERCISE 9.2 (p. 205)

1. could have found
2. am looking
3. had been skating

EXERCISE 9.3 (p. 209)

1. ACTIVE—past perfect progressive
2. PASSIVE—past perfect
3. ACTIVE—past progressive
4. PASSIVE—future perfect
5. ACTIVE—future progressive
6. ACTIVE—present perfect
7. PASSIVE—past
8. ACTIVE—future perfect progressive
9. ACTIVE—present perfect progressive
10. PASSIVE—present perfect

EXERCISE 9.4 (p. 210)

1. may be selling (active voice; be + present participle = progressive aspect)
2. may be sold (passive voice; be + past participle = passive voice)
3. will have been taken (passive voice; be + past participle = passive voice)
4. ought to be going (active voice; be + present participle = progressive aspect)
5. should have gone (active voice; have + past participle = perfect aspect)

EXERCISE 9.5 (p. 210)

1. ACTIVE—Pattern 7
   PASSIVE—The blocks were placed in a tall column by the child.
2. ACTIVE—Pattern 10
   PASSIVE—The poodle was named Hollywood by the actor.
3. PASSIVE—Pattern 8
   ACTIVE—A nurse should give you your medicine.
4. PASSIVE—Pattern 7
   ACTIVE—The painfully loud noise of the machinery damaged Lola's ears.
5. ACTIVE—Pattern 7
   PASSIVE—Any mention of the violent incident on campus was omitted by the newspaper.
6. PASSIVE—Pattern 7
   ACTIVE—I finished my research paper in an hour.
7. PASSIVE—Pattern 7
   ACTIVE—My best friend made the wreath on the door.

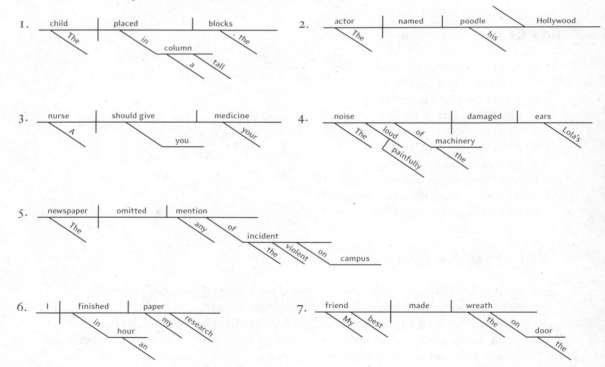

CHAPTER 9 EXERCISE (p. 215)

Part I

1. She is giving
2. She had given
3. She will give
4. She will be giving

Part II

1. An uplifting melody was sung by the choir.
2. Did the choir sing an uplifting melody?
3. The choir could (may, might, would, should) sing an uplifting melody.

Part III

Although sentences will vary, the example sentences illustrate the verb forms that should appear:

1. She *has gone* (or "They *have gone*") to work every day.
2. You *should* obey the rules.
3. Emily *does* enjoy her gymnastics classes.
4. The baby swallowed the marshmallow.
5. The marshmallow was swallowed by the baby.
6. Mrs. Buchanan *had been reading* aloud to the class each day for a month before she realized that no one was listening.
7. The door to the secret chamber *is closing*.
8. You *may* stay out late tonight if you wish.
9. You *can* see the moon clearly through this telescope.
10. The lifeguard *had swum* half a mile before she spotted the child.
11. Carl *drank* all of the beer at the party.
12. I wish I *were* rich. OR My friends have demanded that I *be* more flexible in the future.

Part IV

1. past tense, progressive aspect, active voice
2. past tense, passive voice
3. future tense, perfect progressive aspect, active voice
4. past tense, perfect aspect, active voice
5. present tense, progressive aspect, active voice
6. present tense, perfect aspect, active voice
7. present tense, perfect aspect, passive voice

EXERCISE 10.1 (p. 221)

1. No one wanted <u>to accept Dracula's invitation to the castle</u>.
2. <u>To become wealthy</u> is not the primary objective in life.
3. Elizabeth's dream, <u>to live in England</u>, might become a reality.
4. <u>To be healthy</u> is <u>to possess the first key to happiness</u>.
5. The rabbits wanted <u>to eat the lettuce in our garden</u>.

1.
2.
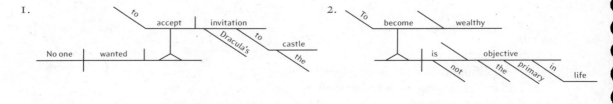

3.
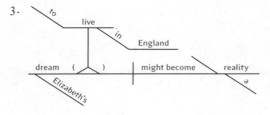

4.
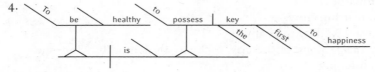

5.
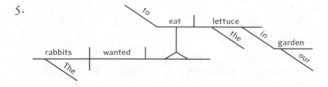

EXERCISE 10.2 (p. 224)

1. <u>To be friendly</u>, we invited our new neighbors to dinner.
2. Sarah enrolled in a review course <u>to increase her chances of a high score on the SAT</u>.
3. The cat was ready <u>to pounce on the unsuspecting mouse</u>.
4. <u>To find your soulmate</u>, you must be open to all possibilities.
5. Some people are unable <u>to smile at adversity</u>.

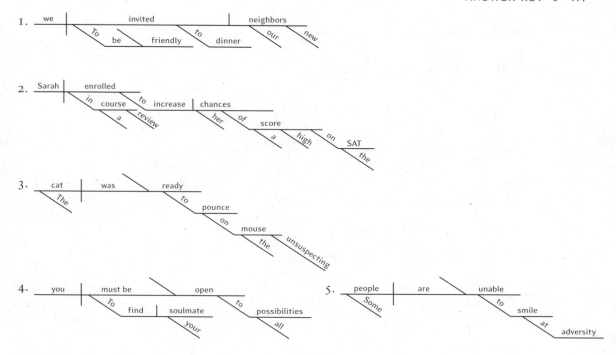

EXERCISE 10.3 (p. 226)

1. <u>To learn his multiplication tables</u>, Mark decided ⟨to construct a math game.⟩

2. Everyone was eager <u>to hear about the new coach</u> in order <u>to determine the team's chances of success.</u>

3. ⟨To be responsible for a pet⟩ is ⟨to demonstrate maturity.⟩

4. <u>To be responsible for a pet</u>, you must volunteer ⟨to make a few personal sacrifices.⟩

1.

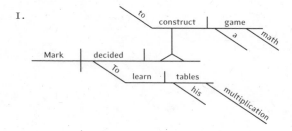

2.
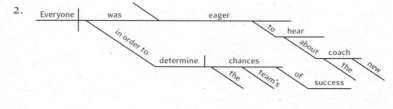

3.
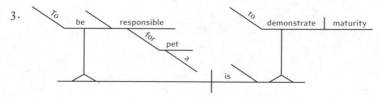

4.
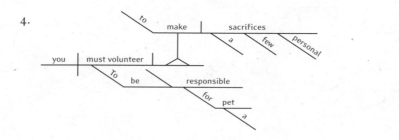

EXERCISE 10.4 (p. 227)

1. The best coffee <u>to drink</u> is this blend of two flavors.
2. Sheila asked a question about which letter <u>to type first</u>.
3. No one told us the password <u>to use for entry into the chatroom</u>.

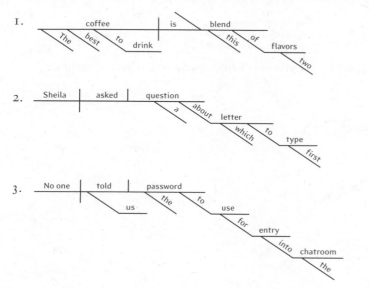

EXERCISE 10.5 (p. 230)

1. No one was going <u>to ask for a favor</u>.
2. No one was going to the concert.
3. Your attitude has <u>to change</u>.
4. Their goal is to increase sales by the end of the month.
5. The salespeople are <u>to increase their quotas</u> in order to receive a bonus.

1.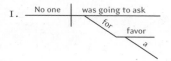

2.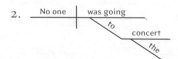

3.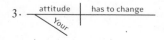

4.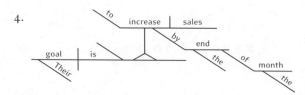

5.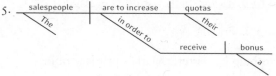

EXERCISE 10.6 (p. 231)

1. Many executives would like <u>to have more free time</u>.

2. Josh wears boots (to appear taller)

3. The best time to study is now.

4. Will was happy (to find his sister.)

5. The best way to eat pancakes is <u>to smother them with syrup</u>.

6. (To stay young,) you have <u>to maintain an optimistic outlook</u>.

1.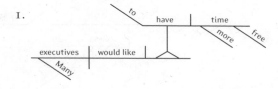

2.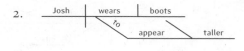

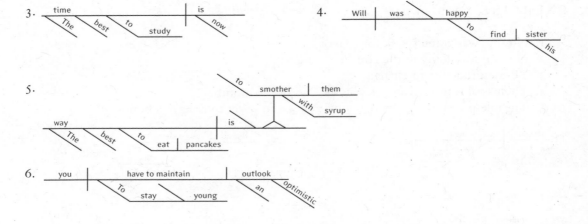

EXERCISE 10.7 (p. 232)

1. To escape from the maze, Tina decided to mark her path with bits of paper.

2. The last day to withdraw from this course is Friday.

3. When she arrived in the United States to help her sister, Maria's primary objective was to establish permanent residency.

4. Whoever has to know this information must prove security clearance to see it.

5. A gardener who waters faithfully will be able to display beautiful flowers.

6. The refrigerator that Jim bought was too big to fit into the kitchen.

7. If you try to complete this crossword puzzle, you will probably fail.

8. My mother read novels to learn about places that she could never visit.

9. Many scholars believe that children read fairy tales to cope with their fears about adult culture.

10. If you are afraid to travel by plane, you should cancel your trip to Europe.

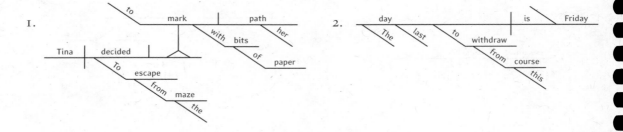

3.

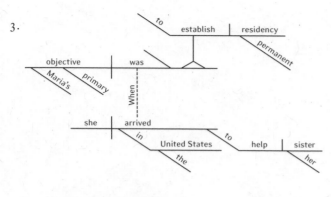

4.

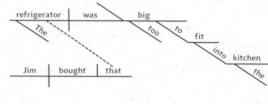

5.

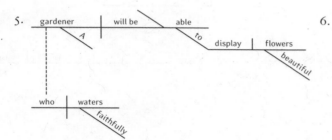

6.

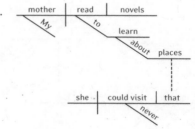

7.

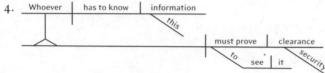

8.

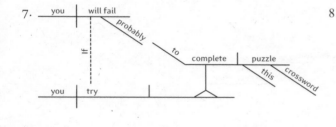

9.

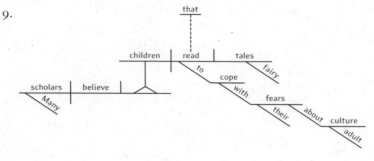

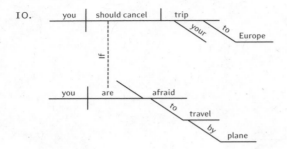

EXERCISE 10.8 (p. 236)

1. Knowing = GERUND; learning = PROGRESSIVE VERB
2. dripping = GERUND; making = PROGRESSIVE VERB
3. visiting = PROGRESSIVE VERB; hearing = GERUND

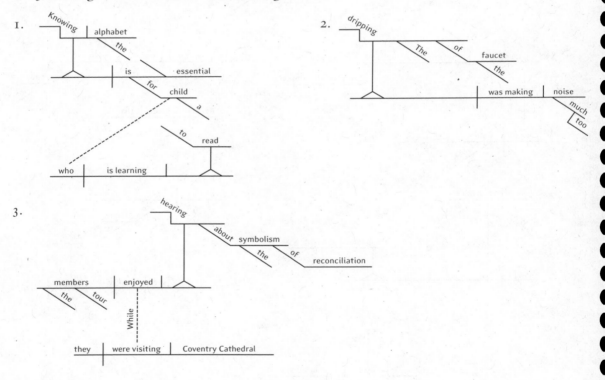

EXERCISE 10.9 (p. 237)

1. <u>Giving her parents headaches</u> is Alison's pastime.
2. His occupation, <u>transcribing medical records</u>, demands special skills.
3. The children were enthusiastic about <u>experimenting with hydrogen</u>.
4. The ancient Romans enjoyed <u>building structures to improve the comforts of everyday life</u>.
5. Tony has been searching for help in <u>tracing his ancestry</u>.

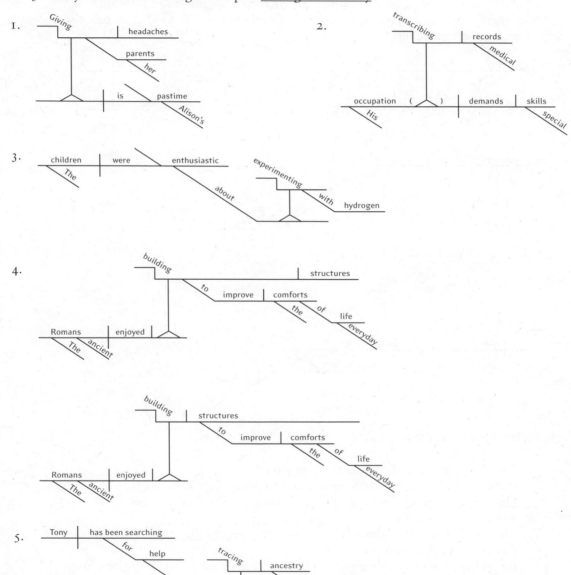

EXERCISE 10.10 (p. 243)

1. <u>Considering her options carefully</u>, Theresa chose the safest course.
2. Everyone <u>saving money at this bank</u> will receive a bonus interest rate.
3. The children found the goat <u>limping on a cracked hoof</u>.
4. The children found the goat, <u>having searched for hours</u>.
5. In the nursery we saw twenty <u>sleeping</u> babies <u>nestled in their cribs</u>.

("Cracked" in sentence 3 and "sleeping" in sentence 5 are pre-noun participles. If you over-looked them, don't worry; it is usually more important to be able to identify participial phrases than single-word participles.)

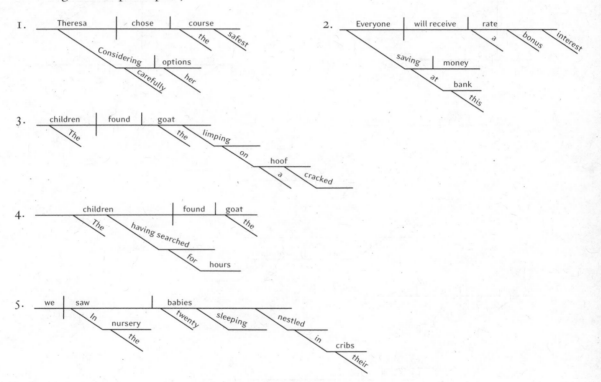

EXERCISE 10.11 (p. 245)

1. The dream of many people is <u>to write a book</u>.
   INFINITIVE USED AS NOUN (subjective complement); Pattern 7
2. <u>Handing the waiter her meal</u>, the irate customer asked for the chef.
   PARTICIPLE; Pattern 8
3. The toddler could not describe the monster <u>hiding in the closet</u>.
   PARTICIPLE; Pattern 6
4. <u>Being happy</u> is a laudable goal in life.
   GERUND; Pattern 2
5. <u>To select Paul as their guide</u>, the tour participants took a vote among themselves.
   INFINITIVE USED AS ADVERB; Pattern 10

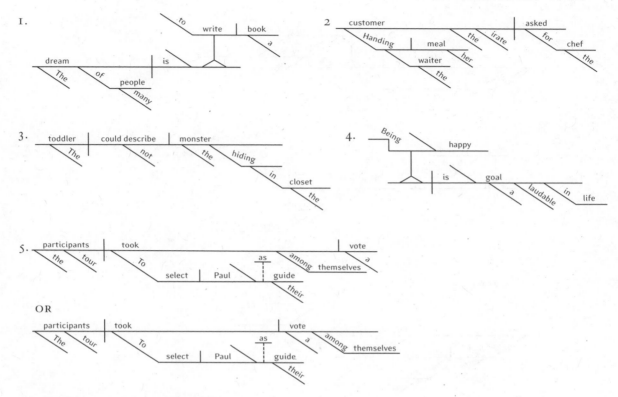

CHAPTER 10 EXERCISE

1. Ignoring the legal drinking age, Rose began to enjoy two glasses of wine with every meal.

2. Drinking wine with breakfast led to arguments with her protesting parents.

3. After a month, Rose stopped causing everyone concern, dropping wine entirely from her diet.

4. To understand this phenomenon, her parents tried to ask questions.

5. Rose, refusing to explain anything, was already experimenting with her next dietary change.

6. Again no one was eager to eat breakfast with Rose.

7. Pouring mustard on her sweetened cereal, Rose managed to make everyone except herself sick.

1.
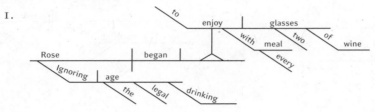

2.
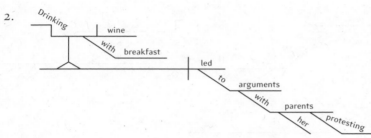

3.
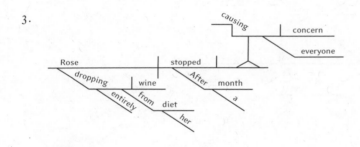

4.
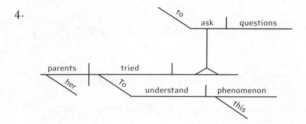

5.
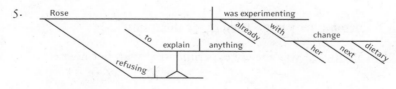

6.
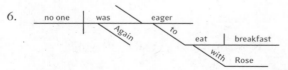

7.

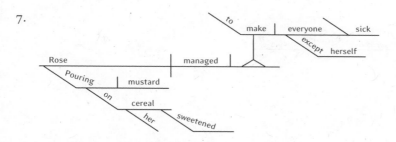

EXERCISES TO REVIEW CLAUSES AND VERBALS (p. 250)

Part I

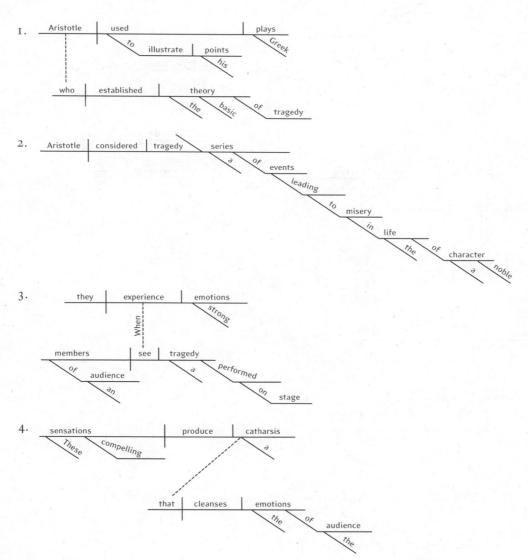

5.

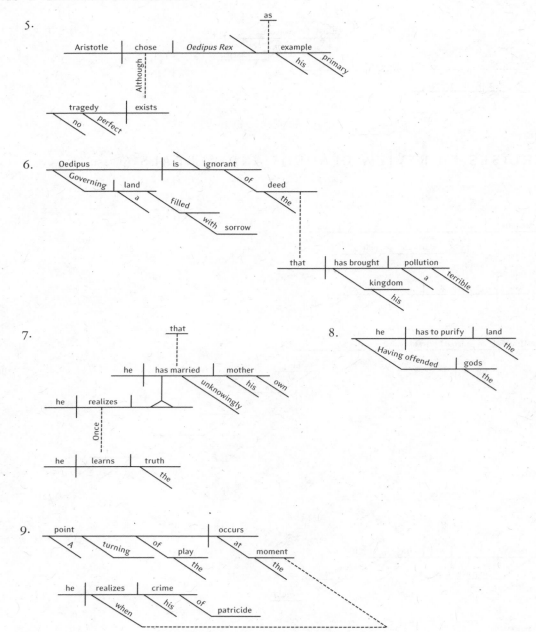

6.

7.

8.

9.

10.

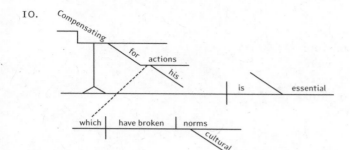

11.

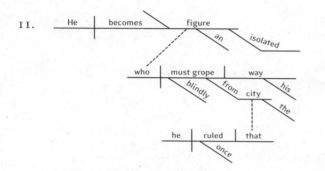

12.

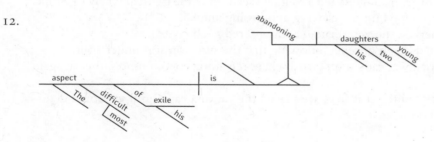

EXERCISE 11.1 (p. 258)

1. were	6. were
2. were	7. were
3. was	8. was
4. were	9. drink
5. come	10. was

EXERCISE 11.2 (p. 261)

1. set	6. lay
2. lay	7. laid
3. rising	8. raises
4. lie	9. set
5. lain	10. sat, lying

EXERCISE 11.3 (p. 263)

1. The veterinarian examined the stray cat limping on a front paw.
2. After the veterinarian administered a routine vaccination, the cat tried wildly to escape.
3. A technician scooped up the clawing and hissing animal.
4. To calm its nerves, the veterinarian administered a sedative.
5. We all breathed a sigh of relief, knowing that the situation was under control.
6. The veterinarian was caught off guard when, regaining consciousness, the cat again attacked us.
7. Although tempted to set it free, we placed the cat in a cage until we could determine what to do next.

EXERCISE 11.4 (p. 265)

1. You must study math for years to understand clearly some of the more complex concepts.
2. All ten siblings in Brittni's family insist that they want to stay close to one another always.
3. To manage a restaurant efficiently, you need to be on the premises constantly.

(Other answers are also possible.)

EXERCISE 11.5 (p. 267)

1. Martha's
2. our
3. mother's

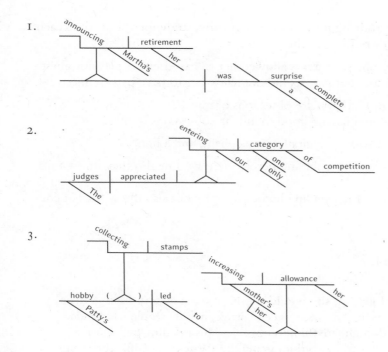

1.
2.
3.

EXERCISE 11.6 (p. 270)

1. The apartment could be rented by the week, by the month, or by the year.
   The apartment could be rented by the week, the month, or the year.
   The apartment could be rented on a weekly, monthly, or yearly basis.

2. Barbara likes to read Tolstoy, sketch landscapes, and run in marathons.
   Barbara likes to read Tolstoy, to sketch landscapes, and to run in marathons.
   Barbara likes reading Tolstoy, sketching landscapes, and running in marathons.

3. Losing his wife to another man, his self-control to liquor, and the custody of his daughter to the authorities brought Andy to the brink of despair.

4. We wondered whether to watch television or to study.
   We wondered whether we should watch television or study.

5. The doctor not only located but also removed the diseased organ.
   Not only did the doctor locate the diseased organ, but he also removed it.

6. The bus driver had to decide either to swerve into the ditch or to risk a head-on collision.
   The bus driver could either swerve into the ditch or risk a head-on collision.

7. The project members drank coffee, smoked cigars, and discussed until dawn all of the near-tragic events of the day.

8. Follow three rules when studying for an exam: start early, study for a short time each day, and get a good night's rest before the exam.

9. When Anna was growing up, her parents allowed her to have neither pets nor guests.
   When Anna was growing up, her parents did not allow her to have pets or guests.

10. Both gourmet food and good friends are obsessions of mine.
    Both eating gourmet food and having good friends are obsessions of mine.

11. No respectable zoo can be without a giraffe, an elephant, and a lion.

12. Not only did the fans cheer as the parading heroes went by, but also they threw tons of confetti into the street.
    The fans not only cheered as the parading heroes went by but also threw tons of confetti into the street.

CHAPTER 11 EXERCISE

If Snow White were a real person, she would not have been able to lie in a deep sleep for many years. As she waited for her prince to arrive, her life would have ended. Because this is a fairy tale, though, anything is possible—his rescuing her, her rising up from an enchanted slumber to marry him gratefully. When we think about the story, the wicked stepmother comes to mind as well. She lays her plans subtly, sets a trap for Snow White, and all the while pretends to be a doting parent. She demands that her mirror tell her every day that she is the fairest in the land. To remove competition, she must remove Snow White, but the wicked stepmother is doomed forever after Snow White returns to life. It is rather disturbing to think that many young girls hear this story as they are lying in their beds. Are they wondering if perhaps they, too, will never be able to wake up? Could a loving mother turn into a wicked stepmother without the daughter's being aware of it? After she argues with her mother, is it possible that this story would come to mind in some way? Perhaps it is time that we either sit down with our daughters to analyze fairy tales more critically or discontinue passing these tales through the generations.

EXERCISE 12.1 (p. 280)

Rule 1

1. That wall clock looks expensive, but it doesn't work.
2. He likes to buy expensive clothes but hates to pay the bills.
3. The lights went out, so the guests had to leave early.
4. The store will have to stay open longer, or it will lose money.
5. John has a large garden, for he loves to grow vegetables.

Rule 2

1. When the snow stopped, we were able to leave.
2. Because I am tired, I am going to bed early tonight.
3. As the stage curtain rose, the audience applauded.
4. Dogs crave companionship, whereas cats prefer solitude.
5. Although English is offered only in the mornings, you can take chemistry at night.
6. Watching television tends to make me passive, while listening to the radio energizes me.
7. George is never aware of what is happening around him while he is immersed in a book.
8. We stayed on the beach until the sun went down.

Rule 3

1. I don't know how to play chess; however, I would like to learn.
2. My brother loves music; in fact, he plays in a local band.
3. Ron is an effective manager; therefore, he has been promoted.
4. I heard a strange howling outside the window; then I buried myself beneath the covers.
5. Jay has poor eyesight; consequently, he cannot play on the basketball team.
6. I would like to learn many things; for example, I have always wanted to take ballet lessons.
7. Historical evidence for the existence of Troy has been found; hence the *Iliad* has taken on new meaning. (NOTE: You are also correct if you insert a comma after "hence.")

Rule 4

1. Wagging its tail, the puppy barked in excitement.
2. By four in the afternoon, everyone wanted to go home.
3. No, I don't want any more ice cream.
4. On every Fourth of July, we salute the American flag.
5. Oh, I love the mountains in the spring!

434 ● GRAMMAR BY DIAGRAM

6. Reluctantly, the students left the classroom.
7. Exhausted by our long day, we fell asleep quickly.
8. During the power blackout, many people tried to help one another.
9. Opening her umbrella, she dashed into the rain.
10. Ignored by the policeman, the town drunk always slept in the park.

Rule 5

1. Contemporary women often try to be wives, mothers, and career professionals.
2. Bill wants to go to the shore, his wife wants to go to the mountains, and their children don't want to go anywhere.
3. I enjoy biking and skating and swimming.
4. The salesman found a television, a blender, and a hair dryer in the used car.
5. Sylvia will be happy to read your poem, comment on it, and return it to you.

Rule 6

1. Emerson gave a short, interesting speech.
2. The green, crunchy lettuce was delicious.
3. The crunchy green lettuce was delicious.
4. The girls were screaming in scared, high voices.
5. The intelligent young woman was interesting to talk to.
6. The bright, creative man was her husband.
7. The impressive brick structure was actually a facade.

Rule 7

1. Susan moved on May 1, 1990, from Fort Lauderdale, Florida, to Cape May, New Jersey.
2. A new store opened at 300 North Road, San Jose, California 95135.
3. People in Charleston, South Carolina, are very friendly toward visitors.
4. I received my first Christmas gift in December 1977 from the man who would become my husband.
   OR
   I received my first Christmas gift in December, 1977, from the man who would become my husband.
5. My teacher taught in London, England, from September 1, 1992, to June 15, 1993.

Rule 8

1. The class feels, Professor Crow, that you should retire.
2. My mother, not my father, disciplined the children.
3. These peaches, believe it or not, were grown in my backyard.
4. Everyone admires Larry, who always sees the bright side of a bad situation.
5. My twin sister, who spends a lot of time at the gym, is in excellent shape.
6. A person who spends a lot of time at the gym should be in excellent shape.
7. Watch out for Phil, a man whose ambition rules him.
8. The movie starts soon, doesn't it?
9. Where did you put my books, Tom?
10. And now, my friends, we will examine the evidence.
11. His wife, Belinda, speaks French and Spanish.
12. Coin collecting, which teaches a great deal about history, is also fun.
13. Her favorite food, much to our surprise, was ketchup sandwiches.
14. Poe died in Baltimore, not Philadelphia.
15. We have the right to complain, don't we?

Rule 9

1. He asked, "Who's there?"
2. "No," she insisted, "there are no monsters under the bed."
3. Henry said, "I'm looking for a mail-order bride."
4. We heard someone shouting, "Help!"
5. "You are lying!" the defendant shouted.
6. "Open the door slowly," cautioned the animal trainer.
7. "By the way," the clerk added, "you have an overdue fine of $500."

Rule 10

1. Learning that we would adopt a baby from Korea led me to make serious changes in my way of thinking about the family unit.
2. The coach shouted to us that we should not give up until the game was over.
3. The coach shouted to us, "Don't give up until the game is over!"
4. Whatever happens in the future is beyond our control.
5. Whatever happens in the future, according to many philosophers, is beyond our control.

EXERCISE 12.2 (p. 284)

1. Our speaker today is a man who needs no introduction.
2. Our speaker today, Mayor White, needs no introduction.
3. The wallet that we found on the sidewalk contained no identification, but it did have a substantial amount of cash.
4. Her instructor, an expert on Egyptian culture, sponsored a trip to Cairo.
5. Believe me, you will enjoy your trip to England.
6. Alaska, which is the largest state, has beautiful mountains and rivers.
7. Before the movie starts, you should buy a bag of popcorn.
8. I can't find my shoes, my socks, or my underwear.
9. I am happy to inform you, Mr. Forbes, that you are the father of triplets.
10. Near a small, quiet pond, the hikers could hear the cries of wild geese flying overhead.
11. The math class that I took last semester was challenging.
12. Algebra II, which I took last semester, was challenging.
13. By Tuesday, June 6, Norwood had already sold four vacuum cleaners.
14. A large man who was smoking a cigar sat down next to me, although there was a "no smoking" sign in the room.
15. What I like about traveling is seeing new places, meeting a variety of people, and eating exotic food.
16. A white cat, especially a Persian, will leave fur throughout your home.
17. I arrived on Tuesday, March 18, 1999, and found that I was in the wrong city.
18. Betty confided in her best friend, whose opinion she valued highly.
19. The meal that was served pleased Uncle Fred, who said, "May I have more, please?"
20. They bought a new painting, a rather beautiful landscape.
21. Stephen King's latest book, by the way, will soon be made into a movie.
22. The crowd that gathered around the accident made the rescue difficult.
23. Having awakened from a nightmare, I found it difficult to go back to sleep.
24. We will rehearse the play at school but perform it in the City Theater, which has just been built.
25. Some plants, surprisingly enough, need no sunlight.
26. By the light of the moon, we could make out a dim, motionless figure near the tree.
27. Pickles, not olives, were in the tray.
28. My youngest sister, who is still in high school, wants to be an astronaut.
29. That package must be sent to 30 Overland Street, Kansas City, Kansas 66102.
30. "I think I'm having an emergency," Catherine said, her voice trembling slightly; then, a few seconds later, she began to scream, "Help! Fire!"
31. Because I have a fear of flying, I seldom take vacations.
32. I have a fear of flying; therefore, I seldom take vacations.
33. Mary Ellen, who asked the question, did not understand the teacher's answer, although she listened carefully.
34. It is important to be polite, but it is also important to be assertive.
35. Answering the telephone, Clark carried on a conversation while he played a computer game.

EXERCISE 12.3 (p. 287)

1. Negotiations have stopped; we will strike at noon.
2. Orphan Annie endured a cruel childhood for a time; then she was adopted by Daddy Warbucks.
3. Stacy's childhood was enlivened by Nutty, a friendly backyard squirrel; Jake, her frisky black poodle; and Minx, her roving tomcat.
4. After buying flour, sugar, salt, and butter, I decided to go home and bake shortbread; but I found, once I checked my telephone messages, that my afternoon was no longer free.
5. At 3:00 on Monday afternoon, Lisa quit her job; at 6:00 the next morning, she could not sleep because she was worried about paying the bills; and at 10:00, just four hours later, she was begging her supervisor to overlook her hasty resignation.
6. The tour group will visit Edinburgh, Scotland; Dublin, Ireland; and London, England.
7. Thinking creatively, the youngster constructed a house out of cardboard, although the wind soon blew it down.

EXERCISE 12.4 (p. 290)

1. After all of the arguments that erupted at Joseph's party, we never again brought up three topics: his failure to graduate from high school, his behavior during his wedding, and the amount of wine he consumed at the party.
2. Dr. Kee, the celebrated botanist, was a brilliant, engaging person; unfortunately, his interns were often crushed by his excessive work demands.
3. Certain qualities should be present in every human, such as a desire to survive, an instinct to preserve one's own species, and an ability to empathize with others.
4. Juices that are exceptionally high in Vitamin C include orange, grapefruit, and tomato juice.
5. Juices that are exceptionally high in Vitamin C include the following: orange, grapefruit, and tomato juice; however, they also contain a large amount of acid.
6. Beth had one unfulfilled ambition: to enjoy high tea in the Pump Room at Bath.
7. The tropical storm damaged everything in its path: houses, trees, and power lines.

EXERCISE 12.5 (p. 293)

1. On my shopping list were four items that I simply had to buy—soap, toothpaste, tissues, and toilet paper.
   OR (more formal)
   On my shopping list were four items that I simply had to buy: soap, toothpaste, tissues, and toilet paper.
2. On my shopping list were four items—soap, toothpaste, tissues, and toilet paper—that I simply had to buy.

3. On my shopping list were the following four items: soap, toothpaste, tissues, and toilet paper.

4. I had to buy soap, toothpaste, tissues, and toilet paper; however, I did not have enough money left over to buy shampoo.

5. The truth of the matter, if you really must know, is that I hate shopping.
   OR (more emphatic)
   The truth of the matter—if you really must know—is that I hate shopping.
   OR (less emphatic)
   The truth of the matter (if you really must know) is that I hate shopping.

EXERCISE 12.6 (p. 295)

1. softly falling rain
2. heart-stopping thrill.
3. faster-than-lightning speed
4. three-part application
5. expensive diamond necklace
6. shy, smiling child
7. shyly smiling child
8. one-of-a-kind costume
9. three-year-old child
10. fast-talking salesman
11. dark brown suit
12. three thousand two hundred ninety-one dollars

EXERCISE 12.7 (p. 296)

1. As soon as Brecken earns her degree, she will be earning about $90,000/year.
2. We could negotiate the details now, and/or we could contact our lawyers.
3. The post of secretary/clerk is now open.
4. The menu indicated that the diner's specials included soup, rolls, ice cream, and coffee/tea with every meal.

EXERCISE 12.8 (p. 299)

1. While it was parked at the curb overnight, Ernie's car was hit.
2. He was fined for contempt of court on the judge's order.
3. The fine china cup had lost its original handle.
4. Mr. Clark's geography class is intimidating for junior high students.
5. On my brother's twenty-first birthday, he gambled and drank for the first and last time.
6. My mother-in-law's recipe for homemade pasta is the best I've ever had.
7. These boys' grades are disgraceful!

8. In my doctor's opinion, I'm overworked and must take a vacation.
9. My mother's job was in the children's department.
10. If you're interested in going on the school trip, you must have both parents' consent.
11. The Simpsons could not decide what to do with their free Saturday evening.
12. The girls' locker room is directly across from the boys' gym.
13. Yeats's (OR Yeats') poetry explains his unique mythological system.
14. It's three o'clock, so I must leave for my best friend's party.
15. The Blakes' car is a classic Mustang.

EXERCISE 12.9 (p. 301)

1. My favorite Hemingway novel is *The Sun Also Rises*.
2. During the holiday season many churches advertise productions of Handel's masterpiece, the *Messiah*.
3. Chapter 12, "Punctuation and Capitalization," is a very long one.
4. Perhaps the most famous plane at the Smithsonian is the *Spirit of St. Louis*.
5. Leonardo da Vinci's *Mona Lisa* is always surrounded by admirers at the Louvre.
6. *Sesame Street* is an enormously popular television series for children.
7. Poe's story "The Fall of the House of Usher" gave me nightmares as a child.
8. The first song to project the Beatles to stardom was "I Wanna Hold Your Hand."
9. Many business executives read *The Wall Street Journal* on a daily basis.
10. *Newsweek* recently published an informative article entitled "What You Need to Know About Political History."

EXERCISE 12.10 (p. 307)

1. "I absolutely must have one of those dolls!" the elderly woman exclaimed.
2. The elderly woman exclaimed, "I absolutely must have one of those dolls!"
3. The client asked his attorney, "What does the Latin word *uxor* mean in this document?"
4. Have you ever heard someone say, "I told you so"?
5. The eager reporter quoted the local official as saying, "I refuse to be intimidated by the corrupt political situation that has prevailed here for years. I predict the imminent arrest or departure of several key figures in the community."
6. The eager reporter misquoted the local official as saying the following: "I refuse to be intimidated by several key figures in the community."
7. "I am a sensitive human," the teenager told her friends. "I simply can't believe that my parents would treat me this way."
8. In perhaps the most famous love poem ever written, Elizabeth Barrett Browning proceeds to "count the ways" in which she loves.
9. To modernize the first line of Browning's poem, Sherry changed the archaic pronoun so that the line now reads as follows: "How do I love you? Let me count the ways."
10. As she walks through London, Mrs. Dalloway muses about her friend Peter Walsh:

For they might be parted hundreds of years, she and Peter; she never wrote a letter and his were dry sticks; but suddenly it would come over her, If he were with me now what would he say?—some days, some sights bringing him back to her calmly, without the old bitterness; which perhaps was the reward of having cared for people; they came back in the middle of St. James's Park on a fine morning—indeed they did. (Woolf 5)

11. As she walks through London, Mrs. Dalloway muses, "For they might be parted hundreds of years, she and Peter; she never wrote a letter and his were dry sticks; but suddenly it would come over her ..." (Woolf 5).

12. "Why do Virginia Woolf's novels remind me of poetry?" inquired Allison.

EXERCISE 12.11 (p. 309)

1. The doctor told the elderly patient to schedule an annual physical.
   OR
   The doctor said that the elderly patient should schedule an annual physical.
2. Harry's wife shouted that he never pays (or paid) attention to her.
3. All of the officers agreed that membership in the club should be closed until further notice.
4. The police officer asked if anyone had gotten a good look at the suspect.

EXERCISE 12.12 (p. 309)

These late eclipses in the sun and moon portend no good to us.... Love cools, friendship falls off, brothers divide ... the bond [is] crack'd 'twixt son and father.... We have seen the best of our time. Machinations ... and all ruinous disorders follow us....

EXERCISE 12.13 (p. 311)

Part A

1. My mother has always loved Italian dressing, but I have always preferred Russian.
2. Dad and Mom would like to sail to Jamaica for Valentine's Day.
3. The local animal hospital has been placing ads in the paper for veterinary assistants.
4. The Pitman Animal Hospital has been placing ads in the *Pitman News* for veterinary assistants.
5. Although our family is from the South, Aunt Jean and her husband have always wanted to live in the Northwest, preferably near Seattle.
6. The Navy does an excellent job recruiting students from St. George's Academy.
7. The Boston Tea Party is an event that almost all American school children can explain.
8. The names in the Old Testament of the Bible can be very difficult to spell correctly.

9. My uncle worked in the summer as a district manager for Pennsylvania Bell.
10. After passing a battery of tests, Kevin rose to the rank of Secretary I in the university system.

Part B

1. *The Origin of All Board Games*
2. "The Best Way to Lose All Enemies and Feel No Fear"
3. "How to Succeed in College"
4. "Cats Are Human, Too"
5. "Learn to Run Your Own Business"

CHAPTER 12 EXERCISE (p. 315)

1. While we were at the Little League game, we bought some candy and soda; however, the game was so exciting that we forgot the candy and spilled the soda.
2. Janet, who is the new president of the Historical Research Club, is a well-organized, efficient person.
3. Some students prefer British literature, while others prefer American literature; each literary tradition has its own unique strengths.
4. The icing on the cake at Boris's (OR Boris') birthday party looked delicious, but it tasted—to our dismay—like glue. (NOTE: The dashes could be replaced by commas or parentheses.)
5. After we had stayed up all night, we decided to have breakfast together at the Regent Café; then we slept until noon.
6. The Smiths used to live in El Paso, a border town with excitement, opportunity, and flair.
7. Sharon's twin sister, who recently took a vacation, decided to move to Honolulu, Hawaii, rather than return to Trenton, New Jersey.
8. My favorite holidays are Christmas, when I receive presents; my birthday, when I receive phone calls from all of my friends; and Valentine's Day, when I receive boxes of chocolate.
9. If I am reading the lease correctly, the rent at Crossbones Apartments includes the following items: gas, electricity, and water.
10. Throughout the years of childhood, most of us develop a strong, sure sense of identity; yet, sadly enough, we may later give up our individuality due to social pressure.
11. The repairman insisted that he could not locate the on/off switch.
12. The three countries that we visited—Sweden, Norway, and Denmark—form what is known as Scandinavia.
13. Jean Smith, the cardiologist; Angelo Martinez, the dentist; and Alan Wilson, the psychiatrist, meet for lunch on the twenty-third of every month.
14. The Payroll Department collects the workers' time cards each week and then prepares everyone's paycheck.

15. Lillian Helman, America's first great female playwright, entitled her first play *The Children's Hour*.
16. The kind, gentle creatures seemed to have descended from the spaceship that was hovering in the background, although I couldn't be sure.
17. Bridge, my parents' hobby; chess, my oldest sister's passion; and three-dimensional puzzles, my favorite pastime, are all time-consuming activities; luckily, though, we all manage our time wisely.
18. During our class on Friday, October 31, three subjects repeatedly came up: ghosts, witches, and vampires. (NOTE: A dash rather than a colon would also be correct.)
19. "Sergio finally proposed to Maria," my mother said, "but she turned him down."
20. Four foods—spaghetti, cheeseburgers, hot dogs, and burritos—constitute Elizabeth's normal diet.
21. That delicately framed portrait is unusual, isn't it?
22. The five-pointed star figures prominently in the book's first chapter, entitled "The Symbolism of Stars."
23. Who said, "A rose is a rose is a rose"?
24. The Victorian period is associated with the Industrial Revolution, middle-class morality, and the foundations of twentieth-century science.
25. When I attended Stetson University, all of the freshmen were required to read *The Great Gatsby*.
26. "Poetry," wrote William Wordsworth, "is emotion recollected in tranquillity."
27. Dan Burns, the coach, made it clear that each member of the team would be held responsible for his/her actions.
28. The police officer asked if the driver had been wearing a seat belt at the time of the accident.
29. In 1895, my grandfather and grandmother settled into a quiet, simple life in the southwest corner of Mississippi.
30. As the fairy waved her wand, the witch disintegrated into dust and ashes, shrieking with horror and rage.

EXERCISE 13.1 (p. 321)

INTERROGATIVE—Does the butler diligently polish the gleaming silver tea set every day?

IMPERATIVE—Polish the tea set every day. [or !]

EXCLAMATORY—How diligently the butler polishes the gleaming silver tea set every day! [or .]

OR: What a gleaming silver tea set the butler polishes every day! [or .]

EXERCISE 13.2 (p. 322)

What the butler diligently polishes every day is the gleaming silver tea set.

It is the butler who diligently polishes the gleaming silver tea set every day.

It is the gleaming silver tea set that the butler diligently polishes every day.

It is every day that the butler diligently polishes the gleaming silver tea set.

EXERCISE 13.3 (p. 323)

1. PASSIVE—The videotape was erased by the mischievous children.
   ACTIVE—The mischievous children erased the videotape.
   This sentence is more effective in active voice because the emphasis should be on the children, not the videotape. The adjective "mischievous" further indicates that the main interest of the sentence is the children.

2. Arthur was crowned king after he removed the sword from the stone.
   PASSIVE independent clause (*Arthur was crowned king*) but active adverb clause (*after he removed the sword from the stone*).
   The independent clause of this sentence should remain in passive voice because the primary emphasis rests on Arthur; *who* crowns him king is not important here.

3. PASSIVE—The lone survivor of the plane crash was besieged by questions from media representatives.
   This sentence should remain in passive voice if the intent is to focus on the plight of the lone survivor.

4. ACTIVE—Someone stole the tooth hidden beneath Amelia's pillow.
   PASSIVE—The tooth hidden beneath Amelia's pillow was stolen.
   This sentence is more effective in passive voice for two reasons: (1) We do not know who stole the tooth; (2) The intent of the sentence is probably to garner sympathy for Amelia, not to blame the thief.

5. PASSIVE—The delicate design was woven into the cloth with threads of gold.
   This sentence should remain in passive because we do not know *who* wove the design.

EXERCISE 13.4 (p. 325)

1. There was a red fox helping itself to the cat food in the Smiths' yard last night.
   There = EXPLETIVE
   Rephrased and stronger version: A red fox helped itself to the cat food in the Smiths' yard last night.

2. There were good reasons for the decision.
   There = EXPLETIVE
   Rephrased: Good reasons for the decision existed. OR Good reasons existed for the decision.
   These versions are not as effective as the original because, although we have replaced the *be* verb ("were"), the substitute verb ("existed") adds no information or force to the sentence; in addition, the rephrased version probably does not sound as natural—as idiomatic—to most people as the original.

3. No one was there when we knocked on the door.
   there = ADVERB ("where")

EXERCISE 13.5 (p. 327)

1. It is important <u>to eat a nutritious breakfast</u>.
2. It has been wonderful <u>babysitting the grandchildren</u>.
3. It is incredible <u>that you survived the accident</u>.

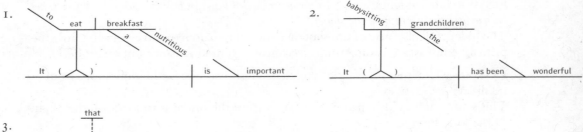

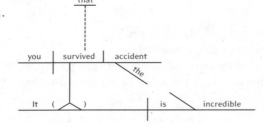

EXERCISE 13.6 (p. 329)

1. No one in class remembered the teacher's birthday—<u>an oversight that led to trouble</u>.
2. All of the players memorized the coach's instructions, <u>an action resulting in victory</u>.
3. The Smiths celebrated their fiftieth anniversary, <u>an extraordinary event in our community</u>.
4. Michael asked when his mother would feel better, <u>a question that no one could answer</u>.

I.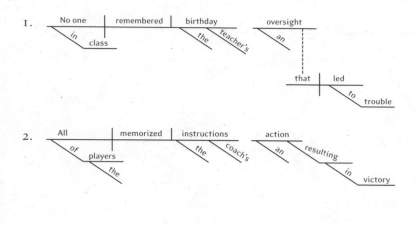

2.

3.

4.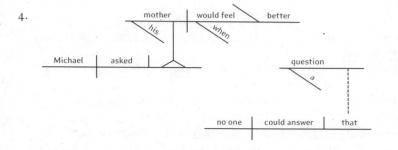

EXERCISE 13.7 (p. 331)

1. <u>The ink spilling onto the table</u>, the words on the document gradually disappeared.
2. <u>Its fur wet</u>, the puppy looked at me hopefully through the open door.
3. The alarm clock rang loudly, <u>its bell near my ear</u>.
4. Marcia walked forward, <u>her hands shaking as she threw the bridal bouquet</u>.

I.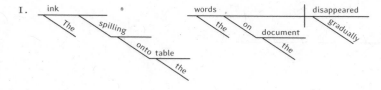

2.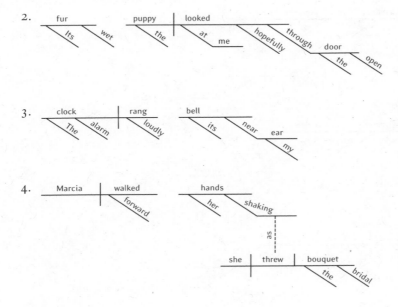

3.

4.

EXERCISE 13.8 (p. 332)

1. My father never completed high school, <u>a fact that he usually concealed from strangers</u>. (sentence appositive)
2. <u>His family in need of income</u>, my father never completed high school. (nominative absolute)
3. My father confessed that he never completed high school, <u>his voice stuttering</u>. (nominative absolute)
4. The package fell to the floor, <u>its contents spilling everywhere</u>. (nominative absolute)
5. <u>Its wings flapping wildly</u>, the bird tried to escape from the cat—<u>a reminder of nature's rule, "survival of the fittest."</u> (nominative absolute at beginning of sentence; sentence appositive at end)

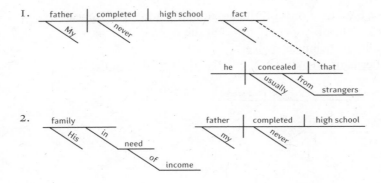

3.

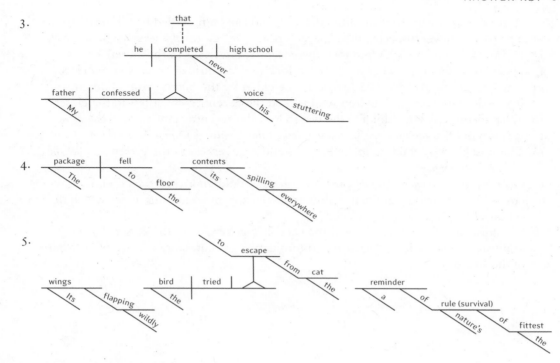

4.

5.

CHAPTER 13 EXERCISE (p. 335)

Although your sentences will vary, here is an example of each type of sentence.

1. The mischievous children locked their eccentric governess in the closet, *but* she escaped.
2. The mischievous children locked their eccentric governess in the closet; *however,* she escaped.
3. The parents did not understand *how the mischievous children had locked the eccentric governess in the closet.*
4. *After the mischievous children locked the eccentric governess in the closet,* they went outside to play.
5. The mischievous children *who locked the eccentric governess in the closet* were sent to bed without dinner.
6. The mischievous children *who locked the eccentric governess in the closet* were sent to bed without dinner, *but they refused to apologize.*
7. *Locking the eccentric governess in the closet* was a shocking action.
8. *Locking the eccentric governess in the closet,* the mischievous children ran outside to play.
9. The mischievous children decided *to lock the eccentric governess in the closet.*
10. The mischievous children were willing *to lock the eccentric governess in the closet.* (Infinitive as adverb here modifies the adjective "willing.")
    The mischievous children used a cruel trick *to lock the eccentric governess in the closet.*

(Infinitive as adverb here modifies the verb and can be preceded by "in order to.")

11. The parents never suspected the children's plan *to lock the eccentric governess in the closet*.
12. Did the mischievous children lock the eccentric governess in the closet?
13. How mischievous the children were to lock the eccentric governess in the closet!
14. The eccentric governess was locked in the closet by the mischievous children.
15. It was the mischievous children who locked the eccentric governess in the closet.
16. What the mischievous children did was to lock the eccentric governess in the closet.
17. It was cruel *that the mischievous children locked the eccentric governess in the closet*.
18. The mischievous children locked the eccentric governess in the closet—*an act she will not soon forgive*.
19. *Her petty ways no longer bearable*, the mischievous children locked the eccentric governess in the closet. (Nominative absolute here explains conditions under which the action of the sentence took place.)
20. The mischievous children locked the eccentric governess in the closet, *her cries for help inaudible to the rest of the family*. (Nominative absolute here focuses on a detail of the situation.)

INDEX